Phenomenology and Ontology

PHAENOMENOLOGICA

COLLECTION PUBLIÉE SOUS LE PATRONAGE DES CENTRES D'ARCHIVES-HUSSERL

37

J. N. MOHANTY

Phenomenology and Ontology

J. N. MOHANTY

Phenomenology and Ontology

MARTINUS NIJHOFF / DEN HAAG / 1970

ISBN   90 247 5053 9

PRINTED IN THE NETHERLANDS

PREFACE

Most of the essays that follow have originally appeared in philosophical journals, Indian and Western. They are reprinted here with the hope that in spite of the wide variety of topics with which they deal there is nevertheless a certain unity of treatment. A few major ideas and distinctions run through all the essays: I need not further single them out here.

For permission to reprint, I have to thank the editors of the journals and books in which the essays originally appeared. My former pupil Miss Manjusree Ray has been kind enough to help me in preparing the book for the press.

J. N. MOHANTY

May, 1968, Calcutta

CONTENTS

PART ONE

CHAPTER I

MODES OF GIVENNESS*

The essence as well as the strength of positivism lies in its emphasis on the *given* as opposed to the constructed. However, in its zeal in favour of the given, positivism – in some of its modern forms – has taken recourse to constructions and reductions. The purpose of this paper is to argue out the case for a positivism which refuses to construct and to reduce and which, instead of dogmatically clinging to one favoured mode of givenness, recognises a hierarchy of such modes. This type of positivism may be named 'higher positivism'; it is opposed to 'lower' positivism which takes recourse to constructions and reductions and which admits some sort of sensuous experience as the only mode of givenness.

One may profitably be inspired by *analogies*, and nothing more than analogies, from other fields of metaphysical philosophy. Philosophers have sought to distinguish between lower and higher naturalism. Seeking to draw this distinction, the late Professor Pringle-Pattison in his Gifford Lectures on *The Idea of God* laid down that the principle of continuity is not incompatible with emergence of real difference. Whereas lower naturalism reduces all phenomena to a dead level of uniformity of the material order, higher naturalism admits continuity of process without losing sight of real qualitative difference where the same appears. This latter insight had led, in the theory of evolution, to emergentism as opposed to the repetitive theory.

Although the area of the problem with which the present paper is concerned is quite unrelated to the above, one can nevertheless draw inspiration from it. It is necessary that the truth

* Presented to Professor Josef König, Göttingen, on his sixtieth birthday, and later published in *Archiv für Philosophie*, Stuttgart, 1958.

underlying positivism be recognised without at the same time losing sight of the aberrations it is suffering from. Positivism, to be revitalised, must be made more comprehensive, less dogmatic in its persuasion and more open to novelties. The attachment to the *given* has to be retained while the prejudice in favour of the sensuously given has to be overcome.

2. Starting with the sense-data as the only given elements in experience, positivism has been struggling with the problem of *things* on the one hand and that of *universals* on the other. Each of these problems is two-faced: it is linguistic and ontological in one. The ontological problem of the constitution of things as also of the reality of the universals is inextricably blended with the linguistic problem of ascertaining the meanings of the corresponding words of the language. Modern positivism has here favoured the reduction of things (and of universals) into sense-data. 'Reduction into' is only the reverse side of 'construction out of'. Things are constructions. Whether this finding has to be interpreted ontologically or linguistically is difficult to decide. No doubt, the linguistic issue dominates. We are given the hope that all thing-words could be eliminated, yielding place to names of sense-particulars. This involves a rule of translation. Underlying all this is the idea of an ideal language in which every word shall be a 'logically' proper name designating immediately given data of acquaintance. But the entire significance of the theory cannot be limited to the linguistic issue: the ontological bearing is undeniably there. *Things* are nothing but families of sense-data. The epistemological basis is also only too obvious: sensation is the only mode of givenness, the rest is construction, arrangement and interpretation. Or, perhaps better, nothing else is there. It is not surprising therefore that positivism should thus be an ally of constructionism and formalism, for these latter are supposed to yield the tool with which what positivism fails to admit has to be made good. Things and universals have to be constructed *formally* out of the material supplied by the senses.

Russell makes use of the principle of Occam's razor to defend his constructionism. This means also a reformulation of the principle. The principle now runs: whenever possible, logical constructions are to be substituted for inferred entities. Reality of the so-called thing could only be established, if at all, by an inference to the effect that sensible qualities require either a support wherein they inhere, or a cause whose effects they are. Such *inference* from the known to the unknown is here sought to be rejected in favour of *constructing* the unknown in terms of the known. Instead of an unknown support or cause of the sensible appearances we have a 'family' of them.

Difficulties of this theory of construction have been pointed out by Stebbing[1] and Black[2] amongst others. Stebbing has insisted that on this theory every proposition about a material object, say, this table, is reducible to a number of *hypothetical* facts about *my* future experience of the sort "If I lean on this table, it won't rise into the air, and so on". As a consequence, every categorical statement about things is in fact hypothetical, involving a number of verifiable predictions. This is however untenable for the reason that though when I know I perceive this table I *also* know certain hypothetical facts, yet the two knowledges are not for that reason identical. Black has rightly drawn our attention to the fact that Russell is perhaps playing on an equivocation with regard to the term 'meaning'. Either, the thing-words (that are not, according to Russell, logically proper names) do mean something for us if we are *not* acquainted with them in Russell's sense, or a new sense of 'meaning' is introduced. In the former case, Russell is accepting the common usage of the term; in the latter case, his argument could be shown to involve *petitio principii*. Further considering the issue from the linguistic point of view, the symbols that are claimed to be completely translatable on the lines proposed by the theory must be demonstrated to be thoroughly *dispensable* which they, in fact, are not. Complete translation of the symbols in question is not possible. Ontologically, we may insist that the *unity* of a thing is totally different from the unity of a family, a series or a nexus of data. Epistemologically, it could be added that things are *given* in a way radically different from that in which sense-data are given.

The application of Occam's razor as suggested by this theory

---

[1] L. S. Stebbing, "Logical Positivism and Analysis," *Proceedings of the British Academy*, Vol. XIX, London.

[2] M. Black, *Language and Philosophy*, Ithaca, Cornell University Press, 1949, Ch. V.

is tempting because the razor is claimed to be rescuing us from a hazardous inference. The danger is imaginary, the rescue is therefore superfluous. The things *are not* inferred; they are given as such, prior to their *analysis* into the data. The application of Occam's razor is carried out against a false enemy. What is given as such needs no replacement.

The fact is that things are not given in that *theoretical* attitude in which the sense-data are given. Taking therefore the attitude of reflection if I approach the things, they fall asunder into those sensory data that now lay claim to be the absolute firsts; the things either recede to the background as unknown inferred entities or else they dissolve into the rarefied logical constructions. The peculiar mode of givenness of things is missed thereby. The sense-data approach to things is destined to end in failure.

Things as such are given in a pre-theoretical attitude. They *qua* things are given in practical relationship with the environment through affective-emotional experiences, through action and practice. Action is a mode of disclosure. It discloses reality as things. The idea of *things* is inseparable from the idea of practice. In fact, the world of things is a world of practical relationships, actual and possible, a horizon of actual and possible activity.

On the other hand, try to understand thing-perception in terms of the theoretical subject, and one is led to that insoluble impasse which ends in the very denial of things and which, not even satisfied with this, goes to the extent of denying that things are at all given.

Theory should know its limits. It should recognise what lies beyond its frontiers. The primacy and irreducibility of the distinction between the theoretical and the practical[3] has to be recognised. This recognition saves philosophy from much intellectual embarrassment. What however is most often lost sight of is that practice is no less a mode of disclosure than theory. It is usual to see in practice a process of making and remaking, modifying, changing, planning, calculating, foreseeing, utilising etc.. But nevertheless through all these the world of things *as well as the thinghood of things* comes to be revealed. To a purely

---

[3] This distinction was brought home to the present author by the lectures of Professor J. König at Göttingen during the years 1953–54. The present use of it however is the present author's own.

theoretical subject there would be no things, but only sense-data, essences, and the subjective. *Given* the thing, it can of course be *analysed*, through subsequent reflection, into sense-data; the temptation therefore to recompose that original unity out of these data is natural for the theoretician. One has only to re-member that, to avoid this temptation, that which is presupposed in analysis cannot be got back through analysis. The unity of the thing as revealed in its original mode of givenness through practice is radically different from that unity – be it that of 'family', series, or of nexus which analysis seeks to substitute for it.

3. The theoretical attitude – presupposing, and supervening upon, the practical – moves through three stages: intuition, thought and introspection. Reflection upon things as given through practice discloses sense-data. Reflection upon the data yields essences. Introspection is a turning away from the objective attitude of the preceding stages. Each of these by itself is a separate mode of disclosure, bringing into givenness the sense-data, essences and the subjective respectively.

3. (1) That the sense-data are given is what lower positivism starts with. It only errs by taking these data as the absolute firsts: it misses that pre-theoretical mode of givenness which as we have insisted, philosophy – in spite of its theoretical nature – should recognise and seek to incorporate into itself. The sense-data are given in the most primitive form of theoretical reflection.

3. (2) We pass on next to the controversial question about 'essences'. These are given in what is rather equivocally called 'thought'. Since Kant it is usual to insist on the constructive and interpretative function of thought at the cost of its intuitive func-tion. What is given – according to this modern view – is the particular, the sense-impressions which thought only welds into judgments. On this view – expressed through Kant's celebrated definition of understanding as the faculty of judgment – thought is the subjective source of *a priori* forms. The *a priori* is held to be subjective and formal, any objective and material *a priori* being ruled out of possibility. Thought becomes wholly discursive, an

endless process of mediation. Within the limits of sense-ex perience it yields constructed appearances; outside of this limit it creates illusions. Nowhere does it have the capacity of presenting or disclosing reality. No wonder that Kant should be reckoned as the father of what we have called 'lower positivism', according to which all other propositions except those that are empirically verifiable and those that are analytic i.e. tautologies are meaning-less. Kant, no doubt, made the synthetic *a priori* the cornerstone of his own philosophy, but his synthetic *a priori* remained a composite of alien elements, material from sense and form from thought – thought having no matter of its own. It was then easy to deny the possibility of this union and to split up knowledge into the sensuous and the analytical-tautological!

As against this conception of thought, we advocate a theory that claims affiliation to the classical Platonic-Aristotelian-Nyāya theory of thinking. Thought on this theory is basically a mode of disclosure. Thought discloses ideas, essences, idealities. Thought thereby gains an ontological significance. It reveals the *ideal* factors and structures inherent in *real* events and processes. It discloses being as essence, to use Hegel's mode of expression.

3. (3) What sense-intuition reveals as accidental and fleeting sense-data, thought transforms into essences, nontemporal and unchanging. Already in sense-intuition, as a mode of theoretical consciousness i.e. as divorced from practice, there is freedom from real existence; sense-intuition can be studied in its essence through phantasy and imagination (Husserl). If ordinary sense-perception pretends to give an existent real thing with its qua-lities, it is because such perception is an admixture of theore-tical consciousness with practice; the possibility however of liberating the theoretical from the practical is there. Just as naive realism commits the error of taking the things as such as given in theoretical sense-intuition, so does the critical realism of George Santayana and others commit the opposite error of taking the essences alone as given. It is not the essences that are the data of sense-intuition; the essences are data of thought while sense-intuition apprehends the accidental and particular sense qualities. It is these latter qualities which thought now reveals as essences but which were *not* given as essences in sense-intuition.

There is a type of philosophical logic according to which if A is given in one mode of experience but if subsequently A manifests itself as B, then A is an appearance of B so that it is really B which formerly appeared as A! In the present case since the data of intuition reveal themselves to thought as essences, it is *really* the essences that - according to this logic – *were* given to sense-intuition. A thoroughgoing application of this logic would lead to a reduction "from above" just as 'lower' positivism is reduction "from below". For if we apply this logic systematically we shall be led to the *metaphysical* thesis that it is *really* the essences that appeared as sense-data, and so on. Ultimately, what are given in the lower modes of experience would be in that case false appearances of what is given in the highest. This is a metaphysical thesis, for it appeals to a distinction between what *is* given and what is *really* given. And yet it is not a purely metaphysical distinction; it is a metaphysical distinction which yet pretends to be phenomenological. For, instead of distinguishing between what is *given* and what *is*, it seeks to distinguish between what is *apparently given* and what is *really given*. This latter distinction between the apparent and the real is untenable. What *is* given is also *really* given. Phenomenology must avoid both types of reduction: "from above" as well as "from below"; it must satisfy itself with distinguishing between levels of givenness and exhibiting, where possible, the transition from one to the other.

4.   A totally new realm opens out with introspection: the realm of the subjective. But even here one has to be cautious not to miss the subtle phenomenological stratifications. One at once faces the thing *as apprehended*, the sense data *as perceived*, the essences *as thought*. Being is apprehended as mental content. As mental contents, things, sense-data and essences are all alike. Even here one is apt to mistake these data of introspection as what *really appeared* as objective. In 3. (3) we have discarded this logic. Besides, the mental content is not wholly subjective. It stands mid-way between the subjective and the objective. The thing *as perceived* is the thing itself; but it is also not the thing itself. It is and yet is not that. Hence the peculiarly evasive character of the mental content, tending to be and yet refusing to get

identified with the object. Introspection of this primary order is not purely subjective; it is subjective-objective.

4. (1) Introspection *par excellence*, that is to say, the mode of givenness of the genuinely subjective begins with the disclosure of the mental *functions*, as contrasted with the mental *states* or contents. From the thing as apprehended, the sense-data as perceived, the essences as thought one passes on to the functions of apprehending, perceiving, sensing, imagining and thinking. This would yield a phenomenology of the noetic functions, the best known example of which is found in Kant's *Kritik der reinen Vernunft*.

4. (2) K. C. Bhattacharyya distinguishes between the above two modes of introspection in the following manner: "The distinguishing of knownness etc. as an abstraction from the object is what is called psychological introspection. The distinguishing of the subjective function of knowing etc. as other than this abstraction of objectivity may also be called introspection and it may be with greater right". In the latter kind of introspection, "the functions represent the modes of freedom from the corresponding psychological abstractions".[4]

Without claiming to be a correct interpreter of Bhattacharyya's rather difficult text, we may distinguish between the two kinds of introspection thus: the one discloses the object as known, as apprehended, as perceived, as imagined, as thought etc., while the other discloses the corresponding functions which on their part represent "the modes of freedom" from the objective character of the first kind of introspection. The two perhaps correspond to the two levels of Husserlian phenomenology: the noetic and the noematic.

5. We have in the above outlined five modes of givenness; what are disclosed through these modes are *things, sense-data, essences, mental contents* and *mental functions*. These five modes fall into two principal groups: the theoretical and the practical. Things are given practically; the rest is given theoretically.

---

[4] K. C. Bhattacharyya, *The Subject as Freedom*, The Indian Institute of Philosophy, Amalner, India, 1930, p. 30.

Amongst these latter, the contents and the functions are said to be given in introspection. The functions alone however are data of introspection in the true sense.

These five however do not exhaust all that we are acquainted with. For there is that immediate self-consciousness which is neither practical nor theoretical, which in fact – so far as its own mode of givenness is concerned – transcends that distinction and yet accompanies both. Each of the other modes of consciousness we have mentioned is an awareness *of* ... ; self-consciousness however which accompanies all our awareness is not itself an awareness of ... It would be wrong to hold that this self-consciousness is an introspective datum. It is an 'enjoyment', not a 'contemplation' – to use a distinction familiarised by Samuel Alexander.

We have thus three levels of the subjective: the mental contents, the mental functions and self-consciousness. The first has a curious status, being also interpretable as objective or at least not distinguishable from the object. The functions are ontologically subjective but epistemologically still objective, for they are 'contemplated', i.e., are made objects of awareness; their awareness is awareness *of*... Self-consciousness is both ontologically and epistemologically subjective; it is not an awareness *of*..

CHAPTER II

THE GIVEN*

I

The purpose of this paper is to suggest a satisfactory account of the chief modes of givenness. From this point of view, contemporary philosophy seems to me to be in a highly unsatisfactory state: it either totally denies that there is at all anything given or, if it accepts the given, restricts the same to one favoured kind of objects. Those who deny that there is at all anything given do so on the supposed ground that all human knowledge is interpretative, though they differ amongst themselves as to the source and the nature of such interpretations: the source may be either the *a priori* constitution of the human mind (Kant), or a metaphysical system (Hegel), or the rules of the language one uses (Wittgenstein). There are on the other hand the sense-datum philosophers who base their philosophy on the notion of the given, but recognise only one mode of givenness, i.e., sensation, and only one kind of objects that are given, i.e., the sense-data. This has led to endless difficulties as to how we come to perceive physical objects. As against this philosophy, some belonging to the first sort of persuasion have formulated the Alternate Language Thesis, according to which since nothing is absolutely given, what has to be regarded as given depends upon the linguistic decision that one makes, so that each such decision commits one to a particular conception of what is given. In short, nothing according to these last mentioned philosophers *is* given, but only anything *may be taken* as given.

It would seem that both these groups of philosophers are mis-

* Read before the Delhi Philosophical Colloquium, 1962, and subsequently printed in the Proceedings of the Colloquium, India International Centre, New Delhi, 1964.

taken. The first group of philosophers proceed to construct conceptual or linguistic systems whose basis remains arbitrary. The philosophers of the second group are dogmatic in holding on to one favoured type, and are inevitably led to reductionism, i.e., to the programme of reducing all other entities to that one type. The errors of both may be traced to a basic misconception about what a philosopher could and should do in such an enquiry as this. The real task of the philosopher here is not to find out which things are given and which not, nor even to recommend which things should be taken as given, but to bring out or make explicit, by analysis and phenomenological description, in the case of those that would ordinarily be regarded as given, the precise meaning, implications and the modes of their givenness. That things and persons are given in unreflective life is beyond doubt, so much so that the word 'given' has its primary application precisely in those cases. If this application be rejected and the word suitably defined so as to exclude from the range of its application whatever one wishes to be excluded, the word would be transformed into a philosophical jargon and in that case any philosophical decision would be but an analytic consequence of one's initial linguistic proposal and would therefore be trivial. There is likewise a sense in which it is meaningful to say that we see colours, hear sounds or taste tastes, and it is again the task of philosophy to explicate this sense. It is only after philosophy has explicated the modes of givenness in all these different cases where we would ordinarily say something is given, that the final *speculative* task of assigning a generic meaning to 'givenness' could be attempted.

II

We may profitably begin with pointing out, as a sequel to what has been said above, what 'to be given' surely does not mean. In the first place, to be given is *not* the same as being analytically the simplest. This has been one of the principal sources of many philosophical errors. It has been wrongly supposed that what is complex, structured and dependent could not have been given, so that it is only the simple, not further analysable *quale* that is given, the rest being only either inferred or constructed. This error is partly due to a faulty psychology, and partly due to a wrong conception of the function of analysis. In the second place, we have to get rid of the only too commonly held erroneous opinion that to be given is to be the content of one's immediate experience. The notions of 'content' and 'immediacy' involved are hopelessly ambiguous. Most of those who hold this view surely mean by 'content' what is a real constituent of one's experiencing so that to be given would amount to be enjoyed or felt in a sense analogous to that in which one enjoys one's pleasure or pain. They however fail to see that the modes of consciousness to which anything is given are all self-transcending, so that to be given to a consciousness is not the same as being a constituent of it or possessed by it. The given may well fall beyond the consciousness. It has again been held that to be given is to be passively witnessed, contemplated and received – a notion that may be traced back to Kant's characterisation of the faculty of intuition as receptive. This is a typically philosopher's error, betraying the philosopher's prejudice in favour of contemplation as against action. It is forgotten that even our most elementary perceptions involve bodily movements and adjustments, not to speak of the more complicated processes of discovery. As we shall argue in this paper, things and persons which confront us (and are certainly given, if the word 'given' is to have any sense at all) – are given not to passive contemplation but to an acting, manipulating, planning, appreciating and evaluating consciousness. The epistemologist's love of certainty has often led him to suppose further that the given must be indubitable. The sense datum philosophers have thus argued that since we may always be in error about physical objects and can never err in our reports about sense data, it is only the latter but not certainly the former that could be said to be given. If to be indubitable means to be free from the very possibility of doubt, it is incomprehensible why reports about sense data are so, for certainly the person who reports "this is green" might very well come to doubt, in a Cartesian mood. "Was that really green, or did I only *think* I saw a green patch?" At the moment when one sees the green patch one may of course be free from doubt and have a feeling of certainty, but surely it is in no greater degree so than at the moment one perceives a physical object. Certainly, this certainty does not as such exclude the possibility of subsequent doubt, and surely the fact that one may subsequently doubt does not rule out the possibility that the thing that claims to be given is really given. We may be in error in thinking that a certain physical object is given in a particular case, but we can be so in error only because there are cases of physical objects being truly given.

There is left yet another misconception to be removed. It is often supposed that the given must be something self-complete, depending upon nothing and leading up to nothing else. More precisely, the experience of having something given to one's consciousness must be a self-sufficient experience, an absolute first presupposing no prior experience and not by *itself* leading up to any. This variety of atomism vitiates not alone the conceptions of the sense datum philosophers, but also the conceptions of the physical object philosophers. A physical object is supposed to be given as a self-complete object, as much an atom as a sensory *quale*, though only complex and structured. Both the sense datum atomism and the physical object atomism have to be rejected if we are to have a satisfactory philosophy of the given.

III

I have made it clear in the first section that for me it is unquestionable that things and persons are given and that the task of philosophy in this connection could only be to explicate the meanings, and the modes of such givenness. I may now proceed to this task in a rather brief and schematic manner within the limits of this short paper. My main contention is, that physical objects and persons are given in a mode that may be called the practical mode. What I mean thereby is that they are primarily given not through passive contemplation but through actual and anticipated practical relationships. I am not denying that we perceive physical objects, but only contending that our perception of physical objects is far from being the contemplative affair that most philosophers would make it out to be.

With regard to the mode of givenness of physical objects, I

would like to concentrate on two points. The first of these may be
developed by way of answering a common objection to the claim
that a physical object is at all given. It is often objected that
when I think I am seeing the yonder tree what I really see is –
if not a patch of variegated colours – certainly only a part of the
tree, this side of the trunk for example. It is surely undeniable
that many of the parts of the tree remain hidden from my view,
and if that be so how could it be maintained that I perceive the
tree at all? In view of the way I have above formulated my task,
I could state the problem posed by the objection in the following
manner: in what sense, could the tree be said to be given, when
some of its parts are surely hidden from my view? Or, how should
my awareness of the tree be related to my awareness of its parts
such that the former awareness should present the tree as a
whole even when some parts of it are not presented to me? It
is to be noted that I am speaking a subjective language, for I am
interested not in the tree and its relation to its constituent parts
but in the relation of my awareness of the tree and my awareness of its parts.

It should be pointed out at once that it is not necessary for a
thing to be given that all its parts should also be given, for if that
were so then only simple *qualia* and relations could be given and
nothing else, for every physical object has its constituent parts,
and if one takes physics seriously, not all the constituents could
after all be given. If we accept this condition, we would only be
drifting towards that mistaken identification of the given with
the simple which has already been rejected.

Phenomenologically, the following seem to be undeniable: the
indispensable condition for a physical object to be given is, that
some of its parts be given. This condition is fulfilled, when the
parts that are given are adequate to awaken a consciousness
intending the object as a whole. There can no doubt be a thought of
a physical object, and that thought also intends the object. But
the consciousness to which the object *is given* exhibits an intention which is founded upon, but goes beyond, the appre-
hensions of its parts. In fact, in such a case, the intention of the
object as a unity forms the principal intention which comprehends
within it the awarenesses of the parts, and this holds good,
notwithstanding the fact that the latter awarenesses form the

indispensable condition of the former. A physical object is thus a unity that is more than the sum of its parts: that would be the rendering of the above in the material mode of speech.

Furthermore, apprehension of a physical object may give rise to further intentions in which a larger unity is presented, and this continuous transition from founding intentions to founded intentions, presenting larger and larger unities, is only interrupted by incursions of fresh interests demanding a total turn of the attention to other directions or to other pursuits. What I have been driving at is this: a physical object is given as the object of a dominating intention that permeates and comprehends the awareness of its parts, and this object again leads up to further intentions, in which still larger unities are presented. As said in the previous section, a physical object is not given as an atom; it always emerges from within an environment and also leads us beyond itself to other objects and relationships. This was the first point that I wished to emphasise in connection with our perception of physical objects.

The second point is this, the physical objects as a 'stubborn matter of fact' (Whitehead) with its *"Härte des Realen"* (Nicolai Hartmann) is given primarily through practical relationships. Heidegger's phrase *"Zuhandensein"* is apt, except for the fact that it suggests as if all physical objects were objects for use. There is no doubt however that it is through action that we recognise the physical object as such, as something which would offer us resistance and so needs manipulation, which has its own laws independent of our plans and so has to be mastered, and so on. The more we take up a contemplative attitude towards it, the more does its unity disintegrate into its component abstractions, *qualia* and relations, patterns and structures: the unity of the object gets lost. It can at best be theoretically represented as a logical construction, or perhaps as a mere *façon de parler*.

It is also possible to cultivate another sort of contemplative attitude towards the physical object, i.e., the aesthetic. In such an attitude, one is interested in an aesthetic enjoyment of *the essence, the rasa,* of an object which, e.g., the painter seeks to convey in painting a still life. Van Gogh's pair of shoes represents a universal essence, but not any particular pair of shoes with its unique particularity. It is quite possible in such an attitude that the sense-data are "abstracted"; the pure *quale* is an "aesthetic abstraction" (K. C. Bhattacharyya). The physical object is given in the primary unreflective practical relationship; the sense-data are abstractions in the aesthetic-contemplative attitude and curiously enough the analyst's favourites. In what sense, and in what mode they also may be said to be *given* is a further question beyond the scope of this paper. The alternate Language thesis which speaks of the sense-datum language and the physical-object language as two alternate languages fails to recognise the undeniable primacy of the physical object language.

IV

Practice may be, according to a distinction made by Kant in his Introduction to the *Critique of Judgment*, either technically-practical or morally practical. The physical object is disclosed through action which intends to use it as means to an end or which meets resistance from it. The person is disclosed through moral relationships whose essence, as Kant rightly saw, lay in acknowledging the other as an end in itself. Just as the physical object disintegrates into abstractions when made a subject of contemplation, so does the person tend to degenerate into a thing as the moral attitude is replaced by the pragmatic, as the end in itself comes more and more to be treated as a means to an end. Happily though, the person never becomes quite a thing.

As we have hinted at before, the two conflicting theories of outer perception could be reconciled (not after the manner of the Alternate Language Thesis, but) by regarding the physical objects and the sense-data as being given respectively in two different attitudes, the practical and the theoretical. Similarly we could attempt a reconciliation also of the two dominating theories about the nature of the self. According to one theory, the self is truly a person, a concrete existent being who is 'in the world' as much as 'with others'. According to the other theory, the self is a pure epistemological subject, a passive witness of the world and the others, detached and contemplative. My contention here is that the person and the subject are *given* in two different attitudes: the former in living, moral, evaluating relationship with others, the latter through contemplation on the implications of the attitude of pure understanding.

In order to bring home the principle on which the suggested reconciliation has to be carried out, I would begin by introducing a distinction between what I would call 'understanding' and 'knowing'. Both that there is a distinction and the point of the distinction would be clear from the possibility that one may simply understand the sentence "S is p" without knowing that S is p. Knowing that S is p however presupposes an understanding of the sentence "S is p", knowing implies that the fact known should be *given*, and not merely thought of. The distinction no doubt is an ideal distinction, for there are cases where the distinction is blurred. The more contemplative a knowing is, the more does it approximate towards the attitude of understanding. The more does knowledge succeed in making unique reference, the more does it approximate towards the ideal of knowing. And the knowledge of the unique individual - whether of a physical object, or of a person – is far from being a contemplative affair: this exactly is the paradigm case of knowing.

Now, one may reflect on the attitude of pure understanding. Such reflection may be a reflection upon the objects of pure understanding: or, it may be a reflection upon the subjective aspect of it. The former kind of reflection leads to the discovery of abstract entities like meanings; the latter reflection leads to the discovery of the detached, contemplative, witness self as the *who* of understanding and as distinguished from the person who is the agent of concrete knowing. As the objects of pure understanding are discovered to be impersonal and outside the context of practical-emotional-volitional relationship, so also the *who* of this attitude is progressively disclosed to be a passive witness and not an active person.

Further, I recognise myself as a person in so far as I recognise the Others as persons as well, so that a plurality of persons – each an end in itself is a not further reducible phenomenological datum in this attitude: the others remain Others to me, and yet ends in themselves.

But I cannot, in the sort of theoretic contemplation mentioned above, realise the others as subjects as I would in my own case. The enjoyment of subjectivity is thus primarily egoistic, whereas the enjoyment of personality is primarily social. We need not discuss here how, in the subjective attitude, the initial ego-centricity may be transcended.

However, the person and the subject are given in two different attitudes. Different spiritual ideals, even different religious faiths, may be traced to these two attitudes. But a discussion of these also falls beyond the scope of the present paper.

V

I have briefly sketched two radically different modes of givenness, the practical and the theoretical. In the former, the external world of physical objects and the community of persons are *given*: there are correspondingly two subdivisions of the practical mode for whom I have suggested the Kantian designations 'technically-practical' and 'morally practical'. In the latter, sense-data, abstract entities, and the passive witness Self are given, and there would be corresponding subdivisions of the theoretical mode. The resulting scheme has no claim to exhaustiveness. The main distinction between the practical and the theoretical however may claim to be a useful and illuminating explanatory principle. It would however lose its value if attempts are made to bridge the gulf separating the two. Using a metaphor, I should say there is no continuous passage from the one to the other: a "jump", a radical change of attitude, is indispensable.

This leads me to formulate what I consider to be a cardinal principle of all phenomenological philosophy. I shall call this principle, "the principle of phenomenological discontinuity". It states that phenomenology should recognise, wherever it comes across, radical discontinuities amongst phenomena and should not seek to blur the distinctions out of a sheer system-building interest.

Keeping this in mind, we may say that no intelligible relation can be formulated between (1) physical objects and sense-data and (2) the person and the subject. With this, many traditional philosophic discussions are rendered pointless, for the things which have been sought to be related are given in two totally heterogeneous modes. They cannot be given "together", and hence cannot be related.

There is surely a difference between the two cases. The sense-data, though "aesthetic abstractions" from the physical object, are yet appearances of it; they are *its*. The subject is not in a like manner an appearance of the person. Nor is the subject either a real constituent or substratum of the person. The person is *also* a subject. It is the same 'I' who is both. The 'I' is thus ambiguous.

The wider and interesting task of ascertaining a *generic* meaning of givenness would not be attempted in this paper.

CHAPTER III

THOUGHT AND ACTION*

1. Two questions, different from each other, are suggested by the title of the present symposium. First, how is the distinction between thought and action to be drawn? Next, how are the two related, as they certainly are? A satisfactory discussion of the second question requires that we have already some clear idea of the answer to the first question. We therefore have to start with the first.

2. Before proceeding with this, let us however take note of some ambiguities in the use of the term 'action' and clarify our position with regard to them. There is, to start with, a distinction between moral action and non-moral action, and any satisfactory philosophy of action must take this distinction into account. Further, we are to exclude all non-human actions, examples of which are bodily (physiological) actions and reactions as well as natural processes (those implied, e.g., in such statements as "the river erodes the bank" etc.). Both moral and non-moral actions are here contrasted with non-human actions. We shall consider only such actions as are accompanied by someone's consciousness of being the doer.

2.1. The distinction between moral and non-moral actions is not however exhaustive, for there are other types of human action that do not fall within either of the two. There are for example religious and aesthetic (creative and appreciative) activities. Karl Jaspers suggests a classification of human actions that ap-

* Presented at a symposium on the occasion of the 32nd session of the Indian Philosophical Congress, Srinagar, 1957. Originally published in the Proceedings of the Congress.

pears to be sufficiently comprehensive – the classification into those that are conditioned and those that are unconditioned. Even if it may be difficult to justify the names given to these two groups of human actions, it seems, in any case, to be obvious that there subsists a radical difference between the two groups of actions. They are not merely different kinds of actions; they are also as actions different. Unconditioned are the moral, aesthetic and religious actions and, may be, many more.

3. The distinction between thought and action is sought to be obliterated in various ways. One of these is only too common. Thought, it is said, is nothing but thinking, and thinking is a mental action, and so generically the same as other kinds of action. First, this view misses the essence of thinking as such, for this essence lies not in thought's being a temporal mental act, but in something else which we have to look for. Secondly, for the purpose of specifying the topic of this symposium, we prefer to exclude from consideration that diluted sense in which thought is an action.

3.1. The pragmatist's contention is different. He is not insisting on the triviality that thinking is a mental act, but is rather pointing towards the practical character of all so-called theoretical activity. All so-called theory serves the purpose of practice. The distinction between the theoretical and the practical is a distinction that falls within the practical. Thought is practical in a twofold sense; it arises out of a practical situation, and again it is a tool, an instrument, to get over that situation.

Much of it may be granted. It may be granted that much of our thinking in daily life as well as in the sciences arises out of some practical situation, and further that much of it aims at solving some practical problem. But at the same time we are also to grant that much of our thinking, in fact, the so-called higher, abstract or pure thinking is free from the urgency of any practical situation. Certainly, such pure thinking is also involved in problems and seeks to get out of them; but all problems are not practical. There are theoretical problems and theoretical situations, the like of which concerns us when we philosophise. But we may even say more. Even in those cases where we

think out of, or rather in, some practical situation, the essence
of thinking is radically different from that of practice or action.
The fact that thought can, and in fact does, attain to freedom
from practical relevance proves its essential freedom. Thought
and action are essentially distinct. That they are nevertheless
found in some cases to be associated with each other has to be
explained otherwise than by any sort of false reductionism.

3.2. Heidegger goes beyond the pragmatists, although it seems
at first as if he is giving nothing other than a pragmatist account
of thinking. Both intuition and thought are, for Heidegger,[1]
derivative from that primitive understanding which characterises
human existence. This primitive understanding (which is not a
kind of knowledge, but a fundamental factor of human existence[2])
is anticipatory and projective in character. Heidegger rejects
the conception of a pure subject. Human existence again is not
a present fact or thing, but an everpresent possibility of existing.
This possibility involves anticipation of, and projection into, the
future. This "being ahead of oneself", this anticipation and projection, constitutes that primitive understanding which has
always a feeling-tone, as it were.[3] The cool and contemplative
theoretical thinking (leading to science and philosophy) as well
as practical action, – both are derivative from this primitive
human existing.

Heidegger is not deriving theory from practice, nor is he plea-
ding for the primacy of practice over theory.[4] Here he avoids the
error of the pragmatists. He is only insisting on the primacy of
human existence. Thinking (scientific or philosophic) is, for
Heidegger, a mode of existence.[5] It is therefore derivative from
the basic existential categories. While we need not, in our present context, pursue this philosophy further, we may safely say
that Heidegger is dissatisfied with the dichotomy of theory and
practice and that he seeks to overcome this dualism not by reducing the one to the other but by deriving them from a higher,

---

[1] Martin Heidegger, *Sein und Zeit*, Max Niemeyer, Tübingen, 7th edn. 1953, p. 147.
[2] Martin Heidegger, *Kant und das Problem der Metaphysik*, Vittorio Klostermann,
Frankfurt, 2nd edn. 1951, p. 210.
[3] *Sein und Zeit*, p. 142: "*Verstehen ist immer gestimmtes*".
[4] *Ibid.*, p. 193: "Das Phänomen drückt daher keineswegs einen Vorrang des 'prak-
tischen' Verhaltens vor dem theoretischen aus ... 'Theorie' und 'Praxis' sind Seins-
möglichkeiten eines Seienden, dessen Sein als Sorge bestimmt werden muss."
[5] *Ibid.*, p. 357.

a more original unity. This too is reductionism, but this type of reductionism is philosophically more satisfying, since it has the courage to look squarely at the initial dichotomy. It shall be our attempt in the present paper to explore some means of overcoming the dualism between thought and action, but we could do that only by a phenomenological receptivity to the facts as they present themselves to us, and not by trying rival metaphysical hypotheses.

4. It is often said that thought is rational and specifically human, while action is irrational. This opinion is so erroneous that it cannot even be adequately formulated, and although it may be considered superfluous to mention such an opinion, there are not a few sensible persons who think along this line. The truth however is the contrary. For just as man alone can think, so also man alone can act[6]. Both thought and action originate in the essential constitution of man. It is a sheer misunderstanding of the true nature of human action to take it as nothing but a succession of real spatio-temporal events. It is as much a mistake to take human existence as a natural fact as to interpret his actions as natural processes. Man is as much a thinking being as an acting one. While on the one hand, he is a subject, he is also on the other a person.

4.1. We have therefore to seek for the distinction between thought and action elsewhere. In this connection, two fundamental questions may be asked: first, who thinks and who acts? Secondly, what is given in thought, and what is given in action?

An answer to the first question has been suggested above. The who of thinking is the subject. The who of action is the person. The relation between thought and action may thereby be illuminated through the question: how are the subject and the person related to each other?

With regard to thought, it is often rightly said that it is no private affair of an individual, but an objective process (thinking) or an objective product (thought). In thinking, I am no more this or that individual person but a universal subject, capable of stepping out of the privacy of my individuality and

[6] Martin Heidegger, *Was heisst Denken?*, Max Niemeyer, Tübingen, 1954, p. 51.

participating in what is common to all. Hence the essential communicability of thought, as contrasted with the utter privacy of sensations, feelings, etc. The who of thinking is therefore not this or that individual, but a subject that is universal.

Whereas it is the universal subject who thinks, it is the individual person who acts. It is not only the who of action that is individual, but all action takes place within a determinate situation. The person in fact is not a thing or substance who acts but could have ceased from acting. On the contrary, the person is essentially constituted by his actions; he is what Max Scheler named an 'act-centre'. Every action affects or modifies the personality of the person, though not all in the same degree. And, conversely, no action is intelligible without reference to the individual person who acts and the determinate situation within which the action takes place. Further, an action requires not merely the doer and the situation but also other persons.

4.2. In thus drawing the distinction we are no doubt describing ideal limiting cases, whereas in fact we have to accept compromise. That is to say, the who of thinking, the subject, does not always attain to complete universality. In such cases, one thinks no doubt, but thinking is motivated, as one says. Action determines thinking. The person pretends to think. The ideal of thought however is to eliminate the person, so that the subject is reduced to a pure zero, a passive witness, '*Zuschauer*'.

To describe limiting cases is however no fault, for it is only through this that one can raise essential distinctions into clear relief. Factual interweaving need not prejudice us against essential distinctions.

4.3. Whereas thought may in fact be practically motivated but is essentially (or, ideally aims at being) universal, action is in fact individual but may ideally aim at universality (as in moral action).

The universality which is thought's and the universality which action may aim at are radically distinct from each other. The subject who thinks is universal inasmuch as it is zero, empty of contents, a bare witness. The person who acts aims at universality by enriching himself in content, by stripping off elements that jar, by attaining to inner self-consistency as well as outer harmony (with other persons etc.).

5. The second of the two questions suggested above is: what is given in thought, and what is given in action? The entire idea of givenness may be challenged in the present context. It may be said that nothing is given in thought, for thought only constructs. Similarly, it may be argued that nothing is given in action; that action only brings about some change, modifies the state of things. As against such contentions we shall here insist on the possibility of considering both thought and action as two different modes of disclosure. Both are modes of givenness in spite of the great diversity subsisting between them.

5.1. That thought is a mode of givenness has been denied by those who insist on the constructive and interpretative function of thinking. What is given is the particular, the sense-impression; thought imposes its conceptual scheme on the impressions, interprets them, and welds them into judgments. This is the view of thinking in vogue since Kant. It makes thought subjective; what is universal and necessary in our thinking is explained as universal form, subjective though. The *a priori* is held to be both subjective and formal, any objective and material *a priori* being ruled out *ab initio*. Thought becomes wholly discursive, an endless process of mediation. Within the limits of sense-experience it yields constructed appearance; outside of this limit it creates illusions; nowhere does it have the capacity of giving reality.

As against this we advocate here a theory that claims affiliation to the classical Platonic-Aristotelian theory of thinking. Thought on this theory gives Ideas, Concepts, Eidos, Essences. Thought does not construct them, but recognises them. Thought gains thereby an ontological significance. It reveals the ideal factors and structures inherent in real events and processes. Thought discloses Being as Essence.

5.2. That however action could be considered as a mode of disclosure is less often recognised. It is one of the services of

Martin Heidegger to have insisted on this aspect of action.[7] Both Max Scheler and Nicolai Hartmann have also recognised some sort of cognitive value of actions.

Max Scheler[8] brings this out in the following way: Thought gives the essential 'what'; sense-perception gives the accidental (the here-now) 'what'; action gives the real 'that'. It is through action and the accompanying feelings of concern and care that we get involved in real situation; in trying to modify this real situation we experience resistance and obstruction; in trying to overcome such resistance and obstruction we are presented with real existence. Thought cannot reach this existence; its intuitions are confined to the sphere of ideality. Nor does sense-perception originally give real existence; it presents only the accidental qualities.

Thought can dissociate itself from real existence. Sense-perception can be studied in its essence through phantasies and imagination (Husserl). But action is so tied to the real situation that to study it in isolation is to miss it altogether.

5.3. We have referred in 2.1 to various kinds of actions. It may be pointed out that each of these kinds of actions has an essential reference to real existence and presents real existence in some aspect or other. The real world is not exhausted by things like tables, chairs, houses and trees, but consists of such diverse entities as the human person, societies of persons etc.... Action brings us face to face with their existence; we can contemplate only their essences dissociated from their existence.

6. We have tried to bring out the essential distinction between thought and action in two ways: (a) The subject thinks, whereas the person acts. The former in its purity is universal, because it is empty of all contents, a passive witness; the latter is an individual that aims at universality by enriching and harmonising its own individuality. (b) Thought gives essences, Ideas, Eidos, the ideal structures inhering in the constitution of the real; thinking is free when such idealities are inspected in themselves,

---

[7] John Wild, *The Challenge of Existentialism*, University of Indiana Press, 1955, p. 98.

[8] Max Scheler, *Die Stellung des Menschen im Kosmos*, München, 1947, p. 11.

bound when they are sought to be discovered within reality. In the latter case, action helps thinking. Action, on the other hand, discloses real existence in all its diversity.

That thought and action, essentially distinct though, are yet factually interwoven may be explained by two reasons amongst others: first, the subject and the person, and secondly, essences and reality, are factually interwoven. The problem of the relation between thought and action may therefore be pushed back to two more original problems: the problems of the relations betwen the subject and the person, and between the essences and reality.[9] We need not carry out this immense task in this paper. It is enough if a line of approach to the topic of our symposium has been suggested.

7. Another line of approach which again could not be worked out here is a study of the time-structures of the two, thought and action. Thought, it could be shown, is backward-looking. Although the essences that are given in thought are timeless, nevertheless thought discloses them only in what has been, in what is past. It is significant that the German word *"Wesen"* (=essence) is connected with the past perfect of *"sein"* (=to be), i.e. *"gewesen"*. Hegel makes this clearer when he defines "essence" as *"das vergangene, aber zeitlos vergangene Sein"*.[10] The timeless essence is recognised, recollected (Plato's amnesia). Action on the other hand, it could be argued, is anticipatory; it is forward-looking. It plans and calculates. It seeks to get out of the present, to build the future. The pragmatists read into thought what holds good of action. This they do when they take our ideas as tools, as plans of action, as programmatic and methodical in significance. Here Hegel is right, and the pragmatists wrong.

[9] The former is ably dealt with in Nicolai Hartmann's *Das Problem des geistigen Seins*, Berlin and Leipzig, 1933; the latter is discussed in ample detail in the present author's *Nicolai Hartmann and A. N. Whitehead: A Study in Recent Platonism*, Calcutta, Progressive Publishers, 1957.

[10] Hegel, *Die Wissenschaft der Logik*, Phil. Bibliothek edn., 1951, Vol. II, p. 3.

CHAPTER IV

MEANING AND TRUTH–I*

1. I have chosen as the theme of my address two questions which to my mind owe their importance in philosophy to the fact that they place us exactly on the borderline between philosophy of language, theory of knowledge and ontology. These two questions roughly formulated are: what is the nature of the meaning of expressions? How is the notion of meaning related to that of truth? The precise implications of these two questions however could emerge only as we proceed with our discussions.

I am aware that in so formulating the two questions, especially the first of them, I am running counter to the prevalent philosophical orthodoxy. One of my main purposes shall be to insist, as against this orthodoxy, that there are genuine philosophical problems about the nature of meaning and about the nature of truth. The problem of meaning has been sought to be dissolved by reducing that notion either to that of synonymity (Quine), or to that of truth-conditions (Carnap) or to that of use (Wittgenstein). Likewise, the philosophical problem of truth has been regarded as superfluous on the supposed ground that 'is true' is no genuine predicate at all (Ramsey and Ayer)[1]. Postponing my defense of the notion of meaning for the present, I would like to examine very briefly the attempt to eliminate the problem of truth.

1.1. It has been argued that since " 'S is p' is true" is equivalent to 'S is p', the predicate 'is true' is superfluous and has at best – as Geach says[2] – the function of cancelling the quotes. (It

---

* Presidential Address, Logic and Metaphysics Section, 36th session of the Indian Philosophical Congress, Santiniketan, 1961 [Proceedings, pp. 27–47.]

[1] A. J. Ayer, "The Criterion of Truth" in Macdonald (ed.), *Philosophy and Analysis*.

[2] P. T. Geach, *Mental Acts*, London, Routledge & Kegan Paul, p. 96.

is at once obvious that this argument closely resembles Russell's elimination of the philosophical problem of existence). As against this one may argue that though the above equivalence holds good, it does not follow that the predicate 'is true' is redundant. The redundancy is wrongly supposed to follow from the equivalence partly owing to the failure to distinguish between the different senses in which the connective 'is' is used in the type-sentence 'S is p' as it occurs on the left-hand side of the equivalence and as it occurs on the right-hand side. As a consequence, it has been wrongly supposed that the 'S is p' remains unaffected by the addition of the predicate 'is true' and that it re-appears on right-hand side unaffected, though only without the quotes. The error in the argument however would immediately be clear if we bear in mind that the 'is' in 'S is p' is not quite the same on both the sides of the equivalence. On the left hand side expression the 'is' is a predicative 'is', whereas on the right hand side expression it is an existential 'is', so that what the equivalence really amounts to is this: saying that the predicative assertion 'S is p' is true is the same as saying that S is in fact p. In that case, the predicate 'is true' far from being redundant fulfils the function of transforming the predicative 'is' into an existential 'is'. Hence the problem of truth is genuine, at least in the sense that it survives the above discussed attempt at its elimination, though as we shall show later on, there is another important sense in which the problem may be replaced by the problem of falsity.

2. Now since one of the questions that I have placed before me concerns the relation between the concept of meaning and that of truth, I should right at this stage begin by clearly separating the two concepts from each other, and in so doing I shall of course be rejecting two diametrically opposed ways of obliterating that distinction. I find no better instance of the tendency to reduce the notion of truth to that of meaning than the following passage from Harold H. Joachim's *The Nature of Truth* (Oxford, 2nd, edn., 1939). "Anything is true", writes Joachim[3], "which can be conceived... Conceivability is the essential nature of truth." Explaining what is meant by conceivability, Joachim goes on to say: "And to be 'conceivable' means to be a 'significant whole',

[3] H. M. Joachim, *The Nature of Truth*, Oxford, 2nd edn., 1939, p. 66.

or a whole possessed of meaning for thought." And with this the reducing of the concept of truth to that of meaning is complete. At the other extreme, we have the more recent attempt to reduce the concept of meaning to that of truth-conditions, which if successful, would go a long way towards eliminating the philosophical problem of meaning. We find a clear enunciation of this principle in Carnap's *Introduction to Symbolic Logic* where we are told that "a knowledge of the truth-conditions of a sentence is identical with an understanding of its meaning".[4] By the truth-conditions of a sentence are meant the circumstances under which a sentence can be used to make a true statement.

Joachim's theory may safely be set aside on the ground that the false is as much conceivable as the true, and if the theory may still seek to maintain itself it must be by giving to the notions of meaning and truth connotations far beyond what their ordinary uses imply. The other reduction, namely the reduction of meaning to truth-conditions is nearer the mark, for it rightly sees the close relation that subsists between the two concepts but errs if it aims at cleanly identifying them.

There are at least two forms of this theory differing in the degree of intimacy that is sought to be established between the two notions. There is on the one hand the Russell-Wittgenstein form of the theory which, rejecting the Fregean distinction between sense and reference, identifies 'having a sense' with 'being true-or-false'. Then there is the Frege-Strawson form of the theory which seeks to retain the distinction between sense and reference, and therefore between meaning and truth, but has curiously enough ended up with the same, though rather diffident, identification of the meaning of a sentence with the circumstances in which the sentence could be used to make a statement.[5]

The following remarks should, I believe, be sufficient to bring out the weakness of this theory in either of its forms: in the first place, expressions that are not sentences are also meaningful and the theory that identifies meaning with truth-conditions evidently does not apply to such expressions. Nor does the theory

---

[4] R. Carnap, *Introduction to Symbolic Logic*, New York, 1958, p. 15.
[5] G. E. M. Anscombe, *An Introduction to Wittgenstein's Tractatus*, London, Hutchinson, 1959, pp. 59-60.

apply to sentences other than the indicative ones. Further, even with regard to the indicative sentences the theory does not apply to sentences other than those that are effectively decidable either as true or false.[6] And finally even with regard to effectively decidable indicative sentences a distinction has to be drawn between meaning and truth-conditions, for in order to be able to decide what the truth-conditions of a given sentence are one must first be able to understand what the sentence means.[7] It must however be said in all fairness to the theory that it does not exactly identify 'having a meaning' with 'being true-or-false', and the notion of 'true-or-false' with the alternation involved in it clearly points to the fact that the notion of meaning is logically prior to that of truth-value or even to that of truth-condition. Phenomenologically speaking, the best evidence for this independence is provided by the fact that one might very well install oneself in the attitude of mere understanding without entertaining the question of truth or falsehood.

There is still another consideration which ought conclusively to prove that the two notions have to be kept separate. We may ask: of what is meaningfulness predicated, and of what is truth or falsity predicated? Of course, it is a linguistic expression, a word, or a sentence, of which alone we could say that it is either meaningful or meaningless. Those who wish to identify meaning with truth-condition also maintain – as a necessary corollary of their contention – that truth or falsity are semantical and metalinguistic predicates of sentences in the object-language. But I wish to maintain as against this that truth and falsity are not predicates of sentences: so far I agree with Strawson,[8] though I would differ from him in holding that they are descriptive predicates. But predicates of what? Once we reject the claim of sentences, there are only two other claimants left: the propositions expressed by the sentences, or the knowledge or *jñānas* as understood in Indian philosophy. Propositions as subsistent entities – what else are they if we at all admit them as distinguished from linguistic expressions on the one hand and the men-

---

[6] Cp. M. Dummet, "Truth" in *Proceedings Aristotelian Society*, 1958–9, pp. 141–162.

[7] W. H. Werkmeister, *The Basis and Structure of Knowledge*, p. 44; Dummet, *loc. cit.*, pp. 148–9.

[8] P. F. Strawson, "Truth" in Macdonald, *loc. cit.*, especially pp. 262–3.

tal acts or attitudes on the other? – are not the sort of things
that could be said to be true or false. Consequently, we are left
with the knowledges and these alone are the proper subjects for
the predication of truth or falsity. We have thereby no doubt
left the conception of knowledge or *jñāna* vague, but our own
immediate purpose in hand would have been served if we can
emphasise that truth or falsity on the one hand and meaningfulness on the other are predicated of quite different sorts of
things – which corroborates our conclusion that the two notions
are really distinct.

3. Before I come to deal with the notion of meaning in particular, a few words on the philosophical method adopted here
would not be out of place. For in matters like those with which
we are at present concerned it is most necessary to start with a
correct perspective in one's mind. This is particularly so with regard
to the concept of meaning. Using Carnap's well-known distinction, we can say that both the material mode of speech and the
formal mode of speech are one-sided extremes. Dogmatic ontology
is as much naive as the modern decision in favour of the formal
mode of speech is. And it must be remembered that the distrust of dogmatic ontology is nothing new: it is in fact as old as
Kant (whose entire philosophy in the First Critique may be
regarded, as Pichler and, following Pichler, Wein have shown, as
an attempt to translate the categories of the old dogmatic ontology into the language of transcendental idealism).[9] Only
whereas Kant sought to transform ontology into transcendental
logic, the moderns have tried to transform it into the formal
mode of speech. As a corrective against the naivety of the material mode of speech, all this is indeed valuable. But if made
into an absolute philosophical method the resulting 'linguacentric predicament' becomes, if less naive, certainly more arbitrary. Faced with such a situation, it seems to me that we are
in need of a perspective – should I say, a mode of speech? –
which would be able to integrate the two opposed and naive

---

[9] H. Pichler, *Ueber Christian Wolffs Ontologie*, Leipzig, 1910; H. Wein, *Zugang
zur philosophischen Kosmologie*, München, 1954. For an account of these see Mohanty,
"The Principles of Modern Kant-Interpretation in Germany" in *Krishna Chandra
Bhattacharyya Memorial Volume*, Indian Institute of Philosophy, Amalner, pp. 104–
119.

extremes, and do so not in the sense of combining them into a unity but in the sense of providing the basis on which both could stand. Such a mode I find in the phenomenological mode which corrects the naivety of the ontological assertion and provides a check to the arbitrariness of linguistic decision, i.e. to the conventionalism inseparable from the formal mode of speech. By the phenomenological mode I mean the appeal to the mode of givenness instead of to the mode of existence or the linguistic usage. I believe that all these three may be regarded as three different approaches to any philosophical problem, but I also believe that of these three the phenomenological one possesses an epistemic priority. The three in their unity constitute the philosophical method.

3.1. Let us see in brief if the above methodological remarks prove fruitful in some other fields before we could confidently carry them over to the problems of meaning and truth. It is well known that many recent thinkers have in their attempts to avoid the ontology either of physical objects or of sense-data come to re-interpret the two traditional theories of perception, the physical object theory and the sense-datum theory, as but two alternate linguistic devices each of which could profitably be adopted, the decision being a matter of convenience and other extra-theoretical considerations. Now, that an ontological theory has a linguistic correlate is an important finding. But to leave the matter at that and to rest content with an ultimate alternation seems to be an escape rather than a solution of the problem of perception. Under such circumstances, the phenomenological method may provide us with the clue: it can help us to reconcile the two theories by exhibiting them not as two alternatives between which one is free to choose but as representing two different but successive modes of givenness, the physical object being given in the primary, unreflective and practical mode, the sense data on the other hand being given in subsequent, reflective and contemplative mode. Detailed explication of these two modes could rehabilitate the two theories to their respective rightful places by freeing them from the arbitrariness of linguistic conventionalism. A similar way out may be suggested from the traditional impasse between nominalism and realism and the modern alternation between the two corresponding languages. In other words, it can be shown that particulars and universals are given in two different modes: the former in sense-perception which is primarily action-oriented in character, the latter in thought. Since it is not part of our present purpose to explore these problems, it is enough to have hinted at the relevance of our methodological remarks, and we may now pass on to a consideration of the question of meaning.

II

4. In no other area of philosophical thinking is the modern philosopher more suspicious of the temptation to ontologise than in discussions about meaning. The main issue here may be formulated as one between Platonism and Anti-Platonism and our need is to find a stable *via media*. Certain forms of Anti-Platonism may safely be regarded as dead. I have especially the so-called image theory in my mind, and Wittgenstein's tirades against it in the *Philosophical Investigations*, just as they are, seem however like flogging a dead horse. Amongst the Anti-Platonist theories, I would consider only three varieties: the theory of meaning as a dispositional property of signs (C. L. Stevenson), Operationalism (the latter Wittgensteinian school); and the meta-linguistic relativism (B. L. Whorf and Hans Lipps).

C. L. Stevenson in his *Ethics and Language* (1944) attempts to avoid the unstability of psychologism without at the same time taking meanings as any sort of entities. Stevenson rightly sees that the problem is to find the constant meaning amidst psychological flux. Psychological reactions to an expression (as to, say, coffee) fluctuate. But one speaks of a disposition or power that is relatively stable. In order to get at the relative identity of meaning, Stevenson undertakes an analysis of the concept of disposition or power. This does not mean that disposition or power is some kind of entity that exists over and above its tangible manifestations. Neither is the disposition the cause of the psychological responses (that would be like saying man's rational faculty is the cause of his reasoning activities). Avoiding such erroneous solutions, Stevenson attempts a definition of disposition in use. This involves detailed complications which we need not examine for our present purpose. Granted that such a definition is possible it becomes relatively easy to say what meaning is. Meaning in that case becomes a dispositional property of the sign. This dispositional property is relatively stable, while the actual psychological effects vary.

The hypothesis of potency, power or *śakti* – whether in the metaphysical or in the positivistic sense – is properly called for to explain only the relation between a word and its meaning. This is how the Mimāmsakas and the Naiyāyikas introduce the notion of *śakti*. But to reduce meaning itself to this potency is not phenomenologically justifiable. Potency or power, on any interpretation of those words, is not felt as being given. It is either inferred as a metaphysical entity or, as with Stevenson, only defined in use. In the latter sense, it may be said to be a logical construction in Russell's sense, but in any case it is not what is felt to be given as such in experience of understanding an expression. Meaning however is felt to be given. What is felt to be given cannot be reduced to what is only either inferred or constructed.

4.2. B. L. Whorf's paper on "Language, Mind and Reality" draws our attention to the supposed fact that the fixation of objective meanings is a process that falsifies the original nature of language. According to Whorf, language has two aspects: the 'patternment-aspect' and the name-giving aspect. In the latter aspect, language gives names to parts of a whole, isolates them and fixes them as self-subsisting entities. In the former aspect, language is not concerned with 'names' and 'forms', but with pure patternments. The reference of words that dominates language in its name-giving aspect is at a minimum in its higher, the patternment aspect. In this higher aspect language is algebraic in nature, the symbols are variables. This algebraic nature persists even in the usual lexical language where "sentences, not words are the essences of speech just as equations and functions, not bare numbers are the real meat of mathematics." [11]

From this follows that word-meanings are not self-subsisting but are isolated artificially from the living patternment-aspect.

[10] Included in B. L. Whorf, *Language, Thought and Reality*, New York, 1956.
[11] Whorf, *loc. cit.*

The identity of meanings is an illusion fostered by the lower mind, the name-giving aspect.

From an allied but different point of view Hans Lipps in his *Untersuchungen zu einer Hermeneutischen Logik* (Frankfurt am Main, 1938) offers a forceful statement of the view that there are no identical word meanings, that the so-called invariable objective meanings are only abstractions cut off from the living linguistic meaning which is determined in each case by the actual conversation and the action and reaction between the speaker and the hearer. That is the living context from which a word could only be artificially cut off. Apart from such artificial separation there are no identical meanings.

In the above arguments there are several points that need be considered separately. In the first place there is the fact that most words change their meanings under circumstances. Besides there are essentially ambiguous expressions including the so-called 'indexical expressions' (C. S. Peirce). Secondly, language consists in actual speaking and hearing and meanings arise only in this context of speaker-hearer relationship. Thirdly, the inner reality of language consists, as Whorf puts it, in a 'pure patternment' and certainly not in that name-giving aspect which comes to the forefront due to the limitations of what he calls the lower mind.

In reply we may point out the following: the supposed ambiguity and fluctuations in meaning may be shown to be rather due to the imperfections of our system of symbols than to the non-availability of identical meaning-contents. For, though an apparently identical expression may convey different meanings in different contexts it is theoretically possible to take hold of each such meaning in each case and tie it to a fixed expression. The fluctuations will then be seen not as fluctuations of meanings themselves but of the use of an apparently identical expression.

Without entering into the distinction between lower mind and the higher mind, we might admit that in its purely formal aspect language does exhibit a "patternment" aspect and that from this standpoint the purely material meaning-contents are of no relevance. But we are presently concerned exactly with these meaning-contents on whose nature the patternment aspect throws but little light. The second of the above facts places before a

Platonic theory of meaning an almost insurmountable difficulty. The living context of conversation or speech may be viewed either from the side of the hearer or from the side of the speaker. Much discussion in Indian philosophy in the context of the *śabda pramāna* takes the standpoint of the hearer. But it may argued that the speaker's standpoint is more fundamental. The expression as spoken may be regarded as the basic phenomenon, so that the expression as heard my be reduced to the former. The hearer understands it as if he were speaking it. The speaker may hear his own expression, but that is a subsidiary phenomenon. If that be so, the apparent relativity implied in the speaker-hearer relationship may be dispensed with. Spoken meaning or, more correctly, meaning belonging to an expression as spoken may be, since it is the basic phenomenon, isolated from the act of speaking as its intended correlate. Such contents then may be regarded as identical entities.

4.3. Another way of retaining the objectivity of meanings without getting involved in Platonism of any kind is that of the later Wittgenstein and the Operationalists according to whom the meaning of an expression is the same as the rules governing its use in a language. We know the meaning of this theory if we know these rules, convention etc., or if we know how to use the expression. This view has the merit that it can explain the objectivity of meanings, for the rules and conventions are objective features of the particular language game under consideration.

But what happens when we grasp the meaning of a word or of a sentence in a flash as it were? Surely it is not the use that we so grasp. Nor is it a set of rules and conventions. Wittgenstein rightly emphasises that what is present before the mind is not a mental picture, for a picture does not force upon us any particular application of the expression under consideration. And yet there is something in the expression *qua* expression and something which the mind grasps that makes possible an understanding of it prior to all applicaion, that in fact in a way predetermines which applications of it are right and which not. Right application may be a criterion of understanding. But should we say in face of the above difficulties that though understanding does not amount to actual application it however does amount to applicability? The switch- over from actual application to applicability is similar to the switch- over from actual verification to verifiability. What these two cases teach us is that a recourse to the language of possibility is indeed inevitable. But the positivists are not able to give a satisfactory account of the possibility and the disposition-words; in doing this they must inevitably come back to actual application (or, verification) thereby completing the circle. It is therefore time that the now fashionable opinion that 'know' and 'understand' are capacity-words should come to be suspected and should be made to suffer the same fate as the one- time fashionable opinion that categorical material object statements are reducible to hypothetical sense datum statements. We have to face the grim reality that though there is an important sense in which they are dispositional, yet the really fundamental sense of these words is episodic. In the case of understanding or meaningfully using an expression this must be an intellectual awareness or an intention whose intended correlate is what we might call meaning in the substantive. Wittgenstein says that an intention "is imbedded in its situation, in human customs and institutions".[12] If there were no rules of playing chess, Wittgenstein argues, I could not even intend to play the game of chess. Wittgenstein's arguments prove only this much – and this can hardly be denied – that certain objective circumstances must be given in order that I could even intend in a certain way. The fact that a conventional system of signs with rules of operation must be given in order that I could even intend constructing a sentence does not decide the issue under consideration. This is not a sufficient reason for holding that the linguistic expression is nothing more than a merely physical sign or that our understanding of it is nothing other than the capacity to operate with it in accordance with custom-bred conventions. Our convention would be that given such a set of signs and rules of operation developed through custom, such a set would not amount to language – nor would the operation amount to an understanding – unless the said intellectual act supervened.

5. W. V. O. Quine has in recent times made the most notable

12 L. Wittgenstein, *Philosophical Investigations*, Oxford, 1954, p. 108e.

attempt in the direction of avoiding Platonism in theory of meaning. With regard to Platonism in general he has, as is well known, suggested that class-names or functions should be prohibited from appearing within the quantifier. Such quantification should be disallowed, for it would amount to an ontological commitment regarding the 'existence' of abstract entities. This particular device meant to limit the 'ontological commitment' of a particular logic need not interest us at present. What we are rather interested in is his suggestion that the problem of meaning, as distinguished from the problem of reference, should be concerned only with one question, namely the question of synonymity. In Quine's opinion, "a felt need for meant entities may derive from an earlier failure to appreciate that meaning and reference are distinct." The hypostatisation of meanings is based on the confusion between meaning and reference. If the distinction between meaning and reference be borne in mind, the question "What sort of entities are meanings?" becomes senseless. Search for entities would then come under theory of reference, while theory of meaning would be left only with one question, how and under what conditions is synonymity possible? There would of course remain the allied notion of analyticity. Platonism would then be entirely ruled out of theory of meaning.

I must confess I do not share the happy optimism of Quine. His diagnosis is not beyond doubt. For both Frege and Husserl have been charged of Platonism even though both of them draw the distinction between sense and reference. The truth seems to be the reverse. The distinction between sense and reference is just what the Platonist can most rely upon. By excluding from consideration the objects referred to, attention may be fixed on meaning as such and now that the meaning cannot be identified with the objects referred to it has to be accorded a distinct ontological status. The problem of synonymity is only another aspect of the problem of identity of meanings. The question which is an empirical one enquires into the criteria by which we could regard two expressions as having the same meaning; but the whole discussion, so much fashionable now, presupposes that the two expressions under consideration have an identical meaning.

6. Our examination of the various anti-Platonistic theories has led us to the conclusion that Platonism in theory of meaning is founded on an incontrovertible phenomenological basis, that there is an important sense in which meanings retain an identity amidst fluctuations of situational and conventional contexts and an objectivity in the midst of varying subjective intentions and responses. This lends to the Platonistic hypostatisation of meanings its point of advantage over against all forms of psychologism and all forms of conventional and operational relativism. But we can accept such a Platonism only as subject to certain provisions which may now be stated as follows:

6.1. In the first place though meanings by virtue of their identity in discourse and their objectivity could be called universals, yet not all meanings are universals. This is especially so in the case of the meanings of the so-called ego-centric particulars like 'I' and 'This'. These expressions make possible reference to unique particulars, and there is something about their sense that refuses to be idealised.

6.2. It has often been pointed out that Platonism in theory of meaning involves the thesis that in understanding an expression, we inspect impalpable meanings. This however is not true. It should be remembered that we have to examine cases of purely symbolic thinking and understanding, not amounting to knowledge. Thinking or understanding as constituent of a knowledge is of course not directed towards the meanings themselves unless in a subsequent act of reflection. But the same holds good also of purely symbolic thinking and understanding. Expressions have not only meaning but also reference, and the intended reference characterises even those cases where the psychological intention to refer has patently been excluded. The function of the meanings is to make reference possible and also to give the reference its determinate character, while they themselves are not the sort of things that could be inspected in themselves: this may be expressed metaphorically by saying that there is a transparency about them so that they serve as the media for reference. Or, if you like, the meanings are at the same time and in the same act given only in the sense of being intended.

But then it could indeed be shown that there is no other gene-ralised sense of being given other than being intended.

To the above it might be objected, following Strawson, that reference is not a function of expressions *qua* expressions, that expressions as such have only meaning and that it is only a ge-nuine use of them that refers. If in the case of a merely symbolic thinking I am not genuinely using an expression, i.e. if I am not using it to make a statement, I am not referring at all, in which case I could then be concerned with meanings not as transparent media for reference but as opaque entities for inspection. But such a theory of reference is not tenable, for Strawson's theory involves as I have shown elsewhere a hopeless circularity.[13] This circularity shows that reference like meaning has to be ascribed to expressions *qua* expressions. This however need not lead us to the acceptance either of the Meinongian ghosts or of Russell's dissection of them. Let us for the moment suppress our interest in ontology. In that case we shall see that every use of expressions refers, though in some cases, owing to reasons which may be either *a priori* or empirical, the reference may remain a merely intended reference, incapable of being fulfilled. Now in the case of merely symbolic thinking or understanding, I may have absolutely no interest in the fulfilment of the intention: my interest may be merely to grasp the intended reference through the intended meaning.

6.3. As has been emphasised in paragraph 3, the objectivity and the ideality of meanings has to be understood against the light of both a linguistic convention and a subjective intention. A linguistic convention, as Wittgenstein rightly saw, is a neces-sary condition of there being a meaning-intention at all, which however by no means implies that the meaning so intended is produced by the convention. A more intimate relation however subsists between the ontological and the phenomenological mo-des, between the objective meaning and the subjective intention. In fact, the "I mean" and the "It means" are correlative aspects and complementary descriptions of the same unitary phenome-non. The former frees the latter from the charge of hypostatisation,

---

[13] J. N. Mohanty, *Edmund Husserl's Theory of Meaning*, The Hague, 1964, pp. 21–23.

while the latter rescues the former from the charge of relativism. To reduce the one to the other for the sake of metaphysical simplicity would amount to a distortion of the phenomenon.

6.4. But there would still arise no doubt the transcendental question: what is the *a priori* condition of the possibility of intending universal and objective meanings? How is it that meanings though they arise out of subjective intentions yet emerge as objective, overindividual, impersonal entities? This transcendental question is parallel in its structure to Kant's problem in his transcendental deduction of the categories. Kant asked, how are the categories though subjective in origin yet objectively valid? He was concerned with the question of synthetic *a priori* truth. Our transcendental question is logically prior and concerns the possibility of universal, objective and impersonal meanings. However, into the solution of this important question we cannot enter here.

III

7. It is now left for us to connect the two notions of meaning and truth. The proper line in which the connection has to be sought has already been indicated in our discussions. It is only in the case of indicative and effectively decidable statements that the question of truth and falsity arises, and it is only in these cases that the relation has to be investigated. But again as we have already said truth and falsity primarily characterise not sentences, not propositions, but strictly speaking knowledges. We call a sentence or a proposition or a statement true only in so far as it is regarded as a constituent of a knowledge of some person or other.

7.1. Modern philosophers are as much suspicious of the word 'knowledge' in the entitative sense or of the verb 'knowing' in the episodic sense as of anything else. But they have only succeeded in analysing it into dispositional language whose interpretation is no easier than that of names of psychic entities or episodes. Indian philosophy also recognises a dispositional sense of the word 'knowledge', and in this sense 'to know' of course means to have the right *samskāra* about a matter. But there is an important sense in which 'to know' describes something that has happened, an occurrence. Perhaps, saying that it is an achievement-verb is nearer the mark. As a more concrete account we uphold the conception of *jñāna* as an occurrent which is propositional in nature, and from which the corresponding proposition is an abstraction.[14] Hence when a statement is said to be true it is so only as an abstraction from a knowledge. But when it is found to be false its claim to be knowledge is rejected: it remains however a statement though still more than a mere sentence. Though more than a mere sentence it is still a sentence and is so far meaningful apart from being referential. Meaning is a presupposition of knowledge for it is only through meaning that reference is possible and in knowledge the referential aspect predominates.

Thus one could say that in any concrete case of knowledge there are three strata, one built as it were upon the other. There is, as logically the most primitive, the sentence as a meaningful expression and with a merely intended reference. Built upon it as the basis we have the statement which *qua* statement might express mere belief, i.e. may be true or false. The final stratum is the knowledge itself as whose vehicle the statement is true and not false, though the knowledge itself is definable only in terms of truth: the very possibility of its being excluded by its very definition.

Our above analysis accords its rightful place to each of the two principal theories of truth in Indian philosophy, the theories of *svataḥprāmāṇya* and *parataḥprāmāṇya*. The former is right in so far as truth is an intrinsic property of knowledge i.e. in so far as they are definable in terms of each other. The latter is right in so far as truth is an extrinsic property of mere statements, i.e. in so far as the latter may be true or false.

This also shows an element of truth in the contemporary denial of the philosophical problem of truth. For truth being a definitional property of knowledge, the problem of truth is the same as

---

[14] For further discussion on this, J. N. Mohanty, *Gangeśa's Theory of Truth*, Santiniketan, 1966.

the problem of knowledge, and in this sense no criterion of truth is called for, though a criterion of falsity is necessary. But with regard to a mere statement the problem is a genuine one of deciding whether it is true or false.

8. The noematic contrast between meaning and truth roughly corresponds to the noetic distinction between understanding and knowing. Understanding a sentence of course as such amounts to knowing its meaning, but we would however prefer to call this sort of knowing 'understanding', for meanings are, as said before, merely the transparent media for reference. In this sense then to understand a sentence 'S is p' is also to understand what kind of facts it refers to, but this does not as such amount to knowing that S is p, i.e. to knowing the fact it is used to refer to. But knowing that S is p presupposes an understanding of the sentence 'S is p'. Understanding the expression which states the fact is presupposed by knowing the fact so stated. Knowing implies a contact – speaking of contact metaphorically though – with the fact referred to by the expression, or in Husserl's language a fulfilment of the intention imbedded in the expression. This is not to say anything regarding the nature of the 'fulfilling' experience. There is in other words a fundamental difference between the way expressions refer and the way knowledge refers. The reference of an expression is a presupposition of the reference of the knowledge which has that expression for its vehicle but which nevertheless exhibits entirely new phenomenological features.

8.1. There are two extreme cases where this fundamental distinction appears to be blurred. In the first place, there are proper names – perhaps Russell's 'logically proper names', the 'this' and the 'I' – in whose case understanding amounts to knowing. There are, on the other, abstract sciences like mathematics and logic in whose case again understanding seems to be the same as knowing. In both cases, the distinction between meaning and reference seems to get blurred: in the former the meaning is assimilated into reference, in the latter the reference into the meaning. But closer examination would reveal that even in these cases understanding may not quite amount to knowing.

In the former case, the "this" has still a theoretical meaning which might be grasped without an identification of the unique reference involved. In the latter case, we might argue – following the intuitionists – that understanding the expression 'the first prime number between 2000 and 3000' need not imply a knowledge of that number: it can be said to amount to knowledge only when the number can be constructed in intuition. The only difference between the two cases seems to be that in the former the passage from understanding to knowing involves a transition from the theoretical attitude to the practical, whereas in the latter the passage is within theoretical consciousness. The really pertinent question therefore concerns the former, and in a way all concrete knowing. Since – as has been said by implication – the gulf between the two attitudes is bridged by intuition and since in all cases of concrete knowing the intuition would have to be such as to involve a unique reference, the question arises, how is such unique reference possible? This question must not be confused with the quite different question, how is extra-linguistic reference of language possible? to which E. W. Hall has devoted two excellent papers in *Mind*.[15] It seems to me however that extralinguistic reference of language is not a real problem, for such reference is an essential character of a language *qua* language. What however is a problem is, how it possible to make unique reference? It must be emphasised that within language purely unique reference is not possible, for even Russell's 'ego-centric particulars' or Hall's 'empirical ties' have an aspect of meaning distinguishable from that to which they may be used to refer uniquely. Unique reference presupposes a transcendence of the attitude of pure understanding. The unique individual must be known. And the knowledge of the unique individual is far from being a contemplative perception. It must be recognised as a radically different mode of knowing, intimately associated with and built upon interests, dispositions, evaluations and practical manipulations. For, the more contemplative a knowing is, the more it approximates towards the attitude of understanding. The more does it succeed in making unique reference possible through a practically oriented approach, the more does it be-

[15] E. W. Hall, "The Extra-linguistic Reference of Language" in *Mind*, 1943, pp. 230–46; 1944, pp. 25–47.

come concrete knowing. Scientific knowledge in its escape from unique reference seeks to transform itself into scientific understanding. It is not for nothing that perception of the physical object and recognition of the other persons, the Thou (but not merely the other mind), have frequently been regarded as the standard type of knowledge. And in both cases, the knower or the subject is not a passive onlooker but an active agent.[16]

8.2. Thus we are led to the conclusion that though, as maintained above, knowledge and truth are definable in terms of each other, yet the confirmation of a belief requires, in cases of relatively more concrete knowing, a pragmatic test whose function cannot be replaced by the merely theoretical consistency or coherence. The close interrelation of concrete knowing with the practical attitude more clearly reveals the gulf that divides it from the attitude of pure understanding.

8.3. Both understanding and knowing however are objective modes of consciousness in so far as both are consciousness of... Meaning as well as truth are, in Husserl's language, 'mundane' notions inasmuch as they presuppose the conception of a world of objects. That they do so is brought out by the fact that philosophizing about them inevitably exhibits an ontologising tendency. They are therefore to be distinguished from the idea of pure consciousness which is not a consciousness of ... , and which therefore represents the idea of the limiting point of our turning away from all ontology, empirical or *a priori*. The notion of such a pure consciousness is not only beyond ontology but also beyond phenomenology, for if phenomenology is concerned with modes of givenness one can always ask what is so given, from which it follows that phenomenology, though the more fundamental of the two, has a correlative ontology. But representing as it does the very negation of the ontological attitude, pure consciousness that is not a consciousness of... cannot be even a phenomenological notion and can at best be postulated only by an act of faith.

[16] For a similar viewpoint, see S. Hampshire, *Thought and Action*, London, Chatto &Windus, 1959, especially pp. 47-53.

For phenomenology, the intentional consciousness i.e. the consciousness of... is the ultimate notion. This intentionality of consciousness develops into two modes: the extra-linguistic reference of expressions through meanings, and the objective reference of knowledge, the former being the presupposition of the latter.

CHAPTER V

MEANING AND TRUTH-II*

The problem of meaning and truth is a vast and widely ramified one, and for our present purpose it is essential to make sure,
at the beginning, what exactly is the problem we would be
dealing with. The central problem, as I see it, is one of distinguishing between, and correlating, the concepts of meaning and
truth. In this context, many other questions otherwise interesting though especially the more familiar ones regarding the
criterion of meaningfulness and the criterion of truth become of
secondary significance. What I propose to do in this paper is to
ascertain, in the first place, the precise nature of these concepts;
then, to bring out certain essential differences between them;
and finally, to throw some light on the way they function together in the total structure of human knowledge. Any enter-
prise of this nature ought to set out, if it is not to be dogmatic, by
considering the many fundamental objections that modern philosophy and semantics have to offer. There is, for example, the
most fundamental objection that there are no philosophical problems of meaning and truth at all. This objection in its various
forms has been considered by me elsewhere,[1] so that I would
prefer not to return to it now. One has also to make initially
clear one's attitude to the linguistic philosophers, especially
to those who seek to replace the concept of meaning by the
concept of use, and those who make 'truth' a meta-linguistic
predicate of sentences in the object-language. On both these
contentions I shall have occasions in this paper to say a few

* Read at the first regional Seminar of the Centre of Advanced Study in Philosophy,
Visva-Bharati University, Santiniketan in April, 1964; and published in the *Visva-
Bharati Journal of Philosophy*, Vol. I, 1964, No. 1, 9–14.
[1] See Meaning and Truth-I of this book.

words. For the present I would rather begin by attempting precise formulations of the two key concepts of this paper.

I

It is of course obvious that "What does the word 'cat' mean?" is not a philosophical question. Nor is "What does the sentence 'The cat is on the mat' mean?" a philosophical question. One answers these questions if one knows the English language, and one expects no special philosophical ability for this purpose. What, then, is philosophical about the question "What is meaning?"? It has also to be admitted that there is no meaning as such and that meaning is always meaning of..., so that the philosophical question "What is meaning?" should really be "What is (the) meaning of ... ?". It is indeed difficult to see why "What is the meaning of 'cat'?" is not, but "What is the meaning of ... ?" is a philosophical question. Asking "What is the meaning of... ?" is, of course, asking the meaning of an expression. What, then, are we asking when we are asking philosophically the meaning of an expression? The peculiarity of the situation is that as soon as we specify the expression whose meaning we are asking for the question ceases to be philosophical. This consideration shows that the two questions – "What is the meaning of 'cat'?" and "What is the meaning of an expression?" – do not have the same logical nature. Nor can it be said that the former alone is a genuine question whereas the latter is a mere dummy question, in the same way as a mere proposition functional is not a proposition but only a dummy.

We may say that in asking "What is the meaning of an expression?" we are asking about what constitutes an expression qua expression. Understood in this sense, the question may be construed as being about the meaning of 'an expression qua expression'. We are indeed asking about the essential and constitutive functions of expressions. We are not expecting to be given a meaning in the same manner in which one gives the meaning of 'cat'.

The philosophical problem, therefore, is to find out the essential functions of expressions *qua* expressions and to enquire into the conditions of their possibility.

Expressions are, of course, used to refer, or to perform many other jobs, but they can be used because they are already at hand as expressions, i.e., as meaningful. Their meaningfulness is not an epiphenomenon of that use, but their usability rests on their meaningfulness. Use is no doubt intimately connected with the determinate job they perform in determinate situations. Use, and all its attendant pragmatic factors, for example, make possible the uniqueness of reference. An expression as such, quite apart from its use, remains at the level of generality. Even if it intends (or tends) to refer, such reference does not quite become fully determinate. What constitutes, then, the essence of expressions *qua* expressions is the generality of meaning.

It is sometimes said that an expression expresses its meaning, as if it were an expression prior to its expressing the meaning. This, however, is false. An expression is in inseparable unity with its meaning, so much so that in meaningful discourse they are not even distinguished. A word as a mere physical event (or object) is, of course, different from the meaning it is used to communicate. But an expression *qua* expression is not to be identified with that merely physical event (or object). The difference would be clear if only one contrasts the awareness of a word as a physical event and the apprehension (or use) of it meaningfully. In the latter attitude the outer sensory perception (that constitutes the former) still remains but it enters into an inalienable unity with an intellectual non-sensory act of a radically different kind. Such an inalienable unity is not merely associational. In a merely associational unity the associated elements are nevertheless distinguished. In the unity of a word with its meaning there is a non-apprehension of distinction or *bhedāgraha*.

Philosophers err here when they start with bare words considered as mere physical events (or objects) and seek to derive their subsequent meaningfulness as a function of their use according to rules. There is no doubt a sense in which words become meaningful through such a process. Use and association determine which symbols are to be tagged on to which meanings, but they neither manufacture the meanings themselves nor do they suffice for a post-mortem analysis of the sort of unity that comes to obtain in effect between the word and its meaning.

Regarding the constitution of expressions *qua* expressions, then, we find the following aspects which are welded as it were into an organic unity:

(a) From the linguistic point of view, an expression belongs to a language system, i.e., to a system of other expressions with which it is related by conventional rules governing their use, rules of formation and transformation. These rules determine the linguistic meaning of an expression, which is what we seem to be giving when we give its meaning in words.

(b) The linguistic meaning, however, is not meaning proper. The real contentual (*inhaltliche*) meaning which is prior to linguistic meaning and is the real determinant of linguistic synonymity is the general sense by virtue of which we succeed (i) in breaking through linguistic relativity as evidenced from success in translation from one language to another, and (ii) in transcending the linguacentric predicament by opening the door to the extra-linguistic world.

(c) It is this contentual meaning which makes reference possible and determines the mode of reference. Language provides us with demonstrative symbols and mechanisms like definite descriptions for the purpose. The referring function is essential to expressions, though (i) the intention to refer may not be fulfilled in experience, and (ii) the reference, in any case, must have to stop short of being unique unless pragmatic factors are taken into consideration.

(d) Subjectively, the apprehension, or understanding of expressions qua expressions amounts (i) in relation to (a) above, to the ability to use them in accordance with the rules of the language system concerned, and (ii), in relation to (b) above, to a grasping of the meaning.

Of these four, (c) is a derivative function of (b). Reference is made possible through meaning. (Even mere ostentation cannot refer, unless it is tagged on to a system of meaningful discourse.) In that case (a), (b) and (d) are the three main aspects of an expression qua expression. These are the linguistic, the contentual (or intensional), and the subjective aspects. It seems to me that three possibilities are open before us. We may start with making the first, i.e., the linguistic aspect basic and reduce the others to it. The success, however, of such a venture is likely to be deceptive, for the language (the word, the sentence, etc.) which it takes as basic is already charged with meaning and is not a mere physical event. We may likewise take the intension, the meaning, to be basic and reduce the others to it. Expressions become accidental vehicles of eternal meanings, and the subjective acts become the means of grasping them. The danger is that thereby we hypostatise meanings and cut off their moorings in language on the one hand, and in the subjective, on the other. Subjectivism is a third possibility – reducing meaning and language to their essential origin in the subjective acts of spontaneous, interpretative, creative thinking. Its risk lies in a possible blindness to the aspect of receptivity, i.e., to the objective restraint that is experienced in operating with a given linguistic system and in the apprehension of meanings. Thus, all the three systems would be one-sided and would err at some point. In order to grasp the essential structure of expressions qua expressions we have to fix our attention on the total nexus of phenomena in their inalienable unity. The three aspects supplement one another.

The doctrine of the ideality of meanings has to be understood in this enlarged perspective, if we are not to be guilty of hypostatisation. The ideality is not an original one. Meanings are not self-existent. They do not constitute an ontological region of their own. Their ideality is derivative. They presuppose both a linguistic system and the spontaneity of the subjective act of thinking. At the same time such is the very nature of human subjectivity that what it generates it also receives as passively pre-given. This gives rise to the transcendental question – how is it possible for a real personal subject to generate meanings that are ideal, impersonal and objective?

The ideality of meanings is purely phenomenological. Of them it holds good that they are as they are given. They are in that sense pure phenomena. They do not point to a noumenon whose phenomena they are. Understanding captures them – if it does this at all – in toto, not in aspects or perspectives. In this last respect they are like sense-data. But they are unlike sense-data in so far as the sense-data point to the perceptual object as their substratum which is presented through them. Meanings, no doubt, make reference to reality possible, but this reference is not to be construed as the reference of a phenomenon to its noumenon. The analogy, often stressed, between perceptual apprehension of sensible objects and intellectual apprehension of meanings breaks down here.

II

One way of determining the nature of the concept of truth is to ask: of what is 'true' predicated? This, as we know, is answered in many different ways. I would outright reject the suggestion that it is predicated of sentences: I think Strawson's arguments against this view are decisive. The other claimants for this position are: propositions (Russell), statements (Austin), beliefs or judgments, and knowledge.

We may be on the way towards a resolution of this controversy if we start by recognising that each of these is in fact called true. The next step would be to see that this fact that so many different things are called true is not an instance of the unreliability of ordinary language, but rather points to the many different dimensions – not unrelated to each other – of the concept of truth. It would be worthwhile, therefore, to distinguish between some of these dimensions (or usages, if you like), and to single out that one with which it would be fruitful to be concerned in the present context.

Beliefs or judgments are either affirmations or denials. By 'proposition' we mean the content of the belief, that which is affirmed or denied. The distinction may be brought out also with the help of the fact that an identically same proposition may be affirmed, denied, doubted, supposed, or even merely entertained. When one affirms or denies a proposition and expresses the affirmation or denial in a sentence, spoken or written, one is said to make a statement. Making a statement is a publicly observable event, but for that reason one should not count it as the only thing that is besides the sentence with which the statement is made. A statement expresses one's affirmation or denial. The latter are about a proposition. A proposition may also be said to be the contentual meaning of a sentence, that which in the last resort accounts for the synonymity of two or more sentences.

Keeping these distinctions in mind we may now proceed to exhibit the different levels at which the problem of truth makes itself felt:

1. When one speaks of the truth of judgments one refers chiefly to the truth (or falsity) of one's beliefs, in other words of one's affirmations or denials. Affirmation is taking to be true; denial is taking to be false. Yet an affirmation may be true or false, so also may be a denial. This shows that truth (or falsity) of beliefs or judgments presupposes another sense of being true (or false). In this latter sense, truth (or falsity) belongs to propositions which are affirmed or denied.

2. In this second sense, there are true propositions (e.g., the propositions meant by the sentences "$2+2=4$" and "Snow is white") as well as false propositions (e.g., propositions meant by the sentences "$2+2=5$" and "Snow is black"). A true proposition deserves to be affirmed, a false proposition deserves to be denied. Designating a true belief by t_1 and a false belief by f_1, and a true proposition by t_2 and a false proposition by f_2, we may then say:

t_1 consists in (a) taking t_2 as t_2

or (b) taking f_2 as f_2, whereas

f_1 consists in (a) taking t_2 as f_2

or (b) taking f_2 as t_2.

It is to be noted that f_2 as such does not amount to error. What is erroneous is the affirmation of f_2 or denial of t_2. Again, it is important to bear in mind that a proposition, t_2 or f_2, need not be affirmed or denied: it may be, as said before, doubted, presumed, assumed, supposed, and finally merely entertained.

3. A statement is true only in a sense that is derivative from the sense in which a belief is so, for in making a statement one expresses the belief in a publicly observable manner. A true statement may, then, be designated t'_1 and a false statement f'_1.

Thus, t'_1 presupposes t_1 and t_1 presupposes t_2 and f_2.

4. In all the above senses truth is opposed to falsity. This opposition is essential to these meanings of 'truth'. There are, however, two other senses in which 'truth' is used without exactly

entailing such a contrast. In one of these senses truth belongs to a knowledge. Whereas a belief, a proposition or a statement may be either true or false, knowledge is only true and cannot be false. A false knowledge is a contradiction in terms. Truth is an essential or a definitional property of knowledge. Thus the truth of knowledge has no meaningful contrast with falsity. When a knowledge, or what claimed to be so, is seen to be false it ceases to be knowledge. Its pretension is exposed.

5. The objective correlate of knowledge is reality, and that also is often called truth. In this sense, again, truth has no meaningful opposite. There is no falsity in reality. The quasi-objectivity of falsity ends with propositions and does not extend beyond it into the sphere of reality.

From amongst these various meanings of 'truth' it is necessary to single out that which is its primary sense. I wish to argue that in its primary sense truth pertains to knowledge. The fifth meaning of truth may be left out of account, for truth is predicated of reality only as a transferred epithet, reality being the objective correlate of knowledge that is true. It cannot be said that there is a circularity involved here, for knowledge is knowledge inasmuch as it is of reality. There is no circularity, for knowledge is not true because reality is the truth, but on the contrary reality is called the truth because it is the objective correlate of knowledge that is true. It is also possible to argue that the sense (1) is derived from the sense (4), for in the first place belief may be regarded as falling short of knowledge and as being true only in so far as its propositional content agrees with that of knowledge. The ideal is knowledge where the true proposition is not only judged (believed, etc.) to be true but insightfully judged to be so, i.e., where the intended meaning is realised, fulfilled – if you like, verified – in intuitive evidence. Belief, even when true, falls short of this, for it terminates in the proposition. A true proposition is the meaning-content of both a true belief and a knowledge, but knowledge does not terminate in it; knowledge is not of the proposition but of the reality whose intuition fulfils or verifies the meaning-intention. Thus the truth of a true proposition, and that of a true belief, derive their truth-character from the truth of the knowledge into which they might possibly enter and in which they are to be fulfilled. The primacy of the truth of knowledge is also suggested by the interesting fact that it alone – leaving aside the sense (5) – is absolute in the sense of having no opposite in the strict sense. I believe that this is the basis of the Mimāmsā theory of *svataḥprāmānya*, the Nyaya theory of *parataḥprāmānya* being based on an assimilation of the concept of knowledge to that of belief which may or may not be true.

We may sum up the very complicated situation thus:

(1) True belief presupposes a true proposition. Hence the truth of the former presupposes the truth of the latter.

(2) A true proposition is the content of a (true) knowledge. Truth of the former presupposes that of the latter.

(3) Truth of knowledge on its own part does not depend upon the truth of its propositional content but consists in the fact that in knowledge reality itself is apprehended.

III

Now that the concepts of meaning and truth have been identified and located we may proceed to investigate the relation that obtains between them. In any concrete knowledge situation, such as when I know an object while at the same time either naming or referring to it by an expression (as when I name what I perceive as "This man here before me"), it should be obvious that meaning and truth are together in an inalienable unity.

Meaning belongs to expressions and is grasped through an act of understanding, howsoever such an act may be interpreted. Truth belongs to knowledge. The difference and yet the interrelation between them is exactly what concerns us here. It must be clear that the two represent two different attitudes. In the attitude of mere understanding I merely apprehend the meaning, and in so far as the meaning determines the mode of reference I also apprehend the type of reference it is capable of being used to make. But all this does not amount to knowledge. When, on the other hand, I know, the general reference is made determinate through intuition or experience; the object, and not the meaning, is what is given as it is really in itself. In this sense, knowledge of

A as A presupposes understanding of the meaning of 'A'. In this sense, meaning is presupposed by truth, but truth goes beyond meaning. Whether truth can be had except through the *via media* of meaning would depend upon whether or not we have a mode of knowledge which is not linguistic. It seems, however, to me – to quote Merleau-Ponty – that we are 'condemned to meaning'. The reference of knowledge to its object presupposes the reference of expressions. The latter reference, however, remains indeterminate. We can think of things that we do not know, and can understand possibilities that exceed the scope of actual knowledge.

Formal logic may be construed as a logic of meanings. It deals with two levels of problems: first, the problem of demarcating meaningful from meaningless sequences of meanings, and, next, the problem of the relations of compatibility, incompatibility and entailment amongst meanings. Accordingly, formal logic falls into two strata: a logical grammar and a logic of non-contradiction.

An incidental point needs to be emphasised. It concerns the distinction between analytic and synthetic truths. From the point of view of a theory of meaning, such a distinction is relevant: there are true propositions which are true by virtue of their component meanings, and there are those whose truth is left undetermined by the relations obtaining among the component meanings.

In a logic of knowledge, on the other hand, such a distinction becomes pointless. For all knowledges are so far alike that their truth consists in the apprehension of their objects as they really are. It is only when the propositional content is abstracted from the knowledge and is treated as a self-subsistent meaning that the question of its analyticity or otherwise becomes significant. This, I guess, would partly explain the absence of this distinction in Indian logic which is a logic of knowledge rather than of meaning.

CHAPTER VI

LANGUAGE & REALITY*

Of the many problems that come under the title of this symposium, two stand out as the most important. These are: 'How is language related to reality?' and 'Is language a suitable medium for knowing reality?'. This paper shall have something to say about each of these problems. However, each of these questions reveals an ambiguity that is due to the ambiguity of the word 'reality'. By 'reality' is sometimes meant real things, events, facts and persons which go to constitute what we in common parlance call the real world. But 'reality' is also sometimes, especially in metaphysical discourse, taken to mean ultimate or metaphysical reality in which case it denotes something that stands behind and beyond the world of things and persons which is but its appearance. One who asks the first question, namely 'What is the relation between language and reality?' may be asking 'How is language related to the real things and persons which constitute the real world?', or he may be asking 'How is language related to the ultimate metaphysical reality, to the Absolute or *Brahman*?'. Similarly, the second question may mean either the same as 'Is language a suitable medium for knowing the nature of the empirical world of things and persons?' or the same as 'Is language a suitable medium for apprehending the nature of the ultimate metaphysical reality?'.

Now of these two sets of questions it seems extremely difficult to tackle those concerning ultimate metaphysical reality. In order to be able even to make a start with them one should have a conception of that reality, which raises a metaphysical problem of the highest order and importance. The term 'meta-

---

* Read at the Centre of Advanced Study in Philosophy, Banaras Hindu University in November, 1965.

physical reality' which is not one in ordinary use has to be suit-ably defined, and it seems our approach to the questions would largely depend upon how we define this key term. But there are at least two difficulties here. In the first place, how can we discuss the relation between language and reality, if giving a meaning to 'reality' is a matter of linguistic decision? What one needs in order to gain a vantage point for commencing the dis-cussion, is to get beyond language to some non-linguistic ex-perience so that it may be worthwhile attempting to correlate *that* to language. The conception of a metaphysical reality does not provide me with such a vantage point. Secondly, dealing with metaphysical reality, I am afraid, any answer I could offer would be trivial in the sense of following from the definition of 'reality' with which I start. I might so define 'reality' that the real is ineffable, and then to contend that language could have no meaningful relation to it, or that it is inaccessible to language would be an analytic consequence of that initial de-finition. It is because of such suspicions that I shall refrain from dealing with this aspect of the problem.

Turning then to the world of things and persons, to the real world as we call it, and its relation to language we find our task no easier. The most difficult and also the most important step in philosophical thinking is a clear formulation of the problem; nowhere is this a more difficult task than in the present case. It was pointed out a little while ago that in dealing with meta-physical reality we run the risk of arriving at a conclusion which is but an analytic consequence of our initial definition of 'reality'. But do we not run the same risk even when we are dealing with the real world of things and persons? Consider, for example, the thesis advocated by many that the world consists in facts (not things and persons). Now what are facts? They are roughly definable only with reference to sentences. A fact is what makes a sentence true. And now to contend further that there is a relation of correspondence, accordance or picturing between language and reality is but an analytic consequence of the way the thesis looks upon reality as consisting in facts. Certainly if you look upon the world to consist not in facts but events, things and persons, you cannot contend that language pictures them, it can at best describe them.

It seems to me therefore that the true problem is the relation of language not to reality but to our *experience* of the real. We call it formulation (1). What we are to call 'real' may to some extent depend upon a linguistic context, not so however our experience of the real. It may however be argued against this contention that there is no experience of the real that does not presuppose a linguistic framework, that there is no merely given that is not conceptualised and therefore not subject to the interpretations flowing from a linguistic system. The crucial question then is, is there a non-linguistic apprehension of the real? I say 'crucial', for upon an affirmative answer to this question depends the meaningfulness of the very problem we are out to discuss.

The contention that what is to be regarded as given depends upon one's linguistic context is closely connected with two other theses: first, that the problem of existence is a linguistic problem, and secondly, that proper names are not indispensable for a language.[1] Taken together they liquidate ontology, or rather assimilate it to a philosophy of language. An assimilation of the one to the other would not do: that would mean a liquidation of our problem.

I have said above that the true problem is the relation of language to our *experience* of the real. At this point it may be asked, does not language refer to the real, and if so is it not worth while investigating the nature of this referential relation? To this I would reply that our problem is in one sense concerned with the referential relation, in another sense it is not. Let me explain my contention.

It has been well established by modern researches in theory of meaning (Frege, Husserl, Quine) that one of the essential functions of language is to refer. This function of referring is different from the other function of meaning. It has been held that the meaning function is an immanent function of language in the sense that it derives from the rules of formation and transformation of a language, while the referring function relates lan-

---

[1] Cp. R. Carnap, *Empiricism, Semantics, and Ontology* included in *Meaning and Necessity*, Enlarged edition, 1956; and W. V. O. Quine, *Word and Object*, M.I.T., 1960, especially 37.

guage to extra-linguistic reality. Whether meaning (even as distinguished from reference) is purely linguistic or whether one can speak reasonably of a non-linguistic meaning is a question into which I need not investigate at present[2]. With regard to the function of reference however it ought to be admitted on all hands that language refers to a real beyond, so that it would not do to reduce even this into an intra-linguistic relationship[3].

Assuming all this to be well-founded conclusions, we may still deny that the semantics of reference is all that concerns us when we are concerned with the relation of language to reality. The following consideration will bear this out. The reference that is intrinsic to language and that constitutes an essential function of language qua language is merely intended reference, and does not by itself carry a guarantee that the reference must find a foothold in reality. The reference does not provide language with a point where it can be hooked on to reality. In believing that it does, Russell was wrong. Russell was wrong in thinking that the sense or meaning of a name is its *designatum*, as also in thinking that meaningful use of names carries with it the guarantee that there must be in reality things which bear those names. Wittgenstein – as Anscombe has rightly pointed out – gave cogent reasons for rejecting this view of Russell,[4] and these need not be repeated here. Language *qua* language refers (and need not picture or even designate, for referring is not always naming), but whether the intended reference is fulfilled in reality, i.e. whether there exists in reality the thing that is being referred to is quite another question. Thus the relation of language to reality is not established through the referring function which belongs to the former. If the question is, how is language hooked on to reality, and if reference fails to do this job, we may further ask, 'What completes the unfulfilled task, and finally nails language to reality?'

My purpose so far has been to formulate the aspect of the problem which seems to me to be of the utmost importance. The vague question 'What is the relation between language and

[2] For further elaboration, see my *"Meaning and Truth"*, *Visva Bharati Journal of Philosophy*, Vol. I, No. 1 (reprinted in this volume).

[3] Cp. my *Edmund Husserl's Theory of Meaning*, The Hague, 1964, ch. II.

[4] G. E. M. Anscombe, *An Introduction to Wittgenstein's Tractatus*, London, 1959, pp. 45-46.

reality?' has now been refined and narrowed down to 'What besides and in addition to the function of referring intrinsic to language *qua* language hooks language to reality?....(2a).

But we should not forget that there is also a reverse side of this question and that may be formulated as 'What makes reality a referent of language?'...(2b). Whereas (2a) is formulated from the side of language and asks how it is tied to reality, (2b) is formulated from the side of reality and asks how reality comes to be the referent of language. It should be noted that the second is the more fundamental question. It enquires into the very possibility of language. It is in fact a part of the question 'How is language qua language possible?'

Taking up now the question (2a) along with the earlier proposed question (1), we may formulate the resulting problem as: 'How is the intended reference of a linguistic expression completed, fulfilled and integrated into a complete experience of the real?' (3). Or, what amounts to the same, 'How is the *gap* between linguistic reference and bodily apprehension of the real overcome, so that there comes about, so to say, a perceptual judgment, a sort of *felt non-distinction* between language and reality, between the name and the named, the sentence and the fact?' (3').

In (3') I have spoken of several things which need to be commented upon. In the first place, it has been suggested that there is a gap between linguistic reference and bodily apprehension of the real. It is necessary to be aware of the full implications of this. Language, of course, *qua* language refers, and the reference is to a reality beyond. But, besides the fact made out earlier that the reference is only intended reference, there is also the supporting consideration that understanding this reference is not the same as knowing the thing being referred to. Talking about an object or understanding the talk about it does not amount to apprehending that object excepting as the object that is being referred to. The existence of the gap may be further exhibited thus: linguistic reference is always through the medium of meaning. Language does not contain an unmeaning mark. Meaning has an unavoidable aspect of universality and *Überzeitlichkeit*. The real however when it is given as real is given as something unique, as a *this-there*. Even the indexical expressions which of all are the most completely referring have an aspect of meaning as distinguished from reference, and do their job of referring only through meaning what they mean. There are no logically proper names in Russell's sense. Now this condition that linguistic reference is determined by the medium of meaning also imposes on it certain limitations. It does not achieve that absolute determinateness and uniqueness which belong to the real referent. This gap has to be filled in. That the gap is in fact overcome is a *conditio sine qua non* of the possibility of our linguistic identification of the reals. But how does that become possible? The question then is not, 'How is it that language comes to refer beyond itself?' (for this reference is a constitutive aspect of language *qua* language), but 'How is it possible to make linguistic identification of a unique real?'.

The existence of the gap may be denied by saying that there is in fact an inseparability between language and reality. This latter contention may be supported by an appeal to the alleged fact of *sahopalambha*, in other words to the fact that a real and its name are never experienced separately. This fact may be taken to entail that the two are inseparable and so non-distinct. If this conclusion holds good then it would further follow that there can be no non-linguistic apprehension of the real, for the real *qua* real is, on this view, a *designatum* of such and such expression. Such a point of view will also liquidate the problem as formulated in (2b), for if to be real is to be the referent of an expression it is pointless to ask how does reality come to be referred to by language. It is pointless then to ask, how is language possible. To vindicate the possibility of the questions we have asked it is necessary therefore to expose the hollowness of this theory.

As regards the alleged fact of *sahopalambha* I think it to be based on several confusions. In the first place, there is a confusion between *mentioning* an expression and *using* it. A name may be mentioned without referring to the named object: there is then no *sahopalambha*. Secondly, even when a name is being used it is one thing to use a name to refer to the named and another to know the named. Mere use of the name does not carry a guarantee that there is an apprehension of the real named excepting as so named. Even if we leave open the question whether the named can be apprehended without apprehending its name it seems indisputable that a name can be apprehended without there being an apprehension of the named.

Although – as argued above – language and reality are separated by a cleavage, yet as our formulation (3') implies, there is in perceptual judgment a sort of felt non-distinction between the two. A sort of identification is *achieved* in consciousness. There is no ontological identity. This non-distinction cannot be explained as a mere associative synthesis, for in association the associated elements are clearly distinguished.

The problem then concerns briefly the relation of language to *perception*, for it is in perception that real things and persons are *bodily* presented. It seems to me that this is a far more important problem than the much discussed one concerning the relation of language to thought. For it is perception – and not thought – which gives us a sense of reality of its object. The fact that perception is sometimes delusive does not go against our contention. No wonder that those who believe in a metaphysical reality and hold both that it is knowable and yet not knowable by thought hold the view that thought leads to a higher, intellectual intuition or perception. The analogy with perception is quite understandable.

But the problem of the relation of language to perception of reality itself presents not one question but a number of them. The non-distinction to which reference was made a little while ago may be studied as a static unity achieved in *savikalpa* perception, or as the limiting point of a dynamic process through which the gap is progressively overcome. Consider the simple perceptual judgment 'This is a pen' in which the linguistic component with its meaning and referential aspects stands non-distinguished from the bodily apprehension of a real pen before me. It is necessary to bear in mind that the apprehension itself is not linguistic, as it is sometimes erroneously supposed to be. Even on the Nyāya theory what distinguishes *savikalpa* perception from the *nirvikalpa* is the presence of certain epistemic contents like *viśeṣyatā* and *prakāratā* and also the fact that the latter cannot be (*avyapadeśya*) while the former *can* be expressed in language.[5] It however stands in a close relation with language,

---

[5] Even on the older view which regarded *savikalpa* as in some sense linguistic, the *padavācyatva* is said to appear only as *upanīta*. Thus, "*viśiṣṭajñāne tattatpada-*

and I do not think the Nyāya is very clear as to the nature of this relationship.

Perhaps it is possible to throw some light on this mystery by studying the nature of the graduated synthesis that leads up to the felt non-distinction. For this purpose let us make a further change in attitude. We transformed the original question 'What is the relation of language to reality?'. This transformation involved a change of attitude from the objective and ontological to the subjective and phenomenological. It was sought to be justified on the ground that the real is what we confront in perception. It is necessary, in order to complete the transformation, to make a similar change in our attitude also with regard to the other term of the relation, namely 'language'. Let us ask the question not about language but about our experience of it. Once we do so then the entire problem gets transformed into the subjective mode. We ask, namely, 'How is the experience of language related to the perceptual apprehension of reality?'. In other words, we ask, 'How is it that in perceptual judgment language and reality both come to achieve a sort of felt non-distinction?'(4).

But how is language experienced? What is the specific and original mode in which language qua language is given? Language *qua* language is certainly not given in outer perception alone. Of course, the speech is to be heard, or the written words are to be seen. But auditory and visual perception, as the case may be, does not constitute the mode of givenness of language *qua* language. If it is the function of meaning that transforms the merely physical shape or sound into an expression, then to apprehend language as such is to understand it or to use it meaningfully. The outer perception provides the basis on which is built up the higher intellectual act of understanding.

Our question (4) may then – in view of the fact that we are to examine graduated synthesis and not the static unity – be restated thus: 'How do we pass on from a bare understanding of an expression to a bodily identification of the real referred to by it?'.(5)

Strawson refers to a class of expressions which may be re-

vācyatvamupanītam bhāsate iti prācīnamatānusāritvāt" (Dinakari on Muktāvali on Kārikā 51).

garded as capable of identifying uniquely the things referred to by them. These are what he calls 'pure individuating descriptions'.[6] An example is 'The first dog to be born at sea'. Now if such expressions can do what they are taken to be capable of doing, then an answer to (5) may be found at least in some cases, on a purely linguistic level. For, in that case an understanding of a pure individuating description would be sufficient to lead us to an identification. But this again is not the case. First, how am I to make sure that there is one and only one individual satisfying the description? There is, in Strawson's words, the possibility of a massive duplication. Secondly, even if I know that there is an individual satisfying the description, knowing this does not amount to knowing the individual itself. What is required is a bodily identification of the uniquely real. And this is what language by itself would seem surely incapable of doing.

Taken as an objective expression there can in fact be no non-distinction between linguistic expression and a uniquely real referent. The objective expression by virtue of its generality of meaning overflows its referent on any given occasion. It is only the subjective speech which achieves the non-distinction, which is felt as non-distinct from the fact being referred to. Perhaps it is here that we may look for an answer.

Identification requires a framework in which to locate, and a field from which to pick out. Mere non-linguistic experience cannot by itself identify. It offers a field from which to choose. But the perceptual field is always relatively vague; it has a fringe and a core of indeterminateness. Language confers determinateness. Linguistic description narrows down the field. Speech as distinguished from objective language, offers not only a framework but also an absolute point of reference namely the speaker himself. Unless there were a speaker the supposed identification of language with reality being referred to would not have taken place. It is the speaker who *uses* language to identify: the result is a non-distinction in consciousness.

It should follow that the non-distinction is more where speech confers more of determinateness in the perceptual field. Contrast the perceptual judgment 'This is red' with 'This is magnificent'.

---

[6] P. F. Strawson, *Individuals*, London, 1961, p. 26.

Though in the former case there is a felt non-distinction between the linguistic expression and the fact being referred to, yet it is also the case that the fact of this being red is a fact independent of my or any one else's saying so. But in the latter case the fact of this being magnificent is a fact only in so far as it is being said so by some speaker or other. Here in a sense speech makes the fact so. Josef König, following Brentano, distinguishes between 'determining' and 'modifying' predicates.[7] I am not sure if an absolute line of distinction can be drawn between the two kinds of predicates. It may be difficult to decide whether a given predicate is determining or modifying. The fact remains however that the non-distinction between speech and apprehension of reality may be achieved in degrees, depending on the degree of indeterminateness of the perceptual field and the degree of determinateness conferred by speech on it.

Communication is not the only purpose of speech. That no doubt is one of its chief uses. Communication is possible because of the generality of meanings, because speech, in spite of its dependence on the speaker, conveys meanings that are impersonal. But it would seem language has another important and perhaps more basic function which consists in locating and identifying reals. It is one thing to have an experience. But if we are to identify the thing experienced and give it a place in a scheme, language is an indispensable aid. In this sense language is like a map. One may know a place, and yet cannot locate it except with the help of a map. Language provides us with a framework in which and in whose terms to locate and identify a real. It is no wonder that sometimes a map is felt as non-distinct from that which is mapped.

By saying all this I do not intend to suggest that language is a picture of reality in any sense. By emphasising the fact that language provides us with a framework I wish to bring to the forefront the aspect of it as a pattern as against the mere vocabulary aspect. This I believe is in conformity with the findings of such linguists as Humboldt, Whorf and Chomsky.[8]

Logical atomism believed that both language and reality

---

[7] Josef König, *Sein und Denken*, Halle, 1937.

[8] A. V. Humboldt, *Menschliche Sprachbau*; B. L. Whorf, *Language, Thought and Reality*, 1956; and N. Chomsky, "Current Issues in Linguistic Theory" in Fodor and Katz, *The Structure of Language*, Prentice-Hall, 1964.

could be analysed down to the simple, not further analysable elements, and it further held the thesis that there is "some real and non-conventional one-one picturing relation between the composition of the expression and that of the fact".[9] This theory fortunately is a dead horse and it would not be worth while flogging it any more. Few remarks in this connection may however be made here.

Meaning of expressions may be simple or compound. But the simplicity or complexity of an expression does not show whether its meaning is simple or compound. Further, we are in no better position in trying to infer the simplicity or complexity of the object being referred to from the simplicity or complexity of the meanings through which reference is being made. For example, 'simple object' which is a compound expression and has a compound meaning refers to a simple object. Nor is there always a one-to-one relationship between a compound meaning and the compound object referred to through it. Bolzano gives the example of 'The country without a hill'. In fact the entire talk about simplicity or complexity is equivocal. It may mean simplicity or complexity of meanings, or it may mean simplicity or complexity of our consciousness of meanings. It may be that a simple meaning is apprehended in consciousness through many phases and stages. Neither expressions nor meanings therefore picture. Expressions refer and meanings make reference possible by imparting to it a certain determinateness.[10] From what has been said it follows that language is neither the same as reality nor a picture of it. Nor is our consciousness, or even our experience of reality necessarily linguistic. But language with both its vocabulary and patternment aspects is a necessary, though not sufficient,[11] precondition of our identifying a real. It in fact provides us with a coordinate system in which to locate the given, so that the real is apprehended as having such and such linguistic designation. This is to know *par excellence*. In this sense of 'know', to know A is to know it as A which entails, amongst other things,

---

[9] G. Ryle, "Systematically Misleading Expressions", *Proceedings of the Aristotelian Society*. 1931–32.

[10] For further elaboration, see my *Edmund Husserl's Theory of Meaning*, Ch. V.

[11] The problem has been further developed in my "On Reference" in *Argumentationen, Festschrift für Josef König*, Göttingen, 1964. (Reprinted in this volume)

knowing it as having the name A. However, knowing a thing as having the name A is not the same as knowing an A.

Heidegger says that the essential function of language is to manifest Being to man; it opens up Being for man.[12] Without taking a stand with regard to Heidegger's peculiar conceptions of Being and openness, we may still regard our thesis as a partial substantiation of his thesis though on a more modest and common sense level.

If now we turn to the question 2 (b) and ask, 'How is it that reality comes to be a referent of language?' and thereby ask, 'How is language *qua* language possible?', we seem to abandon the field of phenomenology to which we had confined ourselves so long and to have entered the precincts of speculative metaphysics. On so large a question, which should not be confused with a genesis of language, we may make only a few, very unsatisfactory, remarks. In the first place, it may be said that the referentiality of language presupposes the intentionality of consciousness. The latter does not depend upon the former but makes it possible. In fact, linguistic reference is one mode in which the intentionality of consciousness is objectified. But to the question why after all a real should come to have designation this is not the answer. An answer, if there be any, may be sought in either of two directions. We may either find it in some need of reality to be made articulate, or we may find it in the nature of human reason i.e. in man's specific mode of relationship to the real. The former shall lead us to a sort of mysticism of the later Heidegger, the latter to a more truly existential philosophy. To choose between these two possible answers, or even to show if they can be synthesised would be going beyond the limits of the present paper.

---

[12] M. Heidegger, *Einführung in die Metaphysik*, Tübingen, 1953, p. 131; and his letter *Über den Humanismus*, Bern, 2nd edn. 1954.

CHAPTER VII

ON REFERENCE*

1. The problem of reference, and that of meaning, first come into clear relief and exhibit their problematic character, only when one has already drawn an initial distinction between meaning and reference. If one fails to make this distinction and thereby implicitly identifies the two, both the problems get watered down to how words or expressions could after all stand for something, – a question to which conventionalism provides a fairly convincing answer. The problem however is much deeper, and for an appreciation of it the Frege-Husserlian distinction between meaning and reference is an indispensable starting point.

1.1. There are many ways of introducing this distinction. The best seems to be by way of showing (a) that two expressions may have different meanings and yet an identical reference; (b) that an expression while retaining its meaning unchanged refers now to one object, now to another; and (c) that an expression does not suffer any diminution or damage in its meaning from the fact that its reference fails. Examples for (a) are 'The morning star' and 'The evening star'; for (b) are the general names like 'man'; and for (c) such cases as 'The present King of France'. The most plausible explanation of such possibilities is provided by the assumption that the meaning of an expression is different from that which it refers to. Once the point of this distinction is seen, one also begins to realise the reality of the problem about meaning: 'What then is the meaning of an expression, if it is not the thing being referred to?'.

---

* Published in Delius and Patzig (ed.), *Argumentationen, Festschrift für Josef König*, Göttingen, Vandenhoeck & Ruprecht, 1964, pp. 159–169.

1.2. The problem of reference cannot however be felt with its full force and with all its implications even at this stage. The question about meaning has to be pursued a few steps further before we could be in a position to formulate the problem of reference which is to be the chief concern of this paper.

There are several answers to the question 'What is meaning?' that suggest themselves to us immediately. One of these has been explicitly rejected by Frege on good grounds, and has fallen into disrepute; another continues to enjoy unabated reputation. The first is the theory that the meaning of an expression is nothing but an image, against which Frege says: *"Die Vorstellung ist subjektiv: die Vorstellung des Einen ist nicht die des Andern.... Die Vorstellung unterscheidet sich dadurch wesentlich von dem Sinne eines Zeichens, welcher gemeinsames Eigenthum von Vielen sein kann und also nicht Theil oder Modus der Einzelseele ist."*[1] An image is private, subjective, i.e. in somebody's mind and therefore is not communicable or shareable. The meaning of an expression however is in an important sense public, objective, not a real constituent of anyone's mental history; it is communicable and shareable. Meaning therefore cannot be an image.

The other theory holds that since meaning has been distinguished from reference, the question 'What is meaning?' does not intend us to produce an entity, be it subjective (an image) or objective (a subsistent entity). All questions about entities being transferred to the theory of reference, meaning as distinguished from reference could only be linguistic (*sprachliche*) meaning. This theory finds support in the undeniable fact that when asked to give the meaning of an expression one produces not a non-linguistic entity but another synonymous expression. Meaning therefore is linguistic. The problem of meaning is really one of synonymity.

As against this, I can do no better than quote the following passage from C. I. Lewis:

"We must express meanings by the use of words; but if meaning altogether should end in words, then words altogether should

---

[1] G. Frege, "Über Sinn und Bedeutung"., *Zt. f. Philos. Kritik*, NF 100 (1892), p. 29. Now also in G. Frege, *Funktion, Begriff, Bedeutung*, Göttingen, 1962, p. 42.

express nothing. The 'language system' as a whole would 'have no interpretation' and there would be no such fact as the meaning of language."[2]

The idea of linguistic meaning is unobjectionable, but it cannot be self-explanatory. It ultimately does refer back to the material (*sachliche*) meaning. This is clear from the recent attempts of account for synonymity on a purely linguistic and conventional level. Convention of course does account for the fact that any two expressions should have been used as synonymous, but that they are so means only that they have been made to express the same meaning.

The meaning cannot also be the same as the use of the expression in a language game. As Wittgenstein himself rightly realised[3], the concept of use is the concept of something extended in time, while there is a sense in which apprehending the meaning of an expression is not an act that is extended in time but an instantaneous apprehension. And it is this sense of meaning with which we are concerned in the present context.

1.3. Any acceptable theory of meaning, it seems to us, should be able to satisfy two criteria: in the first place, it must be able to account for that universality, objectivity and identity of meanings which are the pre-suppositions of all communication of thought, and therefore of all linguistic behaviour. What Husserl calls the ideal-objectivity of meanings is an undeniable phenomenological datum. Those who deny it do so only under the pressure of their preconceived metaphysical prejudices. Maybe this is only one aspect of the phenomena. However, into the question how far and in what manner the phenomenon of the ideal-objectivity of meanings could be harmonised with other aspects of the total phenomenological situation we need not, and cannot enter here[4].

The second criterion to be fulfilled by a satisfactory theory of meaning follows from the fact that meaning also serves as the medium for reference. The possibility as well as the limitations of this function have to be exhibited. It is to this aspect of the problem that we shall now turn our attention.

[2] C. I. Lewis, *An Analysis of Knowledge and Valuation*, Illinois, 1946, p. 140.

[3] L. Wittgenstein, *Philosophical Investigations*, Oxford, 1953, p. 53.

[4] See J. N. Mohanty, "Meaning and Truth", Presidential Address, *Proc. Ind. Philos. Congress*, 36th Session (1961), Santiniketan, pp. 27–47. [Reprinted in this volume]

1.4. The problem of reference is falsified when we regard reference as an intra-linguistic function as does modern semantics when it treats names as designating other expressions. This is not to cast reflection upon the value of semantics as a science, but this clearly implies a serious limitation of its philosophical significance. For the problem of reference is, how in the first place within linguistic discourse we succeed in making extralinguistic reference; and secondly, how does it come about that we also succeed very often in making unique extralinguistic reference although the medium of such reference is provided by the general ideal-objective meanings.

2. One of the contentions of the present paper is that expressions that are names possess, as such, the referring function. Connected with this is the contention that in a very important sense the problem of extralinguistic reference is illusory inasmuch as such reference is an essential function of language *qua* language. Language would not be language and would not serve one of the chief purposes it is meant for if it did not refer to extralinguistic objects. The situation is analogous to – and in fact not unconnected with – the problem concerning the possibility of our consciousness of transcendent objects. How can consciousness, it is asked, apprehend objects that are beyond it? Here again part of the sting of the problem is gone once we realise that such self-transcending reference belongs to the very essence of consciousness, and asking how consciousness could after all perform this miracle is the same as asking how consciousness could be consciousness. That language should succeed in making extra-linguistic reference presents a similar situation, and philosophy could hope to achieve only limited results, if any, here, for the ultimate character of this fact has to be first and foremost acknowledged.

The fact remains nevertheless that such extra-linguistic reference is effected through the medium of ideal-objective meanings, and this perhaps is in need of further explanation. However we may now turn to a possible objection to our basic contention.

2.1. We have contended in the above paragraph that names

possess as such a referring function. Against this it may be objected that reference is not a function of expressions *qua* expressions, for expressions as such have only meaning while it is only a genuine use of them that refers. The purpose of this objection, as is clear from Strawson's celebrated essay from which it is derived,[5] is to steer clear of both the postulation of Meinongian entities and the Russellian analysis of referring expressions with a view to avoiding the Meinongian ghosts. As is well known, on the Meinongian thesis, such a sentence as "The present King of France is wise" could be meaningful only if there is a present King of France, and if there exists no such person there should subsist such a one; whereas on the Russellian analysis the sentence should be further analysed so that the apparent subject is seen not to be the logical subject at all. Both the theories assume, according to Strawson, that a referring expression to be meaningful must stand for or refer to something, against which Strawson suggests that not reference but only meaning is a function of expressions. An expression however may be used to refer. Such uses of it as do not refer are cases of spurious use. Genuine uses alone refer.

There is no doubt that both the solutions that Strawson criticises wrongly assume that meaning is the same as reference. They could therefore be avoided by distinguishing between the two functions of expressions. It is not however necessary to go all the way in Strawson's company. For Strawson's complete separation of the two functions by assigning the one to expressions as such, and the other to their uses is possibly due to his assumption that an expression can only then be said to refer when there actually exists something which is being referred to. This assumption however may be questioned. Before coming to it, however, let us in brief point out what seems to us to be a vicious circularity involved in the solution offered.

The circularity may be brought out in the following manner: How to know that a certain use of an expression does not refer? The reply would be, when the use is not genuine. But how after all can one be sure that the use is a spurious one? Because it does not refer at all, would be the reply.

Now, both Russell and Strawson may be said to assume that

[5] P. F. Strawson, "On Referring", *Mind*, July 1950, pp. 320–344.

an expression (or its use) refers only when there is something to which it refers! In Russell's theory an expression 'A', and in Strawson's theory its use, refers only then when there actually is the A. When there is no such A, Russell would analyse 'A' in the manner outlined in his Theory of Descriptions, while Strawson would say it is not a genuine use of 'A'. I wish to suggest that this need not be so. Russell explicitly, and Strawson implicitly, identify genuinely referring expressions with 'logically' proper names, for is it not so that if I have or use a logically proper name, the something which I so name must exist? To refer is certainly not to designate.

2.3. As against this prevalent attitude, I wish to suggest that reference in the sense in which it is a constitutive function of expressions is nothing but intended reference. Saying that expressions qua expressions refer means only that they contain an intention which as it were is directed towards the extra-linguistic world. But that there is such a directedness or an intentionality does not imply that there is a point in the extralinguistic world where the intention terminates. Whether there is such a point or not, whether in any particular case the intention is fulfilled or not or can possibly be fulfilled, is an empirical question, and therefore falls outside the scope of philosophy. It is also an empirical question to ask what are the causes of the fact that there are such and such intentions and no others in a given language: part of the reason for it may be found in the structure of the language and part in other contingent features. But what belongs *a priori* to the essence of a linguistic expression as such is the fact that there is such an intentionality.

If the above contention is true, then it follows that the possibility of a name or of using it in a language does not imply that there exists in the actual world something which is so named. On the other hand, the expression is made or constituted by an intention just as its use makes a conscious claim upon the world that the intention is fulfilled in a definite spatio-temporal situation. Language or the use of it does not contain within itself the guarantee about what is or is not.

3. The reference which characterises linguistic expressions as

such enters into, and is further reinforced in the different conscious states that make use of linguistic expressions. It shall be
our purpose in this section to attempt a brief sketch of the subjective phenomenology of reference in so far as it characterises
the various modes of consciousness.

3.1. Reference characterises consciousness as such in the sense
that all consciousness is of something, or intends something.
Definite modes of consciousness have definite modes of intending
their objects. If we disregard the various modes and even abstract from any determinate form of consciousness we reach the
idea of pure consciousness, of consciousness as such. To such pure
consciousness we can assign only an indeterminate reference to
something, to what, using Kant' language, could be called object-in-general. Compared to this the reference of an expression
is more determinate, for each expression intends a determinate
possibility. However, subjectively speaking, the intentionality
of pure consciousness constitutes the most primary level which
makes possible all higher forms of reference including that of an
expression. This only shows that an expression considered as such
is not a merely physical event, but is the product of – in a rather
peculiar sense of 'production' – conscious intentionality: the
sense of this could be partly explicated by pointing out that unless there were the intentionality of consciousness expressions
qua expressions would not be possible.

3.2. Presupposing the referentiality of expressions *qua* expressions, there are three distinct modes of consciousness with
their distinct modes of referential character. We distinguish here
between (i) understanding the sentence 'S is p', (ii) thinking of
the fact that S is p, and (iii) knowing that S is p. To be noted in
this connection are the following:
  (a) Knowing that S is p presupposes an understanding of the
sentence 'S is p', but not vice versa. One may quite well understand the sentence 'S is p' without knowing that S is p.
  (b) Similarly, knowing that S is p involves a thought of S
being p, but not vice versa. The latter thought does not as such
amount to the former knowledge.
  (c) The distinction and the relation between (i) and (ii) is

more subtle, and is likely to be overlooked. There is however sufficient linguistic and introspective evidence for drawing the distinction between (i) and (ii). I may be interested only in getting the meaning of a sentence (as for example when I am interested in testing my knowledge of a language I have newly learnt) without getting involved in a thought about the fact being referred to. We may not therefore be unjustified in suggesting that there can be bare understanding of 'S is p' not amounting to a thought of the fact that S is p, though any such thought presupposes the former understanding. We have thus a series of distincts (in Croce's sense of the term) such that (i) does not presuppose (ii) and (iii), and (ii) does not presuppose (iii), whereas (iii) presupposes both (i) and (ii), and (ii) presupposes (i).

3.3. These distinctions may be sought to be denied on the grounds, (a) that an understanding of a sentence presupposes – contrary to what has been said in the above paragraph – thinking of its meaning as also a knowledge of it; and (b) that thinking of anything presupposes a knowledge of it for the obvious reason that one cannot think of something one does not know.

As against (a) we may point out that what we have contended is only that an understanding of 'S is p' does not presuppose a thought of the fact that S is p. Thinking of its meaning may be involved in so far as I do not rest merely in understanding but proceed further to analyse and correlate it to other sentences or meanings. Nevertheless, the point made out in (c) in para 3.2 stands. It may be further pointed out that the objection that understanding involves knowing the meaning rests upon a certain ambiguity of the word 'know'. According to the usage here being followed, 'knowing' the meaning of an expression is the same as understanding the expression, which renders that part of the objection (a) trivial. What is more is that the usage which permits us to speak of knowing the meaning of an expression distorts, in a very important manner, the true nature of the phenomenon. Knowing is either knowing an X, where X is not a that-clause, or knowing that something is the case. In both cases, knowledge has an object, i.e. something (a thing, a person or a fact) that is being known. Metaphorically speaking, it must be something in whom the intentionality of knowledge terminates.

The same however cannot be said of meanings. For when we understand an expression, its meaning is not an object in the above sense. The function of the meaning is to make reference possible, and to give the latter its determinate character. But by itselt it is not the sort of thing that could be inspected. Again speaking metaphorically, the meaning of an expression provides a sort of transparent medium for reference. The intention does not terminate in it, but rather goes through it towards the referred entity. Saying that meanings are known therefore is using the word 'know' in a rather improper sense.

A similar equivocation lingers also in the objection (b). Defining 'knowing' in the strict sense such that knowing that S is p entails that 'S is p' is true, we could easily avoid this point as well.

3.4. The distinctions introduced in 3.2 and defended against some possible objections in 3.3 may now be further explicated in the following manner: –

(a) Understanding the sentence 'S is p' involves:

(i)   knowing the meaning of 'S is p' (in the improper sense of 'knowing' explained in 3.3);

(ii) knowing the type of entity being referred to (in a sense of 'knowing' that is less improper than that in (i) above);

(iii) a predominance of the linguistic meaning (as opposed to the material meaning).

(iv) Added to all these, it must be mentioned, the whole act of pure understanding (which falls short of thinking and therefore of knowledge) terminates in awakening the simple meaning-intention and does not lead to a further attempt at its fulfilment. The referential aspect is thereby thwarted and remains restricted to being the minimum accompaniment of the meaning-intention, i.e. to the broad type.

(b) While understanding terminates in the meaning-intention, the reference being an unwanted but unavoidable accompaniment, there is in the act of thinking ('I am thinking of....') a conscious attempt to go beyond the intention, to sharpen the reference, to reach the material meaning. This partly accounts for the introspective datum that thinking is a more active, self-conscious process than is the mere understanding of another's utterance or writing. Reference comes to the forefront, becomes self-conscious, though still not completely realised or fulfilled. The object of thought not amounting to knowledge is the possibility of S being p, or the ideal construction S-being-p.

(c) In knowledge, taken in the strict sense, the meaning-intention is fulfilled, the material meaning finally swallows up the linguistic, the reference becomes determinate and actual and no more remains at the level of the type and the possible. The meaning aspect is taken up and subordinated to the referential. I do not any more stop with the medium, but succeed in seeing the object through it such that the medium is not itself seen at all, thus completely excluding even the possibility of that improper sense of knowing in which we speak of knowing the meaning.

Thus the two aspects of meaning and reference are present in varying degrees of determinateness exhibited in a rather graded form. In the act of pure understanding meaning dominates and reference is suppressed to the minimum; in thinking there is a more or less even balance: in knowing meaning is taken up into the reference.

4. Knowledge, in accordance with the above analysis, may be regarded as the one end of a scale whose other end is represented by pure symbolic understanding and at whose middle stands thinking of ... The tendency which finds itself realized in knowledge is the demand of reference to be actual and more and more determinate and the necessity of meaning to shade off its opacity and transform itself into what it should be, i.e. a transparent medium for reference.

It is noteworthy however that of all those cases where we do speak of knowing two stand out preeminently. These are our perceptual knowledge of physical objects and of other persons. The reason why these are regarded almost as paradigm cases of knowledge seems to be that in these cases reference is not only actual and determinate but also unique. Here knowledge is of a unique individual, i.e. of this object or of this person here before me. One of the problems we had proposed for ourselves in para 1.4 was: 'How does it come about that we also often succeed in making unique extralinguistic reference, although the medium of such reference is provided by the general ideal-objective meanings?" Now we are in a position to say a few words about this extremely intriguing problem.

4.1. It has been pointed out in para. 2 that according to one of the basic contentions of this paper expressions *qua* expressions refer, so that the simple question of extralinguistic reference is in one sense no problem at all. This does not however amount to saying that the question of unique extralinguistic reference is likewise no problem at all. On the contrary, it is a serious pro-blem, the more so because of the fact that the medium of reference remains the realm of general ideal-objective meanings. But again to solve this problem is really in effect to dissolve it, for the solution could only consist in showing that within a purely linguistic discourse unique reference is not possible. The fact that we nevertheless do refer to unique individuals is to be accounted for by asking, what else supervenes here and gives language the power (or a mere semblance of the power) which it does not really possess?

4.2. The problem may be further precipitated by formulating it in the form of a paradox: Reference in order to be unique requires a total elimination of the medium of meaning. And yet on the other hand without such a medium no reference – and therefore also no unique reference – is possible. The paradox may be sought to be resolved by pointing out that mere ostension does succeed in making unique reference. This however, as Wittgenstein has rightly shown[6], is not true. Ostension to do its job presupposes a context of linguistic discourse.

4. 3. For the same reason as is contained in the first proposi-tion of the paradox, the so-called 'ego-centric particulars' (Russell) or the 'empirical ties' (Hall) fail to rise up to the oc-casion; and yet it is these words – 'this', 'here', 'now', 'I' – if any, that are the likely candidates within linguistic discourse most suited for the task. They no doubt specify and determine, but complete uniqueness is not achieved by them. The reason

---

[6] L. Wittgenstein, *loc. cit.*, pp. 13e–16e.

for this is that they also have an aspect of meaning whose generality transcends the unique referent.

4.4. The problem which almost seems hopeless may be solved on the following lines: –

The total situation in which unique reference takes place may be exhibited as having a stratified structure with these layers:

(i) Linguistic discourse, through the medium of meaning, makes a general reference which delimits the field within which the object of reference is to be located.

(ii) The ego-centric particulars like 'this' effect a further narrowing down of the field, though as pointed out in 4.3, they also fail to achieve unique reference all by themselves.

(iii) What is left over, the unfulfilled part of the job is completed not by anything else within discourse – not even by mere ostension, for that also leaves room for ambiguity as shown above – but by an active participation and communion with the object. This last step, and indeed the most important step from the present point of view, involves a transcendence of the purely theoretical-cognitive attitude.

4.5. The key points in the above analysis may be stated thus: in the first place, linguistic discourse appears to succeed in making unique reference only because it is not self-sufficient, but is tagged on to a non-linguistic, non-theoretical participation in, or communion with the world of objects and persons. Secondly, this latter participation or communion would have been equally ineffective, though in an opposite sense, were it not for the fact that it finds itself within a linguistic discourse. Finally every individual object or person presents itself from within a field which again is possible only within the world. Subjectively speaking, a non-thetic, non-linguistic consciousness of the world is the background from which language serves to cut off a field which is further narrowed down by the linguistic mechanism till the last gap is bridged by a thetic but practical relationship. Uniqueness is the objective counterpart of this practical relationship, and the unique reference of language, even of the 'this', is derived from it.

CHAPTER VIII

REMARKS ON THE CONTENT THEORY*

In this paper I wish to clarify certain points which I consider to be muddles in connection with the content theory. By 'content theory' I mean the philosophical contention that knowledge involves three factors: a subject, an object and a content. Amongst those who subscribe to such an analysis of knowledge there is a great deal of divergence of opinion regarding the more specific problems about the nature of each of the three factors and the exact relation between any two of them. I do not wish to take up these issues in this paper. I only wish to draw attention to certain mistakes which, in my opinion, have characterised the entire discussion for and against the content theory. Once these mistakes are set aside, it would be possible – so it seems to me – to rehabilitate the content theory on a sounder basis than before.

I

In the first place, it would be profitable to state an argument which is most commonly advanced in favour of the content theory, viz. the argument from error and other allied phenomena. It is argued that a two-factor analysis which suits cases of right knowledge fairly well does not, however, apply to cases of error and illusion where there are obviously three factors involved. If, therefore, we start from cases of right knowledge and, taking up a two-factor analysis which they suggest, seek to extend it to cases of error, we are sure to be disappointed. What we should do, then, is to start with cases of error, take up a three-factor ana-

* Published in the *Visva Bharati Journal of Philosophy*, Vol. I, No. 2, 1965, pp. 38–42.

lysis suggested by them and seek to extend it to cases of right knowledge. Success awaits us here, for it is possible to contend that in cases of right knowledge as well the content and the object are distinct but not distinguished as they agree with one another. Hence if we are to have a theory of knowledge which is to apply to all cases of knowledge, true or erroneous, this can only be some form of the content theory.

What I wish to dispute now is the importance accorded to this argument. It seems to me that it is not only not necessary in a theory of knowledge to start from the phenomena of error and illusion, it is positively misleading to do so. It is misleading in so far as in error and illusion the object is not known at all, and this might quite understandably raise the suspicion that the same holds good even in cases of the so-called right knowledge. The point of distinction between right knowledge and error, and the further consequence that the former alone deserves to be called knowledge, are likely to be lost sight of if a theory of knowledge starts from the latter and by analogy with it seeks to explain the former. For, admitting that there is a content in cases of error and illusion, it may still be argued that the same may not be true of right knowledge whose precise point of distinction may be said to lie in this that in it the object is known as it is. If, then, the content theory needs a supporting argument, such argument should take into consideration the very phenomenon of right knowledge.

No knowledge is merely the intentional reference of consciousness to any object, or to an indefinite object-in-general. Consciousness, of course, must be of some object or other, but this indefinite reference is not adequate to constitute a knowledge. Knowledge is of a definite object, and this definiteness is a constitutive character of knowledge. It is, of course, true that knowledge does not confer definiteness on its object. It rather derives its definiteness from its object, it is *viṣayanirūpya*. Not only is a pot different from a cloth, but the knowledge of a pot is different from that of a cloth. This latter difference is derived from but not wholly reducible to the former difference. This definiteness of a knowledge, as the more in it than bare consciousness, is the epistemic content. And its presence is revealed only to reflection on the knowledge whose content it is. For, in reflection a knowledge is recognised not only as a knowledge but also as this knowledge, as having such and such structure. The very fact that a knowledge is capable of logical analysis shows that what is analysed is the content, not pure consciousness nor the object known.

Once the presence of the content is thus discovered, the further question as to how this is compatible with knowledge of the object may be taken up.

II

In most discussions of the content theory it is assumed that such a theory entails some sort of representationism. The advocates of the theory try to show that direct knowledge is not possible. They look upon the naive or direct realist as their chief adversary. Even the critics of the theory have drawn attention to the ruinous consequences of its representationist character and argued that if the content always stands between the subject and the object then the object is perhaps never known at all, so that the knowledge intention should be deemed as terminating at the content and never going beyond it. As a result one may be led even to doubt or deny the very existence of an object other than the content. But then, if there is nothing other, the content is but the object, and there is no point any more in the content theory.

Now it seems to me that the issue between a two-factor and a three-factor analysis of knowledge should not be muddled up with the issue whether knowledge is direct or indirect. The former issue is relatively clear and well-defined; the latter is not so, owing to the fact that there is hardly any clear idea as to what the words 'direct' and 'indirect' are to mean in the present context. It is not true – as I shall try to argue presently – that admission of a content of knowledge entails that knowledge of the object is indirect. The belief that it does so entail has been one of the great stumbling blocks on the way to a clarification of the knowledge situation. This erroneous belief, viz. that admission of a content of knowledge entails that knowledge is indirect, rests, on its part, upon (a) a mistaken notion of the nature of content and its role in a knowledge situation and (b) a mistaken notion about what is meant by 'direct apprehension'.

(a) It is supposed that if there is at all to be content of knowledge then this content, by its very nature, would stand between the subject and the object, and owing to this intermediary position that it would occupy it would not permit the object to be known. It would virtually arrogate to itself the status of the object. At best it would be but a poor representative, perpetually under the shadow of suspicion. Such a theory would no doubt give a plausible account of error, but at what great cost! It would lay every knowledge under the suspicion of being erroneous; and in so far as the object would never be known at all, there would be no true knowledge anywhere.

This apprehension is no doubt genuine if it is directed against the usual conceptions of the nature of the content. The notion of content, however, need not be so formulated. It is necessary at this stage to bear in mind what should be the proper task of a theory of knowledge. A theory has to be true to phenomena; and where there is conflict between a theory and the relevant phenomena, it is the former, and not the latter, that should be discarded. It is not, therefore, within the rights of a theory of knowledge to tell us (far less, to prescribe) what we know and what we do not know. Thus, when some philosophers tell us that we do not perceive physical objects, like houses, trees and tables, but only infer or construct them, they are going beyond the limits of what they are legitimately entitled to say. The philosopher's contention should not be incompatible with our ordinary belief that we perceive physical objects. That we know objects (if we know anything at all) is the fact from which alone we could take our start, which we cannot dispute, and with which, therefore, our subsequent philosophical contentions should not come into conflict. All that we have to do is to analyse such knowledge (but not to dispute it), to discover any new hitherto unnoticed phenomenon implicit in them, to lay bare the presuppositions and implications, if any, of such knowledge and finally, by viewing it in the light of other types of knowledge, to interpret and evaluate it. This being the case, our conception of content should be such that it does not conflict with the phenomenon of our knowledge of objects. There are in fact two phe-

nomena to be harmonised. There is, on the one hand, the undeniable phenomenon (testified by unreflective consciousness)
that we know objects, and there is, on the other hand, the fact,
discovered by reflective consciousness, that all knowledge has a
determinate content. To deny the content in the way the naive
realist does it would conflict with the latter, to deny the object
by reducing it to a system of contents – in whatever manner
'system' may be understood – would conflict with the former.
For, to harmonise the two phenomena is also to maintain the
distinction there is between the two. Where the distinction is
obliterated, the gap bridged, there one of them is just reduced to
the other. Moreover, if the object were a system of contents,
actual or possible – for it could not be a system of actual contents
alone – such a system could not be given, it could only be conceived or anticipated: the object would, in that case, be a Kantian Idea, not a knowable, and certainly not what is known. To
accept the distinction between object and content and yet to set
up the latter as what alone is given – as what intervenes, stands
in between, or even as what represents – is to cast doubt on the
veracity of the first phenomenon which should rather be our
undisputed starting point.

The only way such harmonisation could be effected is to admit that the content serves as a transparent medium for reference.
I would like to contrast this notion of content with the one that
leads to scepticism, by calling the latter a conception of the
content as opaque, and the former the conception of it as transparent. What we need in a theory of knowledge is the conception of a transparent content. It is to the task of elucidating
this conception that we may now turn.

Consider the case of making a meaningful statement, or hearing one being made. The sentence used to make the statement has
a meaning which is the proposition expressed by it. However,
the speaker's primary intention is to refer to the fact it is being
used to state, and not to convey the meaning, though at the same
time the meaning, i.e., the proposition, functions as the medium
which makes the reference possible. The hearer, if his attitude
is a reflective one of understanding the meaning, may simply
entertain the proposition; but in the primary cognitive attitude
the hearer knows or attends to the fact that is being stated,

though understanding the proposition makes this possible. Here the meaning-content, i.e. the proposition, does not thwart objective reference, but renders the latter possible as its indispensable condition.

The same, I would suggest, holds good of all knowledge-situation. The contents are discovered through reflection; but in the unreflective cognitive attitude they are nevertheless there, not as superfluous appendages, but as the necessary media of objective reference. They do not hinder the object from being known by arrogating to themselves its status, for their very function is to make knowledge of object possible. It is to be noted that the conception of content as transparent leaves room for further determination of its status. There remain open such questions as – Is the content an additional entity, or is it the object as known (in the Nyāya terminology, is the *viṣayatā* an *atirikta-padārtha*), etc.?

(b) It may nevertheless be felt that though the concept of transparent content makes room for knowledge of the object it does not leave room for direct knowledge and so cannot avoid some form of representationism. This charge can be avoided only by way of clarifying some misconceptions about what is meant by 'direct knowledge'. It seems to me that the contrast between direct knowledge and indirect knowledge should better be replaced by that between perceptual knowledge (*pratyakṣa*) and non-perceptual knowledge (*parokṣa*). In that case, the issue would be – can objects be perceptually known, or are they always to be inferred? This issue may be settled relatively easily, e.g. by appealing to the principle, as Vatsyayana does in his defence of *avayavipratyakṣa*, that inference presupposes perception, so that if there is no perception of the mark there would after all be no inference either.[1]

If, on the other hand, the issue is formulated in terms of direct knowledge vis-a-vis indirect knowledge, a settlement of the issue is hindered by the difficulty of clarifying the meaning of the key words involved. If 'direct knowledge' means knowledge of an object without mediation by a content or idea, then the contention that knowledge according to the content theory has to be

---

[1] Cp. J. N. Mohanty, "The Nyāya Theory of *Avayavipratyakṣa*" in *The Journal of the Indian Academy of Philosophy*, Vol. II. [Reprinted in this volume].

indirect would be but a naked tautology. The issue, then, is – is there a content or not; and it is advisable not to state it in the misleading language of direct or indirect knowledge. If by 'direct knowledge' be meant knowledge which is not mediated by anything whatsoever, there is no such knowledge, for the mediation or the instrumentality of sense-organs at least is unavoidable. It may be conceded that perception contains a core of direct knowledge, *viz.* the reception of sense-data, while around this core there cluster inferred or associational elements. But against this contention we may say two things. The less important of the two is that such a position entails – as is explicitly held by most of the Western philosophers – that perception contains an element of inference or construction, which, to my mind, amounts to denying the very perceptuality (*pratyakṣatva*) of perception. The other, and the more weighty, point is that this pin-pointing of the directly given to sense-data is based on a very dubious conception of *the given*.[2]

To be directly known is to be perceived. What is directly known is not inferred. In this sense of "direct", admission of a content of knowledge is not incompatible with direct knowledge of the object, provided we correctly formulate the nature of the content. However, it is not necessary that the object should be always directly known. It may be inferred, and in so far as it is inferred it is not directly known, though *known* all the same. The central point is that the content does not hinder the object from being known. It is also necessary to bear in mind that where an object is indirectly known, say inferred, it is nonetheless known, and it is not the case what is known is the content. However, there is no denying the primacy of perceptual knowledge. The object that is inferred could be perceived. One could say, it would have been best if it were actually perceived. Perception, therefore, is the paradigm case of knowledge.

III

We have shown earlier that that in knowledge which makes it amenable to logical analysis is the content. Now this is likely to

---

[2] Cp. J. N. Mohanty, "The Given" in the *Proceedings of the Delhi Philosophical Colloquium*, Indian International Centre, Delhi, 1964. [Reprinted in this volume].

throw light on the nature of the content. It at least tells us what the content is not. The contents in the case of perception are not sense-data, for sense-data are not the sort of things that are capable of logical analysis. Likewise the content cannot be of the nature of sensation or image. For, sensation, sense-data and image are such that if they were to stand between the subject and the object they would themselves be the objects apprehended and would not be the sort of transparent medium for reference which any content *qua* content should be if it is to fulfil its true epistemic function. The content, then, would be of the nature of meaning. It would rather be that from which the proposition regarded as the meaning of an indicative sentence is an abstraction. A logic of such cognitive contents would, then, be in a certain sense prior to a logic of propositions.

CHAPTER IX

PHENOMENOLOGY AND ONTOLOGY

I. PHILOSOPHICAL METHOD

(a) Puzzles: *"Zurück zu den Sachen"*, "Back to the facts" was Husserl's epoch-making slogan. Though I have long since been captivated by this slogan, I have never ceased to be puzzled by it. Husserl's programme attracted me because of his rejection of speculative metaphysics. Philosophy, it seems to me, must in some sense be descriptive. But what should it describe? What sorts of facts are those that philosophy should describe? How are these facts different from the facts described by ordinary perceptual statements as also by the descriptive statements of the sciences? Further, is pure description at all possible? Pure description, it would seem, would be possible only if it were also possible for something to be given without the least admixture of interpretation. But is not all that seems to be given shot through with interpretations? More particularly, is not all givenness subject to the mould imposed by language? Is there, positively asking, any mode of direct i.e. non-linguistic access to the facts concerned? Finally, how is the ancient and age-old conception of philosophy as explanatory and interpretative in function to be accommodated? In other words, should philosophy abandon its age-old function which, as it were, has come to constitute its defining character and assume a totally new role, and if so would not the new science forfeit its claim to be called 'philosophy'?

(b) Hegelians like Bradley and Blanshard, speculative metaphysicians like Whitehead, existentialists like Kierkegaard and Heidegger, and linguistic philosophers like Ryle, Austin and Goodman – all agree in condemning the idea of the unadul-

terated given, though they might differ amongst themselves
as to the nature and the source of the interpretations involved:
the interpretations are tagged on either to an ontological scheme,
or to a conceptual framework, or to a language system. Whitehead expresses the point most forcefully thus: "If we desire a
record of uninterpreted experience, we must ask a stone to record its autobiography".[1] Heidegger writes in the same vein:
*Alles vor-prädikative schlichte Sehen des Zuhandenen ist an ihm
selbst schon verstehend-auslegend"*.[2] The most primitive 'seeing'
is 'interpretative'. It is not therefore surprising that Heidegger
should have subscribed to the apparently paradoxical view that
the phenomenological method of description is really interpretative.[3] Similarly, for the Hegelian there is no absolute immediacy. Immediacy is either a merely logical presupposition
or the consummating goal towards which experience and knowledge are moving and in which they would but commit suicide:
in neither case is it capable of presenting data for phenomenological description. For the later Wittgenstein, even ostension
to be meaningful should presuppose a language system. And
curiously enough, all of them – excluding the extreme Hegelians
alone - recognise the value of description as a philosophical method.
Whitehead speaks of his metaphysics as being descriptive in
character.[4] So does Heidegger also. Wittgenstein writes: "Philosophy may in no way interfere with the actual use of language;
it can in the end only describe it".[5]

The contradiction can be resolved, so it seems to me, by
recognising that what the phenomenological method of description stands for is not the primacy of intuition over understanding. It does not aim at getting hold of the primitive immediacy alone, although it seeks to do that also. The opposition
between intuition and understanding, between the given and the
interpretations is a false one. Reflection and understanding
lead to fresh intuitions. And intuitions may serve to lay bare interpretations that have come to be sedimented in the structure
of phenomena.

[1] A. N. Whitehead, *Process and Reality*, New York edition, p. 22.
[2] M. Heidegger, *Sein und Zeit*, Tübingen, 7th edition 1953, p. 149.
[3] *Ibid.*, p. 150.
[4] A. N. Whitehead, *loc. cit.*, p. 19.
[5] L. Wittgenstein, *Philosophical Investigations*, Oxford, 1953, p. 49.

(c) The idea of a philosophical *system*, understood in the sense of traditional speculative metaphysics, is obviously incompatible with such a conception of philosophical method. For a phenomenological philosophy should neither deduce nor reduce. It should avoid, as Nicolai Hartmann constantly reminded us, both kinds of reduction, *"nach Unten"* nach *"nach Oben"*. There is however another sense in which there is room for system in such a philosophy. Two principles seem to me to be illuminating, and both I owe again to Nicolai Hartmann (though not in the form in which I here make use of them). There should be, in the first place, a minimum of speculative metaphysics. Pure description is an ideal after which we could only strive, and in this striving our heuristic principle should be to make as few speculative-deductive commitments as possible. In the second place, the system should be an 'open' rather than a 'closed' one. A typical example of what is meant by a closed system is the Hegelian philosophy in which there is an explanation for every phenomenon in the sense that phenomena are deductively linked up with each other so as to lead up to the highest Idea. Now by an 'open' system I mean one in which phenomena 'announce' their own status or *'topos'* and, when they are conceptually placed side by side, there are found to be missing links or gaps that can only be conceptually filled in, but need not be. The Advaita Vedānta is a good example of such an open system, though the later exponents of the system no doubt sought to close the gaps arbitrarily. Gaps are to be filled in, as far as possible, by fresh phenomenological data (this is what Sri Aurobindo seems to be doing in his peculiar doctrine of grades of consciousness), failing which they are themselves to be recognised as irreducible.

(d) What are those phenomena which philosophy should describe? It was a common doctrine of the phenomenologists that these are nothing other than essences and essential structures. The full implication however was not as clearly brought out as it should have been. There is no doubt that the different aspects of the situation were seen in different contexts by different thinkers; what is still lacking is a perception of the essential unity and interrelation of these aspects. There were inevitably three different groups of thinkers: the ontologists (Scheler and Hartmann), the subjectivists (the later Husserl, Natorp) and the linguistic analysts (Hans Lipps, Gilbert Ryle). It has not yet however been sufficiently realised that these three groups were concerned with three different aspects of the proper object of philosophical thought. I would now proceed to explicate the above statement.

Critical philosophers since Kant have from time to time suspeted naive ontology, and have sought to reduce ontology either to transcendental logic (Kant) or to some kind of metalinguistic commitment. Quine, for example, following Russell, has reduced ontological commitments to the range of values that are permissible for the variables in the existential quantifier. But more interesting is Carnap's attempt to translate statements in the material mode to those in the formal mode. Now we may broadly distinguish between two different ways of replacing the material mode of speech: the formal mode of Carnap and the phenomenological mode. Whereas the former considers the way the corresponding words are used, the latter considers the mode in which the entity under consideration is given. Thus while the ontological or the material mode speaks of entities and the formal mode of the logical behaviour of the corresponding words, the phenomenological mode considers the mode of givenness of that entity. Now the phenomena that a phenomenological philosophy has to describe are such that with regard to them the ontological mode of speech is inseparable from the formal and the phenomenological modes. This may be clarified with regard to two statements which I quote below: one from the K. C. Bhattacharyya and the other from Edmund Husserl.

K. C. Bhattacharyya writes:

"Speakability is a contingent character of the content of empirical thought, but it is a necessary character of the content of pure philosophic thought."[6]

Referring to the points of distinction between the phenomenological and the ontological attitudes, Husserl writes:

"*Das sind kardinale Unterschiede, die nur Verallgemeinerungen des einfachen Unterschiedes sind, dass Bedeutungen setzen und Gegenstände setzen zweierlei ist..*"[7]

Both Bhattacharyya and Husserl are thus drawing attention

---

[6] K. C. Bhattacharyya, *Studies in Philosophy*, Vol. II, Calcutta, 1958, pp. 102–3.
[7] *Ideen*, Vol. III, Martinus Nijhoff, (Husserliana), The Hague, 1950, pp. 88–89.

to the fact that the essences which phenomenology has to describe are but meanings, and thus any ontological assertion about
them cannot but have an equivalent in the formal mode. Likewise, such an essence has its own mode of givenness which is not
just accidental to its own mode of being. Far from it, the mode
of givenness and the mode of being are but inseparable poles of
the same phenomenon. This equivalence however does not hold
good of empirical facts of whom, as Bhattacharyya rightly sees,
speakability is – and I should add, givability – is only a contingent character.

Thus those philosophers who deny to philosophy any factual
content and assign to it the task of exploring the logical behaviour of words are partly right, as also are those who take up the
programme of bringing to light the subjective constitution of the
objective essences. The former are right in so far as the objects of
philosophical description are, unlike empirical facts, revealed
through meaning analysis. They err however in thinking that
philosophical statements are for that reason of no ontological
significance, and also in concentrating on a therapeutic use of
their linguistic wisdom. We contend on the other hand that
ontology is possible through linguistic analysis, though such
ontology would be very different from naive dogmatic ontology.
The same is also true of the programme of constitution-analysis.
Both meaning-analysis and constitution-analysis are the gate-
ways to a critical ontology, and the three in their unity constitute the *integral* phenomenological method.

The reason why linguistic analysis has been regarded as ontologically unfruitful and why questions of language and questions of fact have been sharply sundered seems to be a mistaken
notion about the nature of language which on its part derives
from a mistaken theory of meaning.

II. MEANING AND REFERENCE

Meaning has wrongly been taken to consist in use. After the
early empiricists' image theory and the latter-day positivists'
verifiability theory were rightly abandoned, the modern analysts
have taken to the view that knowing the meaning of an expres-

sion is the same as knowing how to use it in accordance with the
rules and conventions of the language under consideration. Such a
theory of meaning has, in the eyes of its propounders, two distinct advantages. On the one hand, it renders it impossible to
speak any longer of meanings as entities. On the other hand,
it avoids the subjectivism of the image theory and the verifiability theory, for the rules and conventions that confer
meaning are far from being subjective. Now if this is what constitutes meaning, and if all extra-linguistic facts, objects, events
(whichever language one may prefer) are objects of *reference*, then
analysis of the meaning of an expression should bring to light
its behaviour within the language concerned and cannot by
any means provide us with a basis on which to build an ontology.

Now, such a conventionalist and operationalist theory of
meaning is inadequate for the following reasons: It cannot account for what happens when we grasp the meaning of a word
or of a sentence in a flash as it were. It would not do to say that
what we grasp is a set of rules and conventions for reasons of which
Wittgenstein himself is aware.[8] It is not the bare possibility of
use, for what we grasp is not this possibility itself but rather
that which makes its use possible. Wittgenstein is right[9] that
certain objective circumstances, human customs and institutions
in the present case, a conventional system of signs with rules of
operation – must be given in order that I could intend a meaning.
But this does not imply that a linguistic expression is nothing
but a physical sign or that our understanding of it is nothing
other than the capacity to operate with it in accordance with
rules. We contend on the other hand that given a set of signs
with rules of operation, the set would not amount to language –
nor would the operation amount to an understanding – unless an
intellectual act or meaning intention supervened. Now the meaning in the substantive, the much abused abstract entity, is a
phenomenological datum not to be liquidated by any theory,
though its platonic character would be less appalling if only we
remember that it is but the intentional correlate – as Husserl
would say – of the meaning intending act.

[8] L. Wittgenstein, *loc. cit.*, p. 53.
[9] Cp. J. N. Mohanty, *Edmund Husserl's Theory of Meaning*, Martinus Nijhoff, The
Hague, 1964, p. 40.

In other words, it must be recognised that meanings have an identity and objectivity about them, which all forms of psychologism and conventionalism threaten to destroy. At the same time the 'It means' has its necessary correlate in the 'I mean', and both have a necessary reference to 'in the language L'. Platonism in theory of meaning must therefore be so interpreted as to be the fulfilment of both subjectivism and formalism. The relation between the 'I mean' and the 'It means' is especially intimate: using an analogy which I have elsewhere employed[10], one could say just as in modern physics it has come to be recognised that the wave theory and the corpuscular theory of elementary particles are not rival hypotheses but are really complementary descriptions, so in theory of meaning it has got to be recognised that platonism and anti-platonism, the ontological and the subjective approaches, are complementary, not rival and not even alternate, ways of describing the same unitary phenomenon. The ontological hypostatisation has to be supplemented by bearing the subjective and the linguistic "backgrounds" in mind, just as the subjective and the linguistic relativism has to be overcome by making it subservient to a recognition of the ideality and the objectivity of meanings.

To admit the element of truth that is there in a platonistic theory of meaning is *not* however to betray one's failure to distinguish between meaning and reference, for it is precisely this distinction – kept in mind by both Frege and Husserl – that provides the basis for platonism. It cannot also be said that platonism here implies the unpalatable thesis that in understanding the meaning of an expression we inspect impalpable abstractions. It is particularly against this last accusation that a few words of clarification are needed.

Understanding an expression 'S is p' may or may not be a constituent of the knowledge that S is p. When it is a constituent of the knowledge the intention is of course directed towards the fact referred to, and not towards the meanings themselves. But even when the understanding is a mere understanding not amounting to knowledge, we do *not* inspect meanings, for meanings are just not the sort of entities which could be inspected. They may perhaps be more appropriately described as

[10] *Ibid.*, p. 75.

transparent media through which the intention is directed towards the object of reference. They are not intended in the same sense in which a fact being referred to is: the latter is the object intended, the meaning is the mode of so intending. Our theory that even a mere understanding of an expression not amounting to knowledge is also to refer implies that reference, like sense or meaning, belongs to expressions *qua* expressions, and it should be obvious that with this we are rejecting the view of those philosophers who hold that expressions have only meaning while it is only a genuine use of them that refers. The Meinongian ghosts could be avoided if only we bear in mind that not all intended references are capable of being fulfilled.

A distinction between understanding and knowing may be recommended on the basis of the above considerations. It follows from the above that to understand a sentence "S is p" is also to understand *what kind of facts* it refers to, but this does not – unless the understanding has entered into a knowledge as a constituent thereof – amount to knowing *the fact*. Knowing that S is p however presupposes an understanding of the sentence "S is p". Knowledge in this sense implies a unique identification, in Husserl's language a fulfilment. This is not more than suggesting that the two, understanding with its generality and knowing with its unique identification, represent two poles between which human cognitive endeavour oscillates. Scientific knowledge, in trying to get away from unique reference to generality, aims at pure understanding. Perceptions of physical objects and of other persons are, not without reason, regarded as the standard types of knowing, for they excel just in the unique identification achieved.

III. THE THEORETICAL AND THE PRACTICAL MODES OF
GIVENNESS

How is such unique reference possible? As I have said elsewhere, the extra-linguistic reference of language presents no problem at all, for such reference is an essential character of language *qua* language. The really pertinent problem is, how is it possible to make unique reference? Most philosophers who have dealt with this problem fall back upon such words as 'this', here', 'now'. But the mere fact that even these words have an aspect of sense distinguishable from their reference makes it possible that one can understand them without knowing what precisely is being uniquely referred to. We have to recognise that a knowledge of the unique individual is far from being a contemplative affair. It is necessary to recognise the distinction between two basic modes of givenness: the theoretical and the practical. The unique particular (physical object) and the unique individual (person) are identified not through theoretic con-templation but through practical relationships.

In theory of perception this distinction saves us from much embarrassment. It is well known how the vexed question of the perception of physical objects has been treated in contemporary philosophy. Starting with the sense-data, the qualities or the essences as the only given elements, philosophers have found themselves compelled to regard the physical object either as totally unknown (but believed on 'animal faith') or as merely inferred or even as a construction out of those elements. None of these consequences has proved acceptable for one reason amongst others that they all go against that primary evidence with which things are given in unreflective experience. Things are not given in that theoretical attitude in which one discovers sense-data or essences. Philosophers, as Whitehead rightly saw, have erred in regarding perception as a contemplative experience, and the percipient person as a passive epistemological subject which he is not. In the reflective and contemplative attitude, the stubborn brute physical objects recede to the background and in their place we are confronted with sense-data and essences. This, and not the much discussed argument from illusion, is the real source of the sense datum approach, which is destined to failure as it surreptitiously seeks to replace the data of one mode by those of another. It is not true to contend that the sense datum theory is only an alternate *linguistic* recommendation, the physical object language being another such possibility. The truth seems to be that they are not co-ordinate possibilities but are rooted in two successive modes of disclosure, the phy-sical object being given in the primary, unreflective practical mode and the sense-data in a subsequent reflective and theoretical mode. Each theory, or each language if you like, has thus its own justification. Given the physical object, it can of course be analysed into sense-data and essences.[11] But the theoretician's attempt to recompose that original pre-theoretical unity out of these data is bound to fail.

As with the problem of our perception of physical objects, so also with the problem of our knowledge of other persons. Here again it is an erroneous procedure to begin with my awareness of myself and then to search for some means (inference, empathy or *Einfühlung*) by which I could reach, apprehend or realise other selves. It is again through a system of practical relationships that I discover others as well as myself, in fact both together and as inseparable. This is the element of truth in Heidegger's contention that the person is, in his essential structure, 'with others'. As the practical relationships reveal the person-with-other-persons, so does theoretical reflection lead through various stages to the transcendental subjectivity of Kant and Husserl. Husserl was right when he insisted that even the transcendental subjectivity is intentional, so that the Advaita conception of a pure non-intentional consciousness is beyond phenomenology. Such a purely non-intentional consciousness is *not* given at all in any of the modes of givenness, theoretical or practical. The notion of pure consciousness represents the limiting point of our turning away from the ontological attitude, and since the phenomenological mode has always its correlative ontology, the supposed pure non-intentional consciousness cannot even be a phenomenological datum. It can therefore be postulated only by an act of *faith*.

The practical mode thus reveals on the one hand the world of things and on the other a community of persons, the 'It' and the 'Thou'. Corresponding to this we may draw the distinction, following Kant,[12] between the *technically practical* and the *morally practical*. Both present real existence and conceptually

---

[11] Professor J. N. Chubb (Bombay) tells me that late K. C. Bhattacharyya in an unpublished letter to him expresses the view that the sense-data are results of "aesthetic abstraction". Professor Chubb also recalls a remark once made by the late Professor R. G. Collingwood to him that no intelligible relation could be formulated between physical objects and sense-data since they belonged to two different levels.

[12] I. Kant, *Critique of Aesthetic Judgement*, E. Tr. by J. C. Meredith, Oxford, 1911, Introduction, p. 9.

irreducible unities which, when sought to be grasped by theoretical consciousness, disintegrate into endless series.

IV. A PHENOMENOLOGICAL DISCONTINUITY

Philosophy is generally taken to involve reflection. The suggestion then that the unreflective practical attitude, and the corresponding mode of disclosure, be accorded the recognition that we have given to it may seem to involve a paradox. How can reflection accept the unreflective orientation and its disclosure? And should not philosophy rather challenge the naivity of that primitive attitude, and then shatter it into bits in order to reconstruct it in accordance with reflective categories? Or at least should not philosophy 'transcend' that primitive naivety? Or, if one is in sympathy with that primitive naivety, should not one, as a philosopher, undertake the task of proving or deductively demonstrating – as G. E. Moore sought to do – the beliefs ascribed to it?

Now as is well known, the main point of distinction between a phenomenological philosophy and a deductive metaphysics is that the former "describes" whereas the latter "deduces", "proves" or "explains". Accordingly, a phenomenological philosopher has to face a paradox, a paradox that is involved in his very method. On the one hand he has to install himself in an attitude, be it of unreflective naivety or of reflective contemplation. At the same time, he has to transcend it to be its passive witness (*sākṣin*), to suspend belief as Husserl would say in order to be able to describe. This paradox cannot be resolved, and has to be accepted: this simultaneous participation and transcendence – which in fact provides the key to a phenomenological philosophy. The philosopher therefore need not accept the beliefs of unreflective attitude just as he need not also reject them. Achieving the needed transcendence, his job is to tell the tale. He is not to be a partisan but an impartial spectator. Moore, when he undertook to defend common sense as against speculative philosophers, committed a double error: he ascribed to the pre-reflective attitude beliefs which are themselves only other philosophical theories, and he sought to demonstrate what has a non-demonstrative certainty. He failed thereby to exhibit the nature and the source of that certainty.[13]

A phenomenological philosophy has to accept a radical phenomenological discontinuity, and any attempt to overcome it is to be suspected as originating from a too hasty desire for achieving metaphysical simplicity. One of the beauties of the Advaita Vedānta is that it accepts such a discontinuity between the *vyāvahārika* (the empirical) and the *pāramārthika* (the transcendental), and considers any relationship between them as being logically indescribable. Our distinction between the practical and the theoretical may be regarded as a pale reflection of that spiritual philosophy on the level of secular philosophising.

[13] J. N. Mohanty, "On Moore's Defence of Common Sense", *Indian Journal of Philosophy*, II, 1960, No. 4, 1–10. [Reprinted in this volume].

PART TWO

CHAPTER X

A NOTE ON MODERN NOMINALISM*

I

The purpose of this note is to draw attention to a most perplexing characteristic of some modern nominalistic theories, especially as we find them in the writings of W. V. O. Quine and Goodman.

Before coming to the main point of this note, it would not perhaps be out of order if I recall that I have elsewhere[1] drawn attention to some distinguishing features of modern platonism (using that much-abused term in a very wide sense) as we find it in German phenomenology as well as in Whitehead, Russell (in some phases of his philosophical career) and Santayana. Two such features may be mentioned straightaway: first, platonism has ceased to be a speculative and metaphysical doctrine and has been given a phenomenological, descriptive basis; secondly, the platonic entities are no more taken to be universals in the traditional sense. Whitehead, Santayana and the German phenomenologists refuse to identify their platonic entities with universals. On the contrary, they speak of ideal singularities and of fully determinate essences. I cannot here substantiate these two characterisations. But let me conclude this digression by remarking that in these modern forms of platonism the distinction between individuals and universals has been blurred and that between the real and the ideal has been regarded as fundamental.

---

* First published in the Proceedings of the Indian Philosophical Congress, Cuttack, 1959.
[1] Cp. my *Nicolai Hartmann and A. N. Whitehead: A Study in Recent Platonism*, Calcutta, 1957.

Turning now to the type of nominalism developed by Quine and Goodman, we find another most interesting, and yet perplexing, manner in which the same distinction between individuals and universals is sought to be blurred. What we get at the end is so very different from what has traditionally been called 'nominalism' that we are left wondering what has in the long run been achieved. One even wonders if what has been achieved is not, in some sense, a "meeting of extremes", of the extremes of Universalism and nominalism.

I should now hasten to explicate and substantiate this last remark. Universalism is not the same as platonism. For, what has come to be called 'platonism' consists in the admission of 'abstract' entities into one's ontological scheme; but this admission does not necessarily entail an expulsion of concrete particulars from that scheme. Traditional platonic realism is, in fact, dualistic. Universalism is the ontological theory which denies particulars and reduces them to universals; if a universalist is a linguistic philosopher, he may content himself with a substitution of names of particulars by names of universals. Strictly speaking, nominalism is the exact antithesis, not of platonism, but of universalism. For, just as universalism admits only universals into ontology (or 'names' of universals into the ideal language), so does nominalism admit only concrete particulars; both are monistic. Now, the type of nominalism developed by Quine and Goodman is, in one of its major aspects at least, not far removed from what has been called here universalism. Quine, for example, considers the whole category of 'names' as superfluous and would permit reference to particulars only indirectly over variables within the quantifier. So far as Goodman is concerned, the basic elements of his ontology are identically repeatable *qualia* that are as much individuals as universals, the concrete particulars like tables and chairs being constructions out of such elements. Before considering these two points in some more detail, let me state the main motives, principles and devices of this type of nominalism.

II

Modern nominalism springs from two motives: there is, to start with, a distrust of abstract entities, a distrust that, Quine and Goodman confess, "is based on a philosophical intuition that cannot be justified by appealing to anything more ultimate".[2] One may conjecture that this distrust and this refusal are strengthened by the refusal of 'common sense' to admit such absurd and fictitious entities as 'the present king of France', 'the round square', etc. It would, however, be too hasty to invoke common sense for supporting our refusal to admit such entities as redness or circularity. In fact, one cannot agree with the tendency to huddle together such entities as redness and circularity with such others as the present king of France and round square, to label them all as abstract, and then to banish them together from ontology. This procedure is unjust; common sense rebels against the admission of fictitious entities, whereas it is not common sense but a certain philosophical theory that rebels against the admission of redness and circularity. In the former case, we may call to our aid an intuition that is not further justifiable;[3] in the latter case, what moves the nominalist is not an intuition but an article of faith.[4]

The other motive, clearly stated by Goodman,[5] is the logical incomprehensibility of classes (an incomprehensibility which, as Dummet has pointed out,[6] had puzzled also McTaggart). There may be two classes, A and B, which are as classes different and yet have no difference in their contents.

It is not the purpose of this note to answer this difficulty.

---

[2] W. V. Quine and N. Goodman, "Steps towards a constructive Nominalism", *Journal of Symbolic Logic*, 1947, No. 4, p. 105.

[3] But even amongst entities banished as 'fictitious' one should be able to detect valuable distinctions. The case with 'the present king of France' is different from that with 'round square'. Strawson has convincingly shown that the former expression is not meaningless, even if a certain use of it may have no reference.

[4] Cp. A. Church: "The extreme demand for a simple prohibition of abstract entities under all circumstances perhaps arises from a desire to maintain the connection between theory and observation. But the preference of (say) seeing over understanding as a method of observation seems to me capricious". ("The need for Abstract Entities in Semantic Analysis "in *Proceedings of the American Academy of Arts and Sciences*, Vol. 80, No. 1, p. 104).

[5] N. Goodman, *The Structure of Appearance*, Cambridge, Mass., 1951, p. 108.

[6] *Mind*, 1955, pp. 101–109.

Wang has complained that Goodman does not make explicit what is meant by 'content'.[7] But quite apart from that, a platonist of the modern type may not undertake a defence of extensional classes; he may agree that classes are constructions; he may still insist that the basic entities are fully determinate individuals, abstract or concrete, – the concrete individuals being unrepeatable and spatio-temporally unique, and the abstract individuals being identically repeatable and qualitatively unique.

I am aware that this would not be far from the position accepted by Goodman himself. Qualitative ("abstract") particles of experience and spatio-temporally bounded ("concrete") particles are equally acceptable basic elements for him.[8] Goodman's system is not 'particularistic' like Carnap's. His basic elements are abstract. He is a nominalist in whose system the basic elements are abstract identically repeatable *qualia*. Such a nominalism is welcome to the platonists, for was not the point at issue between traditional realism and traditional nominalism the question if there are or are not identically repeatable common characters?[9]

Goodman no doubt calls his basic elements individuals. But his concept of the individual defies any attempt to assimilate it to any of our common or philosophical notions of it. I would only refer to the two interesting criticisms of this notion by Lowe and Wang.[10]

III

Quine, I suppose, is more thoroughgoing in his nominalism. It seems to me that he would not subscribe to the ontology of qualities, for such an ontology takes predicates as names and is implicitly committed to using variables within a quantifier to refer to universals by "binding predicate letters", a procedure against which Quine's campaign is primarily directed.

---

[7] *The Philosophical Review*, 1953, pp. 413–4.

[8] *Journal of Symbolic Logic*, 1947, No. 4, p. 105.

[9] Cp. H. H. Price, *Thinking and Experience*, London, 1953.

[10] V. Lowe, "Goodman's Concept of an Individual", *The Philosophical Review*, 1953, pp. 117–126; and H. Wang, "What is an Individual?", *The Philosophical Review*, 1953, pp. 413–420.

"To be is to be the value of a variable".[11] Names alone are substituents of variables;[12] the named entities are the values. It follows that whatever is designated is or, better perhaps, is to be the *designatum* of a name. Predicates are not names. But, why? To say they are not names because they are not substituents of variables or that they do not designate any entity is to state that very thing in another language. In reply, we find that a word to be a name must fulfil a condition, namely, the condition that "existential generalisation" with respect to that word must be possible.[13] This means as is well-known that whereas the singular existential statement "Calcutta is a city" entitles me to infer the general existential statement "(∃x) (x is a city)" or "there is something which is a city", the statement "17 is a prime number" does not permit a similar generalisation of the form "(∃x) (x is a prime number)".

Against this argument and this methodological device, let me state my objections as follows:

Firstly, the argument, if intended to prove that predicates are not names, hopelessly fails, because it is incurably vitiated by *petitio principii*. It assumes what it intends to prove, and it conceals that assumption under the mystifying garb of logical symbolism. But let me confess, I am not sure if it is intended by its authors as a proof. Perhaps it is only an explication of the ontological position they advocate; or, perhaps, it is only a prescription of how predicate words should be used.

But, in any case – and this is my second point – it cannot be said that this rule regarding existential generalisation conforms to our ordinary use of predicate-expressions. For, as Warnock has shown,[14] we may, and also we do, use statements of the form "there is something which is ...." with regard to predicate words or the corresponding singular abstract nouns. So the mere use, or absence of such use, by itself does not decide any issue, nor can the ontological issue be decided by banning such use.

Thirdly, (here again I am indebted to Warnock) – Quine's

[11] W. V. O. Quine, "Designation and Existence", *Journal of Philosophy*, Dec., 1939, p. 708.
[12] *Ibid.*, p. 707.
[13] *Ibid.*, p. 706.
[14] G. J. Warnock, "Metaphysics in Logic", *Proceedings of the Aristotelian Society*, 1950–51, pp. 197–222.

insistence on the ontological importance of the existential generalisation "embodies the presupposition that the question whether there are or are not abstract entities is just like the question
there is or is not a city called 'Leeds'." (Warnock). Whatever
else the platonists may have said, they have certainly laid stress
on the radical difference between the way in which particulars
exist and the way in which universals or Ideas exist. To reduce
both forms of existence to a common logical scheme – 'to be is to
be the value of a variable' – is not to do justice to what the platonist wanted to say. The word 'entity' deludes.

IV

To make clear what possibly could have been meant by the
platonist – I am not claiming that any platonist has actually
said this – let me draw upon some of the ideas of people who are
either nominalists or nearer the nominalists' camp. In his paper
"Form and Existence",[15] Geach has sought to bring out the nature of Form according to Aquinas, and has contrasted it with
the nature of Form according to Plato. I am not at present interested in the question whether the contrast as developed by
Geach is historically true, that is to say, whether Plato and
Aquinas held the opinions ascribed to them in that paper. What
interests me is the possibility that the conception of Form may
be formulated in two different ways. For Aquinas, as also for
Frege – so we learn from Geach – what holds good of, or can meaningfully be said of, an individual does not hold good of, or cannot
meaningfully be said of, a Form. For example, manyness cannot
be meaningfully predicated of an individual; it is only Forms
that are repeatable and capable of manyness. An object is never
repeated; a Form alone may be repeated. If we bear this in
mind, the common platonic doctrine that a Form is a single
entity over against its many instances is to be rejected. So far
as this part of the argument is concerned, it seems to me that
there is something deceptive about the concepts of repeatability', 'manyness' and 'oneness'. For it could be replied that a
Form is repeatable just because it is one, and its identity precisely is such as to make room for this repeatability; that no-

thing is repeatable unless it retains its identity through repetitions. Similarly, an individual is one in the sense that its identity does not permit repetition; it does not admit of manyness in the same sense in which a Form does. The two formulations, therefore, the one ascribed to Plato and the other to Aquinas and Frege, are not incompatible with each other. What interests me here especially is the next step in Geach's argument as he goes on to develop the conception of Form as a function. What constitutes an example of a Form is, according to Geach, not 'wisdom' simply, not 'the wisdom of Socrates', but 'the wisdom of...' One has then to admit into the very constitution of a Form a certain openness, a certain indeterminateness, demanding determination. Now, it seems to me that even if the platonist continues to think of 'wisdom' as an entity, he may nevertheless make room for the recognition that it is a peculiar entity of such a kind that it has an indeterminateness about it, an indeterminateness that claims determination.

When Quine tells us[16] that abstract terms are syncategorematic or when he prefers[17] to understand attributes as "open sentences" rather than as propositional functions, he has the same peculiar character of abstract entities in his mind. And platonism may quite well admit this element into its notion of abstract entities. A similar suggestion, though couched in the language of old-day philosophizing, is found in Stout's idea of universal as a "distributive unity of particulars".[18] The universal is a unity, a unity which, as Stout emphasizes, is irreducible to any of the other types of unity including the unity of a substance. To this peculiar type of unity belongs a distributive reference, an indeterminateness demanding determination or individualisation. I should here add that I have already spoken of two kinds of determinateness (and of indeterminateness). The modern platonist speaks of determinate essences; but, again, as I have just remarked, even the most determinate essence has an indeterminateness (in quite another sense). 'Wisdom' is

[15] *Proceedings of the Aristotelian Society*, 1954–55, pp. 251–272.

[16] *Journal of Philosophy*, 1939, p. 708.

[17] W. V. O. Quine, "On Frege's Way out", *Mind*, 1955, pp. 145–159.

[18] G. F. Stout, "On the Nature of Universals", *Proceedings of the British Academy*, Vol. X.

always 'wisdom of....'; 'this specific shade of red' is also 'this specific shade of red of....'

Nothing that Quine has said serves the purnpose of demolishing platonism.

I would conclude this note by referring again to that peculiar, and often perplexing, blurring of the distinction between individuals and universals that we find not only in modern platonism, but also in modern nominalism. Also, we have seen in part how the position advocated by Goodman is a "meeting of extremes", universalism and nominalism. I would now urge that the same strain is also there in Quine's thinking. But for substantiating this point, I can do no better than quote from Strawson's "Singular Terms, Ontology and Identity".[19] Strawson rightly detects in Quine, on the one hand, "a professed nominalism, the acknowledged preference for an ontology of concrete particulars" and, on the other, an "unconscious drive towards platonism, showing itself in the consequences – not, of course, envisaged by Quine himself – of the attempt to discard singular terms as fundamentally superfluous".

This perplexing situation, in which the controversy between realism and nominalism finds itself today, demands that some fundamentally new way of establishing the difference between individuals and universals be found out. But to do that is not the purpose of this note; to have drawn attention to the situation is enough for my purpose.

[19] *Mind*, 1956, pp. 433–454.

CHAPTER XI

A RECENT CRITICISM OF THE FOUNDATIONS OF NICOLAI HARTMANN'S ONTOLOGY*

I

A system of thought, like a house with brick and mortar, has a foundation and a superstructure. It is the superstructure which attracts more attention, applause or censure. The foundation remains unnoticed. Yet it is the foundation which hides the secret sources of nourishment of the entire structure. This foundation consists of a group of basic concepts and assumptions which the thinker brings into play. The greatness of a thinker lies in the originality and strength of these concepts and assumptions. The mediocre build on nothing new.

Most of the attention which has recently been paid to Hartmann's ontology has been concentrated on the various branches of its widely ramified superstructure. The comparative neglect of the fundamentals has led either to an exaggerated applause or to an exaggerated censure.[1] People have found in his philosophy the most comprehensive 'system' of categories. Others confess complete lack of interest and complain of his superficial philosophical genius. Both these attitudes are born out of exclusive attention to the superstructure of his thought. A critical study of the foundation shows that Hartmann can stimulate genuine philosophical analysis, and yet that his 'system' is not the best part of what he has left for us.

---

* First published in the *Journal of the Department of Letters*, University of Calcutta, I, 1957, 1–12.

[1] This neglect may be noticed in the comparatively lesser attention paid to N. Hartmann's best philosophical work *Möglichkeit und Wirklichkeit*, Berlin, 1939. For example, a volume exclusively devoted to his work (*Nicolai Hartmann, der Denker und sein Werk*, Göttingen, 1952) contains no study of his modal doctrine. Yet it is the modal doctrine which, in Hartmann's case, constitutes the basis of the entire thought-structure.

That the modal doctrine constitutes the innermost basis of Hartmann's thought has been most successfully demonstrated by Josef König, Hartmann's successor at Göttingen. König has attempted to canalise his own critical study of Hartmann's ontology in a novel creative line. It is this Hartmann-König controversy which the present paper seeks to present. The controversy would throw light not only on the basis of Hartmann's ontology, but on the basis of ontology in general.

II

How to get at the basis of Hartmann's ontology? Let us sketch the superstructure, and then descend into the depths of the foundation.

Following the Aristotelian tradition, Hartmann takes ontology as the science of beings as beings. Ontology is concerned with what first makes beings beings. The word *"Sein"* gives rise to the illusion, as if there is some entity or attribute corresponding to it, something over and above, may be, underlying or pervading the various beings. Hartmann rejects this thought. A science of beings as beings is not a science of any such entity or attribute as *Sein*. On the other hand, it can only be a science which lays bare the various spheres of being along with their general and special categories and inter-categorial (hence, inter-sphere) relations. Hence, ontology becomes a doctrine of categories, a *"Kategorienlehre"*.

There are two primary spheres of being: the real and the ideal. The real consists of the chain of temporal events. The structure of the real sphere is a stratification of various levels: the material, vital, psychical and spiritual. The stratification consists in the relation of "founding". The higher level is "founded" on the lower. The lower provides the basis for the higher. The real sphere has its general categories, those which determine the entire sphere, irrespective of the differences of strata. Such categories are, for example, the modal categories. But each stratum of reality has also its own special categories. The relation in which two levels of reality stand to each other is concretely illustrated in the relation in which the categories of the two stand to each other. The inter-categorial relations thereby gain a new significance.

The ideal sphere consists of such elements as the essences (compare Whitehead's 'eternal objects', Santayana's 'essences') and the mathematical entities on the one hand, and the values on the other. Hartmann's uncompromising realism rejects any attempt at subjectivising. The ideal sphere has its own general and special categories, just as there are also such categories as are common to the two primary spheres: the real and the ideal.

Besides the two primary spheres, there are two secondary spheres of being – the spheres of 'logic' and 'knowledge'. These are mid-way spheres inasmuch as they share the categories of both the primary spheres. (Compare Whitehead's 'hybrid' entities.)

To keep these primary and secondary spheres along with their general and special categories before the mind, in their distinctions as well as in their interrelations, is essential for an understanding of Hartmann's ontology. Hartmann displays great acumen in drawing these distinctions and in keeping clearly apart what he considers to be distinct. Through these distinctions, he claims to have the clue in hand for avoiding many of the errors of the traditional ontologies.

The key to this entire discussion lies in the formulation of the nature of the ideal sphere. In setting aside what he calls the errors of tradition, Hartmann shows here his capacity at its best. We shall do best to catalogue the errors which Hartmann rejects and then pass on from this negative consideration to the more positive aspect of the situation.

1. The distinction between the ideal sphere and the real sphere is not the same as the distinction between Form and Matter. Neither is the ideal sphere a realm of mere Forms, nor is the real that of mere Matter. The idealities are also material in character and the real is also formed content. The Form-Matter distinction thus reappears within each of the two primary spheres and so cannot be identified with the distinction between the spheres.

2. The real-ideal distinction is not identical with the distinction between 'concretum' and 'category'. The ideal sphere does not determine the real as the categories determine the 'concre-

tum'. On the other hand, within each sphere, the 'concretum'-category distinction reappears. There are real categories (i.e., categories of the real world) as well as ideal categories (i.e., categories of the ideal sphere). Further, the idealities possess a primary mode of being, being for themselves (*"Für-sich-sein"*), whereas the categories have no independent mode of being, but are only in the 'concretum' which they determine or constitute.

3. Similarly, it is also wrong to identify the ideal with the *a priori* and the real with the *a posteriori*. The distinction between the *a priori* and the *a posteriori* is a gnoseological distinction, a distinction between two modes of cognition, whereas we are here concerned with an ontological distinction, a distinction between modes of being. While the two pairs cannot be identified, neither can we claim an exact correspondence between the two. For there can be *a priori* knowledge both of the real world (as in mathematical physics) and of the ideal, whereas it is true that the real alone is apprehended *a posteriori*.

4. More plausible, but not any more tenable, is the identification of the real with *Dasein* (existence, or *'that'*) and of the ideal with the *Sosein* (*'what'*). The distinction between *Dasein* and *Sosein* is a distinction between the two aspects of being and should be kept apart from that between the spheres. The relation between the aspects is conjunctive (that is to say, any particular being has both *Dasein* and *Sosein*) whereas the relation between the spheres is disjunctive (that is to say, any particular being is either real or ideal). Ideal being, like the real, has its own *Dasein* and its own *Sosein*.

5. There is another tradition, wrongly attributed to Plato but first explicitly championed since Leibniz, according to which the ideal sphere is a realm of mere possibilities whereas the real is the world of actualities. To this the tradition adds as self-evident that the actual is a selection from the many possibilities, so that the real can be seen as an actualisation from amongst the ideal. This tradition arose historically, as Faust shows[2], in connection with the theological doctrine of creation and later on

[2] A. Faust, *Der Möglichkeitsgedanke*, Heidelberg, 1931, 2 volumes.

gained plausibility from the rise of abstract formal logic and of alternative systems of logic and geometry. Hartmann devotes much of his analysis to the task of demolishing this tradition and as we have said, one of the principal results of his modal analysis is that he has provided us with an alternative conceptual scheme which demonstrates the illusory character of the self-evidence which this tradition claims on its own behalf. A brief summary of this modal analysis is of central importance for our purpose: –

Each sphere, according to Hartmann, has its own modal category. The real sphere has its own modes of possibility, actuality and necessity, just as the ideal sphere has its own modes. Meaning by 'real-possibility' the mode of possibility in the real world and by 'ideal-possibility' the mode of possibility in the ideal sphere, we could say that the two are radically different modes. By saying that they are 'radically different', we mean that real-possibility and ideal-possibility are not species of a common genus 'possibility', as their names illusorily suggest. On the other hand, they are not only different possibilities, but are, as possibilities, different. 'Real-possibility' has meaning and significance only in connection with a real being, just as 'ideal-possibility' is meaningful only in connection with an ideal being. Only a real being can have real-possibility, whereas an ideal being alone can have ideal-possibility. The suggestion of a common genus is illusory, so that the term 'possibility' becomes devoid of any meaning of its own.

The same can be said of 'real-actuality' and 'ideal-actuality', as well as of 'real-necessity' and 'ideal-necessity' (by construing these terms as in the case of the pair in the above paragraph).

We are at present concerned directly with the modes of actuality and possibility. 'Real-possibility' is to be defined as the completion of the series of conditions necessary for generating a real event. A real event X is then and only then possible (that is to say, 'real-possible') when the series of conditions required for X's coming into being is complete, i.e. when the completed series is given. 'Ideal-possibility' consists in compatibility, logical non-contradiction being a special case under it.

With this new conceptual scheme in hand, we readily begin to see through the illusion which lends support to the tradition. It is wrong to say that the ideal sphere is a realm of possibilities out of which the real is a selected actualisation. The ideal sphere has its own modes of possibility and actuality, just as the real world has its own. There are the modes of 'ideal-actuality' and 'real-possibility' which the tradition overlooks. And, the real-actual is an actualisation of 'real-possibility', but not of 'ideal-possibility'.

Neither in the real world nor in the ideal, is there mere possibility, that is to say, possibility which is not actualised. In the real world, an event is possible only when the series of conditions is completely given. But when this series is complete, the event is also actual. That is to say, what is 'real-possible' is simultaneously, at that very instant, also 'real-actual'. Similarly, in the ideal sphere actuality being only a secondary mode, a mere shadow of the mode of possibility, what is 'ideal-possible' is already 'ideal-actual'. As such, the usual notion that the range of possibility is wider than that of actuality is false. It does not hold good of either of the primary spheres of being.

By rejecting the above errors of tradition, Hartmann gives a new form to the two-world theory which ever since Plato has been a recurrent philosophical motive. This novelty may be stated with regard to the problem of the relation between the two spheres.

The alternatives in terms of which the tradition of philosophy has formulated its answer are the following: –

Either, the relation is one of determination, the precise nature of the determination being conceived mainly in two ways. The ideal sphere may determine the real world as the categories determine the *concretum* they constitute. Or, the ideal sphere may be the *telos*, the perfection towards which the real aspires. Both forms of determination – whether categorial or teleological – are rejected by Hartmann as being distortions of the situation. The identification of idealities with categories has already been shown to be erroneous. Teleological determination again is out of place in a purely ontological situation. The ideal and the real are two primary spheres of being and there is no degree of being, no scale of perfection in order of being. Not only is the ideal sphere not more perfect than the real, but one can rather say the reverse, if one can at all speak of more or less perfection. Hartmann does suggest a reversal of the usual judgment of value by demonstrating the superiority (?) of the real world over the ideal.

Or, the real may be conceived as being a selection from the ideal. This again may be supplemented by the theological appeal to a God who chooses the best of all possible worlds. The above modal doctrine has already exposed the fallacy underlying this.

With this, room is left only for a phenomenological approach. To talk of determination – causal, categorial or teleological – is to indulge in speculation. Phenomenologically, we have the following before us: – firstly, we have the *Für-sich-sein* of the two realms of being. Secondly, we have also a certain degree of inter-weaving of the two realms. This is illustrated, for example, in the possibility of mathematical physics, in general, of *a priori* knowledge of the real world.

Allowing for the least measure of speculation, how are we then to formulate the relation between the spheres? Hartmann attempts this in his own doctrine of partial categorial identity. The two realms, being autonomous and primary, have their own categories. What we have said to be the phenomenon of inter-weaving of the two realms is nothing but a partial identity between the categories of the two.

To ask further about the rationale of this identity, as to its 'why' and 'how', is for Hartmann, to ask those ultimate meta-physical questions which offer a limit to solvability. Such questions point beyond phenomenology, but cannot be themselves answered.

III

The significance of all this for ontology is great. The separation between the two spheres is now complete. The autonomy and independence of each from the other is established. With the radical separation between the modalities of the spheres, the crux of the situation is reached. The modalities are the most fundamental categories. They are the categories which along with the inter-modal relations bring into concrete relief the mode of being (*Seinsweise*) of each sphere. With demonstration of the radical difference between the modal categories of the two spheres, absolute separation between the spheres is set on a sure footing. This is further strengthened by rejection of the possibility of any 'influence' or 'determination' of the one by the other.

Ontology, therefore, divides itself into two special branches: an ontology of the real world and an ontology of the ideal sphere. Let us call them for the sake of convenience – without however attributing the terminology to Hartmann himself – '*Realontologie*' and '*Idealontologie*' respectively. Since the two spheres are now separated radically from each other, each has its own mode of being, its own categories, each of the two special ontologies must be autonomous. The categories and structures of the real world can be described without reference to the categories and structures of the ideal sphere. Hartmann thus aims in the first two volumes of his ontology, at laying the foundation of an autonomous *Realontologie*. More and more, it is the real world which comes to be the principal theme of his philosophizing. The dignity of the real world forces itself upon him in contrast with the shadowy airiness of the idealities. After the general considerations of the first two volumes have laid the foundations, the special *Kategorienlehre* in the last two volumes is devoted entirely to the real world. In all this, Hartmann's motive is to develop an autonomous *Realontologie*, an ontology of the real, independent of, and without reference to, the ideal considerations.

Is such an autonomous *Realontologie* at all possible? This is a question which is of central importance for ontology and for philosophizing in general.

IV

In *Archiv für Philosophie* (1948), Josef König (then of Hamburg) published a paper entitled "*Über einen neuen ontologischen Beweis des Satzes von der Notwendigkeit alles Geschehens*", which is meant to be a criticism of a very special doctrine of Hartmann's ontology, but which lays down the principle for questioning the very foundations and possibility of an autonomous *Realontologie*.

The special doctrine which König's paper seeks to examine is the doctrine of thoroughgoing necessity in the real world.

The modal analysis which keeps apart the modalities of each sphere makes the distinction between "ideal-necessity" and "real necessity". "Ideal-necessity" is the necessity with which one essence includes or excludes another, a mathematical conclusion 'follows' from its premise, or with which a logical system hangs together. "Real-necessity", on the other hand, is the necessity with which the chain of real events is constituted, so that nothing in the chain is fortuitous or accidental.

The thoroughgoing necessity which characterises the real world is not to be identified with any particular type of necessity, either causal or teleological. To say that the real world has thoroughgoing necessity does not mean that there is strict causal determination all through the real process. The real world has a stratified structure and it may be reasonable to suppose that the various strata exhibit differing types of necessity. But all through the various strata there runs a common thread, a thoroughgoing determination which allows no accident, a *Realzusammenhang* which makes of real events a continuum-like interconnectedness.

Hume missed this basic *Realzusammenhang*. Hume's inquiry failed, because he was searching for the wrong thing at the wrong place. He was searching for "ideal-necessity" in the real process, – a search which, by its very nature, is doomed to failure.[3]

König's criticism was directed against this doctrine of *Realzusammenhang*. The starting point of this is an examination of what Hartmann means by a real being. A real being of Hartmann is a real event as happening here and now. It is only with regard to such a real event as happening here and now that the idea of real-necessity meaningfully holds good. Precisely this is what König contends to be absurd.

The idea of necessary connection between A and B implies the idea 'if A, then B'. This latter implies the repeatability of both A and B. But if A and B be real events of Hartmann's conception, they cannot by their very nature be meaningfully thought as repeatable. Since, as said before, the real event of Hartmann is thought of as happening here and now, which means that the idea of A's existing here and now is included within the very idea of A's being a real event, the idea of repeatability and hence also the idea of necessity cannot be meaningfully predicated of A.

That his own criticism of Hartmann's doctrine of Real-necessity is but an exemplification of a more general principle of criticism is suggested by König himself. This at once brings

---

[3] Cp. Whitehead's criticism of Hume.

out, according to König, the novelty as well as the absurdity of Hartmann's ontology.

Traditional ontology since Aristotle had as its subject matter for theorising the scale of being from the summum genus down to the last species which is also a genus. This means that the particular, the individual was always excluded from the subject matter of theory. The particular as such was recognised to be a limit to theory.

The novelty of Hartmann's ontology lies in an attempt to make this particular as such the subject matter of theory. Hartmann's real being is a particular taken as such, i.e., with its transient particularity. This novelty is also the highly paradoxical character of Hartmannian *Realontologie*.

König seeks to clarify this situation with the help of a distinction whose importance for logic and ontology he has been emphasizing through his published papers and university lectures. This is the distinction between 'theoretical this' and 'practical this'.

The 'this' may mean 'such and such', or it may mean the 'this-there' (identified ostensively). In the former case, 'this' also means 'this sort of'. In the latter case, the 'this' implies a 'pointing out', – an act which involves somebody for whom the 'pointing out' is meant. For these two kinds of 'this', König chooses the terms 'theoretical this' and 'practical this'. If A be a real being of Hartmann, A is a 'practical this'. By its very nature, A can only be pointed out as 'this-there'. Of such an entity, no theoretical statement can meaningfully be made.[4]

The principle implied in König's above-mentioned paper (whose explicit intention was to question Hartmann's doctrine of real-necessity) has been developed by the present author in his Göttingen thesis entitled "An inquiry into the problem of ideal being in the philosophies of Nicolai Hartmann and A. N. Whitehead"[5] with a view to extend its scope to cover the entire

---

[4] The corresponding distinction in logic is between 'theoretical sentences' and 'practical sentences'. This distinction was laid down by König in his *Vorlesung* on '*Theoretische und praktische Sätze*' during the summer semester, 1953, and the winter semester, 1953/54 at the Göttingen University.

[5] Now published under the title *Nicolai Hartmann and Alfred North Whitehead: A study in recent Platonism*, Calcutta, 1957.

basis of Hartmann's ontology. Thereby, the very task of ontology is questioned from a fresh point of view.

We can interpret König's suggestion in our own language thus: – Absolute separation between the two primary spheres of being leads to an attempt to build an autonomous ontology of the real world. The real, when it is robbed of all ideal elements and structures, is nothing but the transient particular, the mere 'this-there', König's 'practical this', Hartmann's real being. The elements and structures in the real world which are essentially repeatable and recognisable are all ideal. In the stream of real events, taken as real happenings, nothing is repeatable. Of such events, no theory can be made. And yet Hartmann's concepts of 'real-possibility' and 'real-necessity' are elements of such a theory which Hartmann seeks to build up.

This is supported by a critical examination of Hartmann's philosophy of ideal being and the way the two spheres have been kept asunder. It becomes clear that the way the spheres have been kept apart depends upon and, in its turn, influences Hartmann's formulation of the nature of ideal being.

V

Comparison with the cosmology of A. N. Whitehead affords us with an important case of the principle involved here. Whitehead's distinction between actual entities and eternal objects is a parallel to Hartmann's two sphere theory. But also like Hartmann, Whitehead recognises two secondary spheres of 'hybrid' entities: propositions (corresponding to Hartmann's sphere of logic) and feeling (which includes Hartmann's sphere of knowledge). Thus the ontology and the cosmology present the same external pattern. But their inner motives and executions show great differences and these differences illustrate the principle of criticism suggested in the above section.

To bring this out, the course of development of Whitehead's platonism must be mentioned. The early works on natural philosophy had introduced the distinction between 'events' and 'objects'. 'Objects' were those elements in nature which were 'recognisable', which are the same. 'Events' on the other hand

were the passing, transient, spatio-temporal factors. Whitehead's account of 'objects', which cannot be elaborated here,
shows that in this early formulation, the separation between
'objects' and 'events' was absolute. 'Events' were what 'objects'
were not; 'objects' were what 'events' were not. When one re-
views the different classes of 'objects' ('sense-objects', 'perceptual objects', 'scientific objects') which Whitehead admitted,
one realises that the 'events' were nothing but the passing 'point-
instants', so that every other content of our experience was
itself an 'object' or composed of factors which were themselves
'objects'.

In the later cosmology, the nature of this distinction under-
goes a significant change. The category of 'events' is now replaced and enriched by the category of 'actual entity'. The
'objects' are raised to the dignity of being 'eternal objects'.
Whereas in the earlier natural philosophy, 'events' were only
'thin slabs of duration', 'point-instants', now the actual entities
are recognised to be enduring, to have all the richness of content
within themselves. The 'perceptual objects' and the 'scientific
objects' of the former phase are no more now eternal objects,
but actual entities. The only eternal objects are the so-called
'sense objects' (the eternal objects of the 'subjective species')
and the mathematical entities (the eternal objects of the 'objective species').

While thus the two categories underwent a change, what is
directly relevant for us is the following: –

Whereas the 'events' and 'objects' mutually excluded each
other so that the 'events' were what the 'objects' were not and
vice versa, now the actual entities and eternal objects stand in
organic relation with each other. The actual entities are what
they are because of the eternal objects which have found 'in-
gression' in them, so that no description of the actual entities is
possible without referring to the constituent eternal objects.

Hartmann's distinction between real being and ideal being is as
radical, as absolute as Whitehead's early distinction between
events and objects. We have seen that this way of keeping the
two spheres asunder makes it impossible to theorise about the
real sphere. In spite of his two entity theory, Whitehead's later
cosmology avoids this error. Whitehead realises that any des-

cription of the actualities must necessarily take into consideration the eternal objects ingredient in them. Whitehead's cosmology therefore, though eminently concerned with the real
actual world, is no autonomous '*Realontologie*' in the above
specified sense.[6]

The real as such, as merely real, as the stubborn matter of
fact, "*die Härte des Realen*" is not a subject matter of theory.
Theory always transcends this stubborn matter of fact and, in its
attempt to come back to it, always falls short of the ideal. Actuality, in Whitehead's language, must be described in terms of the
eternal objects and yet cannot be exhausted by them. This is the
significance of Whitehead's doctrine of "infinite associate hierarchy of eternal objects", developed in the chapter on "Abstraction" in *Science and the Modern World*.

The real as such, as merely real, as the stubborn matter of
fact is reached through practical relationship, vital-emotional-
organic situations. Both Whitehead and Hartmann recognise
this. That this also imposes a limit upon the scope of theory is not
recognised by Hartmann.

A significant suggestion is made by Whitehead when he tells
us that 'theory' is a 'hybrid' entity. That the ontological '*Fra-
gestellung*' can and should be extended to ontology itself is not
seen by Hartmann. Hartmann's blind faith in the capacity of
intentio recta covers up this vision. Direct access to reality is
possible only through vital-emotional-organic relationship.
In theory, language intervenes. It is interesting for this purpose
that Whitehead does not distinguish between 'proposition' and
'theory', and hurls them together as constituting one class of
'hybrid' entity. Hybrid entities are constituted of both eternal
objects and actual entities. Hartmann recognises this of logic,
but not of ontology.

Theorising about actuality must involve reference to possibilities. Theory moves in the realm of meaningful possibilities. The
so-called ideal-possibility is the only theoretical possibility. The
so-called real-possibility of Hartmann is no meaningful concept

---

[6] The *Process and Reality* also makes a distinction between 'general' possibilities
and 'real' possibility, but the latter is not an independent and autonomous mode,
but only a limitation of the former.

within the realm of theory. It may be designated practical possibility[7], – a concept which is in need of further elaboration and specification.

[7] This suggestion was given to the author by Josef König inthe course of a private conversation, although the responsibility of using it in the present form is the present author's own.

CHAPTER XII

REMARKS ON NICOLAI HARTMANN'S
MODAL DOCTRINE*

I

In his *Möglichkeit und Wirklichkeit* (Berlin 1937, 2nd ed. 1949), Hartmann gives us an ontological theory of the modes. He starts from a distinction between the modes of the various spheres of being, primary and secondary. The two primary spheres of being, according to his ontology, are the real and the ideal. The two secondary spheres are those of logic and knowledge. The modes of the real world are accordingly contrasted with those of the ideal realm; the modes of the realm of logic are again different from those of knowledge. The modal doctrine is thereby divided into four parts. But there must be also a part on the relations between these different spheres.

Traditional discussion of the problem of modality did not see clearly through these distinctions. This gives to Hartmann's treatment of the problem its originality. Further, these modes of the various spheres are distinguished from the naive day to day consciousness of modality.

The ontological point of view requires specification. For this purpose, we are to distinguish between three different approaches to the problem of modality:

First, it is possible to consider the modalities as criteria for classifying all objects in the three groups, those that are merely possible, those that are both possible and actual, and those that are possible, actual and also necessary.

Secondly, it is possible to consider the modes as if they were different stages of a process. Thus, it may be said that a thing

* First published in *Kant-Studien*, 54, 1963, pp. 181–187.

first becomes possible, then is made actual, and further may or may not be necessary. The process however may not be carried to the end; what is possible may never be actualised.

Thirdly, the modes may be taken neither as criteria nor as stages of a process, but as the constituent aspects of the existent or the subsistent, as the case may be. This is the point of view which we may call the critical point of view, because we may trace it to Kant. Kant starts from the given object of experience and then asks how the same is possible, actual and necessary.

Hartmann rejects the first two approaches. Modes are for him neither criteria nor stages, but the most primary characteristics of the being of anything. As such, given an object of experience, we can ask: what makes it possible? What makes it actual? What makes it necessary? Thus in an important sense, Hartmann's treatment of the problem is similar to Kant's, even though Kant's own solutions are rejected by Hartmann. For Kant, the given is possible when considered in relation to its form and actual when considered in relation to its matter. Hartmann finds this not only inadequate but also misleading: to this however we shall turn later on.

The second approach is attributed to Aristotle. Both the first and the second approaches attribute to the merely possible which is not 'or has not yet become actual' a sort of ghostly existence – a position in between being and non-being. Aristotle's doctrine of dynamis and energia is further criticised as an illegitimate extension of the categories of the sphere of organic being to the entire domain of being. Further, if a prior stage of mere possibility is admitted, the question arises as to what must be added to it in order to render it actual. Kant had shown that any answer to this question is absurd. For that which must be so added, argued Kant, must be other than the possible, that is to say, must be impossible.[1]

As such, we come back to the critical formulation of the question. This is one of the points where we begin to see the influence of Kant on Hartmann's ontology which claims the name of critical ontology.

---

[1] I. Kant, *Kritik der reinen Vernunft*, Kant Werke III, p. 206, ed. by Cassirer.

II

Hartmann's entire discussion of the mode of possibility sets out from a distinction between disjunctive and indifferent possibility. There are two kinds of possibility. The one always implies its contradictory: that is to say, the possibility of A always implies the possibility of non-A. If it is possible that it rains, it is also possible – we could even say that the first possibility implies this – that it does not rain. Or, the possibility of the being of A implies the possibility of the non-being of A. Hartmann calls this kind of possibility disjunctive, because it hides a disjunction within it. The other kind of possibility is called indifferent because from the possibility of A nothing can be said about the possibility of non-A. Thus the indifferent possibility does not completely exclude its contradictory, but neither does it necessarily contain the latter within itself.

Now, when the possible becomes actual, it does not cease to be possible. In the language of the critical point of view, we can say that an actual A also contains its own possibility. That is to say, possibility and actuality are not mutually exclusive modes but go together. An A which is given in experience is at the same time actual and possible, actual from one point of view and possible from another.

At this stage, the question arises: which of the two kinds of possibility above enumerated is so compatible with actuality? Hartmann shows that the so-called disjunctive possibility cannot remain contained in an actual A. That is to say, when A is actual, it can contain only its own possibility but not that of its contradictory. The actuality of A is incompatible with the possibility of non-A. The so-called disjunctive possibility is not therefore admissible into a critical philosophy of modality. On the other hand, it is connected with the view of possibility as a state, in which case the modes exclude each other and no question of compatibility arises.

At least in the real world the reis no disjunctive possibility. At least in the real world the actuality of A contains the possibility of A but not that of non-A. In the real world therefore the so-called disjunctive possibility is split up into two different modes:

the possibility of A and the possibility of non-A. These are, in the real world, two different modes and not members of an inseparable disjunction.

With this splitting up of the so-called disjunctive possibility into two different modes, the ground is prepared for Hartmann's most important doctrine in the *Möglichkeit und Wirklichkeit*, i.e., the doctrine of *"Real-möglichkeit"*. This doctrine finds its best expression – for Hartmann formulates it in diverse ways and from diverse points of view – in his short formulation of the so-called *"Realgesetz der Möglichkeit"*: *"Was real möglich ist, das ist auch real wirklich"*. What is possible is also actual: this holds good of the real world[2]. This law, according to Hartmann, is *"die kürze Formel für einen umständlichen Revolutionsprozess im philosophischen Denken"*. *"Man kann diesen Prozess als die Austreibung der Gespenster aus dem Weltbilde des Menschen bezeichnen."*[3] This ghost is the merely possible in the real world. The real world does not contain mere possibilities that are not also actualised. On the other hand the real world is such that here possibility is only a structural element of the mode of being of an actual.

This doctrine of Hartmann, revolutionary as it is, has been variously criticised. We shall however concentrate on understanding what exactly Hartmann aims at. The conviction which he carries in his exposition of the doctrine is certainly based on some bit of truth. We shall aim at finding this out. For this purpose, the so-called *"Spaltungsgesetz"* puts us in a favourable vantage position.

The above mentioned *"Realgesetz der Möglichkeit"* is proved (or, rather demonstrated) by Hartmann in two different ways. The one is called the formal proof, the other is called the material proof.

The formal proof starts from a law which Hartmann claims to be self-evident. This is the so-called *"Spaltungsgesetz"*. His task consists in demonstrating that the *"Realgesetz der Möglichkeit"* follows analytically from this self-evident *"Spaltungsgesetz"*. Hence the proof is called formal.

The *"Spaltungsgesetz"* runs thus: *"Was real möglich ist,*

---

[2] N. Hartmann, *Möglichkeit und Wirklichkeit*, Berlin, 2nd edn. 1949, ch. 21.
[3] *Ibid.*, p. 176.

dessen Nichtsein ist real nicht möglich". If something is possible in the real world, its non-being is not possible in the real world. The so-called disjunctive possibility being split up, the possibility of A and the possibility of non-A are now two distinct, mutually incompatible, modes. Though this *"Spaltungsgesetz"* is claimed to be self-evident, nevertheless it requires to be clarified. This is done by Hartmann in the following way: actuality presupposes possibility; "presupposes" means here "contains". Only the possibility of A can be contained in the actuality of A; the possibility of A's non-being cannot be contained in A's actuality, for if that were so then what is already actual could also be non-actual which is impossible.

Once the *"Spaltungsgesetz"* is accepted as valid, Hartmann claims, the *"Realgesetz der Möglichkeit"* follows by formal implication. Let us therefore examine the meaning and the validity of the *"Spaltungsgesetz"*:

The argument is this: because the possibility of A is contained in the actuality of A, the possibility of non-A is excluded therefrom. Is this an immediate inference? No. The inference is rather indirect, mediated by another premise: the possibility of non-A implies the non-actuality of A. Since the actuality of A and the non-actuality of A exclude each other evidently, the possibility of A and the possibility of non-A also must exclude each other. Is this new premise, i.e., the proposition that the possibility of non-A implies the nonactuality of A self-evident? Hartmann does not demonstrate this premise. He takes it as self-evident. On the other hand, the absurdity which he brings out in the supposed coexistence of positive and negative possibilities in the actuality of A depends upon the truth of this premise.

We may suggest a vindication of this proposition. It may be argued that this follows from the very nature of the critical approach to the problem of modality. The critical approach as we have seen, considers possibility not as a phase preceding actuality but as a structural element in the mode of being of anything. If that be so, one cannot meaningfully speak of the possibility of non-A unless non-A is actual. And when non-A is actual, A is certainly non-actual. From the critical point of view, therefore, the possibility of non-A implies the non-actuality of A. Hartmann's *"Spaltungsgesetz"* follows.

III

In the face of the above results, the following questions may further be raised:

1. Granted that Hartmann's 'real-possibility' is a defined term, we may still ask – as we are entitled to ask in case of every defined term – if there is really anything corresponding to it. This question may be answered affirmatively. The ontological situation corresponding to this term has been brought to light.

2. But we also ask: is this term in accordance with the meaning of the term 'possibility' as used in ordinary language? This is a difficult question. And it is interesting to find that Hartmann recognizes it. The common usage of language is not fixed enough. Hartmann would suggest a double answer: first, he would say that the common language has disjunctive possibility as its meaning. But, secondly, Hartmann would suggest that his own use of the term is not totally strange to common usage, that we do often use the term in his sense without being sufficiently conscious of the fact that that would involve a radical change in the philosophical point of view. That Hartmann tries to establish this harmony with common usage gives to his doctrine a large degree of plausibility.

Hartmann asks: ,,*Was eigentlich meint man, wenn man sagt 'Was nicht ist, das kann doch sein', oder ,es ist vieles möglich, was nicht wirklich ist'? Meint man denn im Ernst, dass dieses ,Mögliche' auch zur Zeit schon wirklich sein ,könnte'? Oder auch nur, dass es unter beliebigen künftigen Umständen wirklich werden ,könnte'? Man weiss ja doch sehr gut, dass dem nicht so ist. Man weiss, dass es nicht wirklich werden kann, ohne dass noch mancherlei Voraussetzungen dafür sich verwirklichten. Man weiss dass eine ganze Kette von Bedingungen erfüllt sein muss, bevor es wirklich werden kann. Und wenn man sich die Sache zum Ziel macht und sie aus eigener Kraft verwirklichen will, so weiss man nur zu wohl, dass man die noch fehlenden Bedingungen erst beschaffen muss*"[4]

---

[4] *Ibid.*, p. 155.

In this paragraph, Hartmann tries to show that his doctrine is already contained in the popular use of language. Let us examine what this means for the understanding of Hartmann's doctrine and its validity as a modal doctrine.

It seems that here Hartmann plays on a certain ambiguity of language. No one denies that the possible cannot be actualized till the necessary conditions are all there. But does this mean that the so-called possible is in fact impossible so long as the necessary conditions fail?

The really decisive question which one must ask is whether possibility as such is possibility of being actual. Is *"Möglich-keit"*=*"Wirklich-werden-können"*? To be actual is to be actual at a definite time and place, so that the *"Wirklich-werden-können"* really breaks up into as great a number of *"Hier-und-jetzt-wirk-lich-werden-könnens"* as there are here-and-nows in the process. In Hartmann's modal theory, possibility is a relational mode and actuality is the fundamental mode: since the relational mode presupposes the fundamental, possibility as such is also possibility of being actualized. Something can be actualized only when the necessary conditions are all there. It follows that something is possible only when the conditions are all there ("is possible"= "can be actualized").

We can see that in our common language there is this ambiguity. Sometimes we say, "It has not yet been possible on my part to arrange the affair". In this case, we really mean that the arrangement of the affair has not yet been actualized by me. Hartmann's theory conforms to this ambiguous use.

Let us consider some other possibility-sentences:

(a) "It is possible that it rains to-morrow": Hartmann may say that this statement conveys not ontological possibility but epistemological possibility, and is due to ignorance or partial ignorance on our part of the actual conditions.

(b) "Wood may burn" or "Poison may kill": Hartmann may say wood may burn only under certain conditions, and poison can kill only under certain conditions. No one denies this. These conditions however may be included within the judgment of possibility without implying the actuality of those circumstances. We could then say: "Wood may burn under circumstances x, y..". We are not speaking of any particular actual piece of wood.

Hartmann would then say that the judgments express essential-possibility, *Wesensmöglichkeit*, and not real-possibility.

(c) What about such an event as the death of a man X to-day at this moment? Hartmann would say that this death has been made possible by a completed chain of conditions. Before this moment of his actual death, his death was really impossible. It is clear that in this case "has been made possible" is a phrase which is also used in language but is supposed to mean "has been made actual". Hartmann is playing on the ambiguity.

If that be so, can we further say: (a) while the chain of conditions have brought about, i.e., actualized the death of X today at this moment, (b) the possibility of his death was always there (imbedded in the essence of X's being a man)? The absence of the necessary conditions did not make it possible only in the sense that it could not be brought about. It is clear that (b) would be called by Hartmann *Wesensmöglichkeit*. Hartmann agrees that this *Wesensmöglichkeit* underlies real-possibility. But where, in common usage, is the idea of real-possibility implied if not in the above mentioned ambiguity?

3. We may now pass on to a further question. It has been said above that Hartmann's theory of real-possibility is not a purely modal theory. What does this mean? What is a purely modal theory?

We should for this purpose clearly separate two questions. The one is the empirical question, if and when something will or can happen. This question may variously be answered. The talk of chance or of probability may be explained as being due to imperfect knowledge of the real situation. Whether there is an objective probability or objective indetermination arises here and is to be discussed. The predictions of the sciences are on this empirical basis. They answer questions as to whether and when a certain anticipated event will happen. Similarly, when a certain event happens, we can consider the conditions which have actualized it.

On the other hand, there is the purely modal question, whether something is possible or not. Or, to state it in the language of critical philosophy, in what sense something given in experience is to be regarded as possible?

The answer to the empirical question is independent of the modal enquiry. The working scientist who is deciding such empirical questions need not have a modal theory to work with. On the other hand, granted that something satisfies the requirements of modal possibility, the question arises as to whether it is going to be actualized, and if so, under what conditions.

Hartmann's doctrine of real-possibility is an empirical theory. Hartmann would probably say that to the above two questions corresponds his own distinction between real modes and ideal modes. But, a purely modal analysis does not require Hartmann's division of modal enquiry according to the ontological spheres. The modes must be common to the spheres. A purely modal theory must demonstrate the unity between the spheres and be a unified one. We are to ask: in what sense is it meaningful to speak of the possibility, actuality and necessity of anything – without consideration of whether this something is a real event or an ideal entity.

We thus see that Hartmann's own doctrine of real-possibility still leaves room for a more comprehensive, more truly modal doctrine of possibility. Hartmann's theory of real modes serves the purpose of giving us a picture of the inner structure of the real world. But it does not satisfy the needs of a genuine modal analysis.

CHAPTER XIII

THE 'OBJECT' IN EDMUND HUSSERL'S PHENOMENOLOGY*

Phenomenological enquiry concerns two main questions. First, there is the enquiry into the nature ofpu re subjectivity and the problems bearing on it. Second, there is the problem of the 'constitution' of objectivity "as referred to its subjective source."[1]

In a paper on "Husserl's Phenomenology and Indian Idealism",[2] we had the first question principally in mind. Our interest there was to examine the consistency and success with which Husserl found room in his philosophical system for the idea of pure subjectivity. Husserl's treatment of the second problem received only a secondary consideration i.e., only so far as it corroborated the main thesis of that essay. We were considering how Husserl was struggling – though in vain – to free himself from the shackles of objectivity.

But just as at times Husserl would have the courage to make extreme assertions in favour of the single principle of subjectivity, so also at other times he would explicitly refuse to limit phenomenological study to the investigation of pure consciousness alone. More Hegelian at such moments, he would ascribe to phenomenological enquiry as its main task the study of the relation of the principle of objectivity to its source in the subjective realm. Phenomenology is not merely a study of immanent formations of the pure consciousness, but also of the intentionality of such conscious formations and conversely of the 'constitution' of the objectivities corresponding to such intentional experiences.

---

* First published in *Philosophy and Phenomenological Research*, XIV, 1954, pp. 343–353.
[1] E. Husserl, *Ideas*, E. Tr. by Boyce Gibson, (paperback edition), p. 234.
[2] In *Philosophical Quarterly*, Amalner, India, Vol. XXIV, No. 3.

In any case, as our previous study has emphasized, there lurks a fundamental contradiction in this way of looking at the problem[3]. On the one hand, there is the recognition of consciousness as constituting a self-contained and self-sufficient realm by itself. On the other hand, intentionality is said to be a necessary and universal feature of all consciousness; every consciousness must be *of* something. This something may, of course, be some other experiential process, as in the case of what Husserl calls 'immanent experiences'. But it is, in most cases, some object. How a self-contained system can get associated with an object is thus a problem of major importance in this context and we have seen how Husserl's solution or for that matter any consistent solution on such premises – tends towards an extreme variety of Idealism on the lines of the Vedanta of Sankara.

But we should be true to Husserl also. If he does evince any such tendency, our dealings with him must yet be true to the basic ideas of this thought. And even if we did follow him on the lines of this particular tendency of his thought, we are yet obliged to follow him right through the basic concepts guiding his philosophic excursions. And that we propose to do in the present essay.

II

Husserl's treatment of objectivity starts basically from the recognition of intentionality as the principal feature of conscious life. This doctrine of intentionality had been handed down through Brentano. The distinguishing feature of conscious life had been recognized as lying in the fact that all consciousness is of some object. Recognition of this feature opens up, for Husserl, a great variety of complex problems of phenomenological importance. What is the meaning of this 'of' relation, when it is said that consciousness is always 'of' some object? If consciousness constitutes a realm of its own, how does it come to be related to the object? Further, what meaning are we to attach to the 'act'-hood of conscious acts, when we bring under this general name a great variety of processes from presentations

---

[3] I do not any longer think this criticism to be correct – J. N. M.

and judgments to willing and desiring? The problem of 'meaning' creeps in when we are asked how this reference to object is to be intelligible.

The straightforward doctrine of intentionality is transformed phenomenologically by Husserl into the more complex doctrine of noetic-noematic structure of experience. 'Noesis' is a general name for all objectifying acts; 'noema' for all objects of such acts. The two terms respectively cut across a great variety of 'acts' and a correspondingly great variety of 'objects' of these 'acts'.

The problem of objectivity is, however, the other side of the intentionality situation. If all conscious acts refer to some object, it is no less true that all objects are 'constituted' by some objectifying act or other. This, as we shall see, gives a predominance to the act over the object, to the noesis over the noema. The relation is not merely one of equal partnership.

Helmut Kuhn[4] finds two arguments which exhibit this primacy of the noesis over the noema in Husserl's philosophy. First, analysis of 'act' shows that the act as a whole does not become visible to us till we free ourselves from absorption in the object as independently given; we are, instead, to look at the object as 'intended' by the act, as an element in the act, as the intentional end or *telos* of the act. The second argument carries even more weight. The very objectivity of the object cannot be defined except in terms of the objectifying act. How this is so we shall see later on. The two lines of argument, however, point in the same direction, i.e., towards establishing the supremacy of the objectivating striving over the object, as ready-made.

Recognition of this primacy gives to Husserl's thought its basic idealistic character. But the distinctive nature of this idealism will be clearer if we enquire into the exact nature of this objectivating activity. The most important question in this context is this: What is precisely meant when it is said that the object is 'constituted' by the act? Further, what does Husserl mean by 'objectivity', and how is it that this objectivity is not definable, as we saw, except in terms of the objectivating act?

---

[4] H. Kuhn, "Concept of Horizon" in *Philosophical Essays in Memory of Edmund Husserl*, edited by M. Farber, University of Buffalo Publication.

III

To come to the second question first, we are to see in what 'objectivity' consists and what we mean by 'object'. Husserl's reply is developed on the following lines: There is one consideration which is clear to us *prima facie*. The same object can be the object of perception, of judgment, of inference, of love or hate, of desire or aversion. Thus there is a certain *independence* from the varying modes of apprehension. This independence, however, is but the negative aspect of a positive character. Positively, an object possesses an *identity* amidst all variations of acts. The same object appears as the *telos* of various intentional processes. It is around this problem of identity that our consideration of objectivity shall mainly center.

Where is the place of this identity in the general noesis-noema doctrine? The noetic-noematic structure of experience implies a strict parallelism between the two aspects; every noesis has its corresponding noema. Thus for every conscious (or noetic) act, there is a different noema. What then is the meaning of saying that an identical object persists as the objective of varying acts?

Every noema has a nucleus, its own 'noematic' meaning, through which it gets related to the object. Husserl, in this context, introduces elaborate considerations regarding the problems of 'meaning' and 'content'. This is not the place to go into those details. We need only to remember that this noematic nucleus is the central core around which gather all subsequent phases. Now the different noemata of the varying acts, no doubt, possess different nuclei. But, Husserl goes on to tell us, these various nuclei "close up together in an identical unity, a unity in which the 'something', the determinable which lies concealed in every nucleus, is grasped as self-identical."[5]

How do we grasp this self-identity? Is it really given in intuition? If all that we get is a series of perspective variations, where do we get the identical something, the point of unification?

Husserl suggests that this problem of identity needs a solution on a transcendental level. The problem of identity is, according to Husserl, a problem of Reason; and its solution demands phe-

[5] *Ideas*, p. 338.

nomenological clarification. Husserl does not leave the solution
where Hume left it by denying any identity; nor does he assert
such identity naively in the manner of the realist. The phenomenological solution proceeds on lines akin to Kant's. "How in
the spirit of phenomenological science we are to describe, 'noe-
tically and noematically', all the connections of consciousness
which render necessary a plain object (and this in common speech
always means a real object) precisely in its character as real"?[6]

Phenomenological clarification considers objects not as independently given but as intentional correlates of conscious
experiences. Now, intentional objects may be either themselves
other experiences, or what are called 'things'. Hence the distinction, which is discussed by Husserl in great detail, between
immanent and transcendent perception. In the former case,
the object is an immanent constituent of the process; in the latter,
the object and the conscious process do not constitute a natural
unity. The distinction, however, which is relevant to our present
purpose is this: in the case of immanent perception the object is
given completely and absolutely, while the object of transcendent perception is capable only of perspective variations.
In the latter case, we can have only a series of variable perspectives; and this series is infinitely determinable in infinitely
various directions. But however far we extend these series in all
possible directions, a margin of indeterminacy is still left over,
so that in this case the object can never be completely given.

The problem of identity is therefore to be solved in two different ways in the cases of the two different types of intentional
experience. In both cases, we are to keep in mind, Husserl
makes use of the same criterion. True Being, in phenomenological analysis, reduces itself to adequate givenness (*Ideas*, pp.
365f). This adequacy, however, is to be differently conceived in
the two different cases. In the case of immanent experiences,
adequacy means complete givenness of the object itself, with
all its possible and actual determinations; there is not the least
shade of indeterminacy left over. The object is just that which is
grasped.

In the case of transcendent perception, the solution is truly a
problem of Reason. Since we have never here complete given-

6 *Ideas*, p. 348.

ness of the object, in its full determination, since a margin of determinable indeterminacy is always left over, a principle of Reason is invoked to make up for the deficiency.

Husserl's solution comes up to this. Though complete givenness of the object itself is not possible in this case, Reason nevertheless prescribes an idea of complete givenness as an *a priori* determination of the continuum of appearances.[7] What is given is this Idea. The Idea of an infinity is not itself an infinity; "the insight that this infinity is intrinsically incapable of being given does not exclude but rather demands the transparent givenness of the Idea of this infinity".[8] Thus though the objective factor itself is not given, what is given is an Idea of this objective factor; and Idea serves as "an *a priori* rule for the well-ordered infinities of inadequate experiences".[9]

We are to recall here how closely the phenomenological point of view resembles Kant's account of our apprehension of object.

Husserl is explicit in his indebtedness to Kant on this point. The reference to Idea is a Kantian heritage. The term 'Idea' is said to have been used in the Kantian sense.[10] "I understand by Idea," says Kant, [11] "a necessary concept of reason to which no corresponding object can be given in sense-experience." The completed series of perspective variations, in other words, the full determination of the objectivity cannot be given to intuition. Hence the Idea of such a completed series serves as an *a priori* rule to make the incomplete givenness adequate.

But it is clear that the status Kant accords to the Ideas of Reason is different from what Husserl confers on them. Kant distinguishes between the concepts of understanding and the Ideas of Reason. The former constitute objective knowledge; the latter yield only pseudo-knowledge. Knowledge requires a basis in sense-intuition. Ideas refer to transcendent things which can never be given in intuition. Objective knowledge starts from representations and is completed by synthesis of a concept.

---

[7] *Ideas*, p. 366.
[8] *Ideas*, p. 367.
[9] *Ideas*, p. 367.
[10] *Ideas*, p. 366.
[11] I. Kant, *Kritik der reinen Vernunft*, KW III, edited by Cassirer, p. 264: "Ich verstehe unter der Idee einen notwendigen Vernunftbegriff, dem kein kongruierender Gegenstand in den Sinnen gegeben werden kann".

In the Deduction of the first edition, Kant gives an analysis of our awareness of object. Apprehension of the manifold is followed by reproduction in imagination and is consummated in Recognition through concept. It is easy to see that the purpose this concept of an object serves here in Kant's Deduction is exactly what the Idea yields in Husserl's philosophy. Since for Husserl sense is not the only source of intuition, and consequently since he considers rational explication as equally intuitive, he does not distinguish between the concepts and Ideas in the Kantian manner. This is also corroborated by Husserl's recognition that Kant is treading on phenomenological ground in the first edition Deduction, though he is also accused of having retraced his steps in the second edition Deduction.[12]

We have seen that corresponding to the Kantian Idea of Reason, no object can be given in sense-experience. Husserl's use of it is not unwarranted; for though in apprehension of objectivity, experience does provide a series of perspective variations, yet the completed series, the object in its full determination is never given. An Idea of this completed series is therefore an Idea, whose object cannot be given. The Idea, therefore, serves a purpose, which may be, not illegitimately, interpreted as not being un-Kantian in spirit. And yet there is no question of this Idea's yielding here a dialectical illusion, for a specific sense-core is already there. Further like the Kantian Idea, here also the Idea of the object does prescribe an *a priori* rule for the completion of a series, which is infinite, and which is, in principle, indeterminable by any empirical experimentation.

IV

We have, thus far, considered in some detail the second of the two questions that we placed before ourselves. Now we may revert to the first question. Husserl speaks of the 'constitution' of objectivity, of the object-world, as being 'constituted' by its subjective 'sources'. What could he mean by these phrases, 'constitution' and 'sources'? They are certainly important,

---

[12] *Ideas*, p. 166.

inasmuch as they concern the metaphysical status of the object-world.

The reference to 'constitution' is not to be interpreted onto-logically; that is, it contains no implication of 'creation'. The object is not 'created' by some subjective process; nor do certain subjective processes, by working together, result in an objective formation. The idea of such 'creation' does not strictly belong on the philosophical level. Kantian analysis of knowledge is often wrongly interpreted by people unaccustomed to philosophic reflection as an account of the various stages by which subjective processes conjoin to terminate in a unity, which we call the object. That is fundamentally a non-philosophical approach. Philosophical reflection proceeds on a level which is only indirectly concerned with temporal sequence of processes. And 'creation' is a matter of temporal attainment through process. Philosophic analysis is a reflective analysis. Both Kant and Husserl distinguish between true philosophic reflection and other pseudo-philosophic reflections. The latter include psychologizings and historicizings. Both name true philosophic reflection 'transcendental reflection'; Husserl calls it also 'phenomenological reflection'. It is from this higher point of view that we are to consider the present question.

Phenomenological analysis is also functional analysis. The point of view of 'function', Husserl tells us, is the essence of the phenomenological standpoint.[13] Indeed, all epistemological analysis is functional. It is the correct philosophical standpoint. Kantian analysis is more so. Functional analysis of object is not an analysis on the same objective level. Psychological or historical analysis moves on the same objective plane, and hence does not completely satisfy our reason, which aims at grasping completely the principle of objectivity. Functional analysis is regressive in the sense that it leads us back to more fundamental principles; it is also transcendental in the sense that it takes us back to principles which account for the very possibility of the datum.

Now, 'constitution' of objectivity is a functional phrase and is to be understood accordingly. In Husserl's view, the greatest problems are the functional problems or those of the 'constituting

13 *Ideas*, pp. 230f.

of the objective field of consciousness'. "By 'function'," Kant says, "I mean the unity of the act of bringing various representations under one common representation."[14] The Kantian account of objectivity is an account of how objectivity resolves itself into several functions of the transcendental subject. The categories are such functions, inasmuch as they can be understood as the modes in which the transcendental subject 'acts'. To call these the modes of 'activity' of the transcendental subject does not carry the sense of any temporal process in which the transcendental subject issues forth. They are called 'modes of activity', 'modes of synthesis', etc., because they do not stand for static faculties. Kant is not speaking about psychological faculties, but is undertaking a transcendental reflection, the next outcome of which is a perception that the principle of objectivity is no ultimate principle, which can be conceived as adequate to itself, but is resolvable into certain basic functions of a higher unity. Husserl's point of view is similar, though he does not sketch it in such detail as we find in Kant. Objectivity is 'constituted' within the field of pure consciousness, inasmuch as the former represents a 'function' of the latter.

It is interesting to see that this functional point of view is not really foreign to the doctrine of intentionality which forms the basis of Husserl's philosophy. The doctrine of intentionality recognizes conscious 'acts' as being directed towards some 'objective' reference. Now, to call these 'acts' is not to introduce any sense of temporality. Here 'act' means nothing but 'function'. Even Meinong means by 'act' only such an element in experience as exhibits a variability independent of the reference to a given object. Thus, the 'act' involved in an idea is the function of presenting, the 'act' involved in a judgment is the function of judging, and so on.[15]

It is true that Husserl does not go so far with Kant. He believes Kant to have abandoned the true phenomenological point of view in his second edition Deduction. But it is really in the second edition Deduction that the Kantian analysis comes to a maturer grasp of the functional point of view. The first edi-

---

[14] I. Kant, *Critique of Pure Reason*, A 68–B 93 (Kemp Smith's translation).
[15] J. N. Findlay, *Meinong's Theory of Objects*, Oxford, 1933. p. 25.

tion sketch of what may be called a transcendental psychology is a prelude to this more mature undertaking.[16]

V

In this section, we are to consider the philosophical significance of what Husserl calls 'phenomenological reduction'. Phenomenological reduction 'brackets' the entire natural world. Things of the outer world and events of the psychological world – all go together. All objective formations, aesthetic, cultural, social – suffer the same fate. The phenomenologist is relentless in the use of his weapon, till he attains to pure immanent experience. The least shade of transcendence is repugnant to this motive.

We need to examine the arguments that underlie Husserl's censure of the objective world. Are they new or are they only old wine put into a new bottle? Novelty in philosophical argument is a rare treat; and what passes for novelty is, in most cases, not so in fact. There are two main arguments in Husserl's sketch of phenomenological reduction in his *Ideen*; and with regard to both of them, doubt arises if they are but modern versions of the same old idealistic arguments, that had drawn Kant's attention.

1. First, the absolute being of the immanent is contrasted with the contingency of the transcendent. Being as Consciousness is presented to us absolutely in immanent perception, while Being as thing is presented in transcendent perception only through perspective variations.

It may be that the argument contains something new; but it certainly contains a restatement of the old idealistic faith that the inner world is knowable with far greater certainty than the outer. This is one of the fundamental convictions of the idealist, who has, with this faith, always looked inward for knowledge and enlightenment. Kant, in his *Refutation of Idealism*, challenged this postulate to the extent of making inner knowledge dependent on the outer. Kant's argument is well-known. Our so-called self-knowledge presupposes knowledge of something outer.

---

[16] Again, I do not think the interpretation of 'constitution' given here to be adequate: it may even mislead. – J. N. M.

Even apart from that, it is strange how Husserl seeks to censure the natural world by establishing the contrast between immanent and transcendent perception. Husserl has rejected psychologism simply because he had the courage to see that inner events are no less natural or objective than are the things or events of the outer world. The objects of immanent perception are no less natural or objective.

2. The second argument follows from the first and has more obvious affiliation with the idealistic thought of the past. Here is a revival of the Cartesian doubt, may be, as its author claims, with profounder implications. Phenomenological reduction starts with something like the Cartesian doubt, but it is not exactly that. Nor is it a negation of the starting point. Midway between thesis and antithesis is the neutral. Phenomenological reduction 'brackets' the thesis, sets it 'out of action', 'disconnects' it, makes no use of it, suspends belief in it without yet generating disbelief. Since we are not to pass straight off into the antithesis of the naturalistic thesis, we are not required to doubt all Being. To doubt the Being of anything, Husserl recognizes, is a self-contradiction. I can doubt any object of awareness only in respect of its being actually there. This amended form of doubt necessitates not a negation of Being, but a suspension of the naturalistic thesis.

The whole philosophy of doubt, of which the present is a modern version, is based on the faith, examined above, that inner experience alone yields certain and indubitable knowledge.[17] Kant's *Refutation of Idealism* is a direct challenge to this belief.

But there is quite another way in which the very fundamentals of Kantianism throw out a challenge to this type of philosophizing. According to Husserl, as according to most idealists, no awareness of objects gives anything absolute. That may be correct. But from this to pass over to the contention that the non-

---

[17] "To every stream of experience, and to every Ego as such, there belongs ,in principle the possibility of securing this selfevidence: each of us bears in himself the warrant of his absolute existence (*Daseins*) as a fundamental possibility ... That which floats before the mind may be a mere fiction; the floating itself, the fiction-producing consciousness, is not itself imagined, and the possibility of a perceiving reflection which lays hold on absolute existence belongs to its essence as it does to every experience. (*Ideas*, p. 130). Is this not Cartesian?

existence of the objective world is always thinkable, and then to use this latter possibility as a weapon for idealistic censure of the outer world, involves an unjust philosophic procedure. Kant makes out a strong case against such a procedure. Here is a confusion, a very subtle confusion indeed, Kant points out, between the logical possibility of the concept and the transcendental possibility of things. "For to say that the non-being of a thing does not contradict itself, is a lame appeal to a logical condition, which though necessary to the concept, is very far from being sufficient for real possibility. I can remove in thought every existing substance without contradicting myself, but I cannot infer from this their objective contingency in existence, that is, that their non-existence is possible".[18]

The logical basis of the controversy gets a clearer relief as we probe a little deeper. Eidetic study of empirical connections reveals, Husserl goes on, that " '*the real world*', as it is called, the correlate of our factual experience, then presents itself as *a special case of various possible worlds and non-worlds*, which, on their side, are no other than *correlates of the essentially possible variations of the idea* 'empirical consciousness'."[19] The actual world is the realization of one amongst infinite possibilities. So also with actual experiences: All actual experience refers beyond itself to possible experiences, which themselves again point to new possible experiences, and so on *ad infinitum*. [20] The existence of this world is accidental. Not only is it possible that this world were non-existent, but Husserl even goes so far as to assert that there might not be a world or anything of that sort. The possibilities might never be realized owing to irreconcilable oppositions.

This whole logic of possibility is opposed to Kantianism. For Kant this logic of possibility struggles under an illusion. The question "whether my perceptions can belong, in their general connection, to more than one possible experience," whether other forms of intuition than space and time, other forms of understanding than the discursive categories are possible is inadmissible. Kant is not concerned with mere logical possibility, but with real possibility, and the latter belongs to the realm of possi-

[18] *Critique of Pure Reason*, A 244 = B 302 (Kemp Smith's translation).
[19] *Ideas*, p.134.
[20] *Ideas*, p. 135.

ble experience. Possible experience for Kant denotes not abstract conceptual possibility, but real possibility under the universal conditions of experience; Kant is concerned with the actual and the valid, not with the possible.

Kant has another weighty argument against this logic of possibility, which sees in the actual an accidental formation out of many possibilities. On such a view, something must be added to the possible to constitute the actual, "But this alleged process of adding to the possible I refuse to follow. For that which would have to be added to the possible, over and above the possible, would be impossible."[21]

Thus Husserl's censure of the objective world for the purpose of effecting the phenomenological reduction is based on quite dubitable postulates, which cannot afford a stable foundation for the idealism which his system in the end aims at. What Husserl calls 'transcendental reflection' is a surer basis than the method of 'phenomenological reduction.'[22]

VI

If the natural world is 'bracketed,' if all transcendence is rejected, how is it that phenomenology has yet to do with a study of the 'constitution' of the objective realm? If nothing but pure immanent experience be relevant, real and not intentional analysis of such experience should have been the only subject matter of phenomenological study; but that is not so, and we have seen in some detail how phenomenology is yet directly concerned with the explication of the principle of objectivity.

The reason is important and with a consideration of this point, we will be concluding the present study. Husserl states the principle thus: "This disconnection (i.e., the phenomenological reduction) has also the character of a change of indicator which alters the value of that to which the indicator refers, but if this change of indicator be reckoned in, that whose value it serves to alter is thereby reinstated within the phenomenological sphere."[23]

---

[21] *Critique of Pure Reason,* A 231, B 284 (Kemp Smith's translation).
[22] Though I think some of the above criticisms to be still valid, I do not think that they could justify a final disposal of the Reduction. – J. N. M.
[23] *Ideas,* p. 194.

What is disconnected is the naturalist's thesis. Phenomenology is opposed to the naive assertion of thing-transcendence. But such transcendence is also a phenomenon to be explained, never to be explained away. To undertake this responsibility, the phenomenologist admits a concession, a very significant concession in any case. From the higher point of view, from the standpoint of transcendental reflection, the same 'content', which as the subject matter of naturalist thesis had received censure, is admissible for consideration, though only under a 'change of signature'. This 'change of signature' is the effect of rising to the new level of reflection.

Phenomenological reflection, as we know, considers things as 'intended', as intentional correlates of experiences. Under the 'change of signature', therefore, all transcendents must be "represented in the phenomenological spheres by the whole nexus of corresponding meanings and positions" "within the limits of real and possible consciousness... In other words, all objectivities must be traced to their "constituting in the subjective sources."[24]

[24] *Ideas*, p. 345–46.

CHAPTER XIV

INDIVIDUAL FACT AND ESSENCE IN EDMUND HUSSERL'S PHILOSOPHY*

1. The purpose of this paper is not, as its title is likely to suggest, to reopen the discussion on a distinction familiarized by Husserl. What I intend doing is to examine critically some of Husserl's attempts to bridge that gulf between fact and essence with which he himself starts. For the purpose of this discussion I shall single out two notions of Husserl and examine whether with the help of these two we may not succeed in connecting facts with essences in such a way as to overcome the original distance. These are the notions of 'individual essence'[1] and 'an individual fact's own essence'.[2]

2. Before we take up these key notions, it is necessary, however, to prepare the ground by introducing certain well-known ideas of Husserl that are relevant in the present context:

(a) To begin with, it may be mentioned that notwithstanding the radical distinction between the two realms of being, facts, and essences, Husserl also evinces an awareness of a certain parallelism between them. Just as what is given in empirical perception is an individual, so what is given in essential intuition is an essence. Husserl even cautions us against treating the above as a merely external analogy; what we have here is rather a *"radikale Gemeinsamkeit."*[3] In both cases the terms 'perception' or 'intuition' and the correlative term 'object' are used with equal

* First published in *Philosophy and Phenomenological Research*, XIX, 1959, 222–230.

[1] *Ideen*, Vol. I, p. 75. The references to Husserl's works are to the new Husserliana editions, except in the case of *Erfahrung und Urteil*, the *Logische Untersuchungen*, and the *Formale und Transzendentale Logik*.

[2] *Ibid.*, p. 35.

[3] *Ibid.*, p. 14.

justification. In empirical perception what is revealed is the individual spatio-temporal fact; so is an essence revealed, given, 'bodily' presented in eidetic perception. Eidetic perception is also an original mode of perception in the sense that it has its own specific type of objects that are primarily given through it.

The parallelism holds good between two modes of original givenness. Essences are given in thought, that being the only way they are given. Husserl is thereby treating thought as a mode of disclosure, and not as mode of construction or analysis as other philosophers have taken it to be. In this sense thought is intuitive, but it is not so in any other mystical sense. 'Intuition' is nothing but a generic name for all modes of original givenness. Thought being one such mode may be said to be intuitive. What Husserl calls *"Wesensschau"* is not a mystical vision of essences, but it is nothing but thought purified. Thought, though it discloses essences, is ordinarily tied to sense perception and practice. Ordinary thought discloses essences, but only as they are in facts. To attain to a pure awareness of essences is to render thought free from this naturalistic attachment. One way of doing this, much emphasized by Husserl, consists in varying the factual circumstances, in taking recourse to fantasy, etc., through which the identity of the essence as well as its indifference to fact comes into clearer relief.

Husserl no doubt courts the risk of overemphasizing the *"radikale Gemeinsamkeit"* and thereby is partly responsible for that bugbear of *"Wesensschau"*. Amongst the limitations of this parallelism, let us bear in mind one: awareness of the essence is founded on a prior perception of the individual fact while empirical perception on its own part is not so founded, it being the absolute first.[4]

(b) Facts presuppose essences in a twofold way. The individual fact is accidental; it could have been otherwise. This accidentality is relative to an essential necessity. It is only from the point of view of essences that the individual fact could be judged as accidental. Otherwise, considered in its factual interconnections the fact is determined and thoroughly necessitated. What more this relativity means and entails Husserl does not make clear in § 2 of the *Ideen*, Vol.I, where it is introduced. The argu-

---

[4] Josef König, *Der Begriff der Intuition*, Halle, 1926, p. 303.

ment as it stands seems to be circular in nature: a fact is judged accidental only when considered from the point of view of the universal, there being nothing in the fact taken by itself to betray its accidentality. A fact by itself does not reveal its own accidentality, which could point to that essential necessity of which Husserl speaks. On the other hand, it is the awareness of essential necessity which reveals the fact as accidental.[5]

(c) The relation between facts and essences however is said to be more intimate and ontologically founded. Every individual fact has its own essence,[6] just as again every essence has its own range of possible individual facts.[7] Leaving aside the latter point for the present, let us turn to the former. An individual fact is not only a mere 'this-there', a *'dies-da'*, but also a so-and-so.[8] There are essential predicates that hold good of it. It has no doubt accidental properties, but these accidental properties presuppose the essential ones.

Considered from this point of view the word 'essence' is now taken to mean *"das im selbsteigenen Sein eines Individuum als sein Was Vorfindliche."*[9] Every 'what' or content of an individual is an essence. This seems to be the familiar doctrine that the qualities or features of a thing are all universals. There is however a difference between this old doctrine and what Husserl intends telling us here. Husserl is not telling us that what we perceive in an individual fact are essences, as they are according to critical realists like Santayana. If that were Husserl's opinion, that is to say, if he held that every 'what' of an individual fact as given in the mode in which the individual fact itself is given were an universal or an essence, then it would be difficult to explain why he should have followed up the above account with the statement: *"Jedes solches Was kann aber 'in Idee gesetzt' werden."*[10] Explaining this last statement, Husserl continues: *"Erfahrende oder individuelle Anschauung kann in Wesenschauung (Ideation) umgewandelt werden."*[11] It is only when the empirical

---

[5] Nicolai Hartmann seeks to overcome this kind of ontology by his own modal analysis laid down in the work *Möglichkeit und Wirklichkeit*, Berlin, 1949.

[6] *Ideen*, Vol. I, p. 12.

[7] *Ibid.*, p. 21.

[8] *Ibid.*, p. 13.

[9] *Ibid.*, p. 13.

[10] *Ibid.*, p. 13

[11] *Ibid.*, p. 13.

perception is 'transformed' into eidetic perception that the content of the former is also 'transformed' into an essence. This is far from saying that the essence itself was given as the content of empirical perception. In *Beilage* V to the new edition of the *Ideen*, Vol.1, Husserl notes that the essence lies implicitly in the individual fact.[12] This notion of implicit existence is phenomenologically questionable, for the distinction between what is given and what is really given is a metaphysical distinction pretending to be phenomenological. It is therefore phenomenologically unsound to say that the essences were really given in sense perception, although they were not then recognized to be so given. On the other hand, what we are phenomenologically justified in maintaining is that every content of empirical perception can be 'transformed' into a corresponding essence. It is only then that *"Das Erschaute ist . . . das entsprechende reine Wesen oder Eidos."*[13]

(d) Before we take up the key notion to be examined in this paper, let us try to understand the only definition of individual fact which Husserl suggests in the *Ideen*. The definition however has to be developed through stages for it involves certain other distinctions.

i. Distinction is made between independent and dependent essences. "Dependent objects are objects of whom the essential law holds good that when they at all exist they exist only as parts of a more comprehensive whole of a definite correlative kind."[14] The color of this paper is a dependent part, for it is not only factually part of a whole, but even essentially can exist only as part of a whole. "A part is dependent, if it belongs not merely to a factual but also to an essentially necessary (*'idealgesetzlichem'*) connectedness."[15] On the other hand, if there is a part that has only a factual membership of a whole, but essentially need not be so, then it is independent. This distinction holds good of essences and is an ontological distinction.[16] Dependent contents are called abstract; independent ones are called concrete.[17]

---

[12] *Ibid.*, p. 387.
[13] *Ibid.*, p. 13.
[14] *Logische Untersuchungen*, Vol. II, Part 1, p. 240.
[15] *Ibid.*, p. 251.
[16] *Ibid.*, p. 248'
[17] *Ibid.*, p. 248; also compare *Ideen*, Vol. I, p. 15.

ii. Another distinction is required before the '*Individuum*' can be defined. This is the distinction between formal essence and material essence.[18] Formal essences are those that form the subject matter of formal logic: concepts like 'one', 'many', 'whole', 'part', etc. The highest regional essence of the sphere of formal essences is 'object in general'. Formal essences are said to be empty, while material essences are essences in the strict sense.[19]

iii. Husserl now defines an '*Individuum*' as a 'this-there' whose material essence is a concrete one. [20] An individual is not a bare 'this-there', but is a so-and-so-constituted one. Its 'what' again can be 'transformed', in eidetic intuition, into a complex material essence. This complex essence in the case of an individual is an independent, hence concrete, essence. One immediately sees that this definition holds good only of things and not of determinate qualities. The shade of green here before me as I write this is a 'this-there' whose material essence is a 'lowest difference', an 'eidetic singularity', which however is not an independent or concrete essence in the sense defined above, for a shade of color must with a priori necessity be coupled with an extended surface.

3. We may now take up the notion of 'an individual fact's own essence' and critically examine whether it is to be retained. It is no doubt one of Husserl's well-known doctrines that every individual fact is an 'index' for an 'essential structure'. Corresponding – using 'correspondence' in a rather odd sense – to every individual fact there is a definite structure of essences. This means that a group of essences of varying orders of generality – eidetic singularities, species and genera – arranged in a definite pattern of combination and subsumption are 'in' that individual fact. This structured whole is a complex essence.

Husserl however goes further than saying this. He speaks of an individual fact's own essence, seemingly meaning thereby that each individual has its own essence which a priori cannot be the essence of another individual. Taking up suggestions of this sort, Jean Hering[21] distinguished between the individual object (fact),

[18] *L. U.*, Vol. II¹, pp.252 ff.
[19] *Ideen*, Vol. I, p. 27.
[20] *Ibid.*, p. 36.
[21] Jean Hering, *Jahrbuch für Philosophie und phänomenologische Forschung*, Vol. IV, pp. 496–543.

its essence, the *'Wesenheit'*; and the *'Idee'*. Leaving aside for the present Hering's distinctions between *'Wesen'*, *'Wesenheit'*, and the *'Idee'* – which by the way could be given up without setting up serious difficulties in clarifying Husserl's texts (the single word *'Wesen'* would do!) – let us consider what Hering calls the 'individual object's own essence." Such an essence, according to Hering, is the essence of something, *"und zwar Wesen von diesem und keinem anderen Etwas"* (i.e., is the essence of this something, not of any other thing).[22] This essence, Hering continues, is the *'Sosein'* ('what') of the object, taken in the complete fullness of its constitution (*"Sosein des in der ganzen Fülle seiner Konstitution genommen Objektes"*).

Now it is true that the palm tree that I see through my window as I write this 'has' a complex essence 'corresponding' to its own 'what'. But in what sense is it meaningfully possible to maintain that the complex essence concerned is the essence of this palm tree, and not of any other possible object? In order to be able to say so, it must be possible to demonstrate that the essence in question contains within itself the principle of individuation of facts, so that this fact and no other can possibly have this essence as its own. If this were so, the very distinction between facts and essences would stand obliterated; the world of facts could in that case be deductively derived from the world of essences. This would amount to a denial that facts are facts; they would, in fact, be individuated essences. And yet how could essences determine without 'residue' the this? Why should it be a priori impossible that the same complex essence be 'illustrated', 'realized', 'ingredient', etc., in that also? Besides, to maintain that the entire individual fact could be 'transformed' into an essence that is only this individual's and none other's would go against phenomenological evidence: individual facts are given in an attitude totally different from that in which essences are given.

3.1 It is in *Erfahrung und Urteil*[23] that Husserl attempts a fruitful discussion of the problem of individuation as well as of the question of 'this individual's own essence'. Here Husserl clearly

22 *Ibid.*, p. 497.
23 *Erfahrung und Urteil*, pp. 429–430; compare also *Beilage* I.

shows his recognition of the truth that an individual fact as such cannot be 'transformed' into an essence that would be its own essence. 'The same' object, no doubt, can be empirically given; it can also be given in fantasy. Cannot an essence of 'this same' object, and of this object alone, be brought into evidence through the process of imaginative variation? Yes, Husserl would say. But what is 'the same object'? By 'the same object' is not meant, Husserl cautions us, simply the object as such (*"der Gegenstand schlechthin"*), for when one speaks of the simple object one means it as actually given here and now. What alone can identically be given in experience as well as in fantasy as 'the same object' is "a content that can be identically separated for intuition" (*"als identisch herausschaubaren Gehalt"*), the "full meaning" (*"voller Sinn"*) that has now the character of actuality, and now the character of "fantasized", etc. This content is *"der noematischer Wesensbestand"* which is identically the same in full experience as well as in quasi-empirical fantasy. This is the "individual essence" of the object concerned.[24] This is nothing but what is common to the intentional correlates of the acts of perceiving, imagining, remembering, and calling up in fantasy this very palm tree here before me.

In order however that the essence thus gotten hold of may be this individual's own essence we must have in the essence the correlates of those elements that impart to this object its uniqueness. The source of this uniqueness, Husserl is well aware, is the unique temporal character of the 'now'.[25] The essence of this individual as such must therefore contain the noematic correlate of this 'now'. Husserl intends no doubt to show that this is possible. For example, he says: *"Die Zeitdauer ist hier aber ein identisches Wesen, so gut wie die Färbung....."*[26] But this is doomed to failure. Husserl himself has elsewhere emphasized the truth that the idealities are not temporally individuated.[27] The uniqueness of the this-now refuses to be absorbed into or derived from an essence, however articulated and structured that essence may be. This is another aspect of the truth that 'in-

[24] *Ibid.*, pp. 460–461.
[25] *Ibid.*, p. 464.
[26] *Ibid.*, p. 461.
[27] *Formale und Transzendentale Logik*, p. 139.

dexical' expressions or 'ego-centric particulars' are irreducible.[28]

We must, therefore, conclude that though corresponding to an individual there is always discoverable an essence, simple or complex, such an essence cannot in any sense be meaningfully spoken of as this individual's own essence.

3.2. This does not preclude us however from recognizing the phenomenological truth in speaking of 'individual essences' in quite another sense. Not all essences, Husserl saw rightly, are as such universals that are instantiated in facts. There are also essences, the 'lowest eidetic differences,' that are not instantiated, but are themselves identically present in those facts which they characterize. These are what Husserl calls the 'eidetic singularities'. These, it is obvious, fail to bridge the gulf between facts and essences in the same way in which the notion of 'this individual's own essence' pretends to do.

4. Does the notion of the 'extension' of an essence serve this purpose any better? Just as every individual fact has its essence, we are told, so has every essence its range of possible individuals.[29] It is obvious that to ascribe to an essence *qua* essence a range of possible individuals is not to curtail that freedom from the realm of facts which belongs to the essences as such. An essence *qua* essence cannot have a purely factual extension[30]; if it has an extension, that extension can only consist in possible facts. Possible facts are not facts *qua* facts. Nor are they the given facts, only considered not as facts but as instances of the essence concerned, for the idea of 'possible facts' is logically prior to that of given facts.

Husserl in fact distinguishes between the 'eidetic' extension and the 'empirical' extension of an essence. [31] The eidetic extension of an essence is constituted by the specific eidetic differences coming under it; members of such an extension are themselves essences. To the eidetic extension of 'color', of course, belong essences like 'red', 'blue', etc., and also in the long run eidetic

---

[28] Compare Bar-Hillel, "Indexical Expressions", *Mind*, 1954.
[29] *Ideen*, Vol. I, p. 21.
[30] *Erfahrung und Urteil*, p. 426.
[31] *Ideen*, Vol. I, p. 33.

singularities, i.e., lowest specific differences like 'milk-whiteness'. It follows that only material essences that are not themselves eidetic singularities have such an extension.

To be contrasted with this 'eidetic' extension is the 'empirical' extension, consisting not of actual individuals but, as we saw above, of possible individuals, of *'einen Gesamtinbegriff von möglichen Diesheiten'*. As has been emphasized, this extension is not empirical in the strict sense, for its definition involves the concept of possibility which is not an empirical concept. This notion therefore fails to annul the distance between the two spheres.

5. Connected with the above is the distinction between 'eidetic' judgments and judgments about 'eidos'.[32] Essences may be intuitively apprehended without yet being the objects of *('Gegenständen-Worüber')* such apprehension. This is so in the case of judgments that have for their objects not the Ideas themselves, but the totality of possible individuals constituting the 'extension' of the essence concerned. Thus, for example, when in geometry we say something about 'all triangles' or, in general, when we form a universal judgment, we are of course having an eidetic judgment, but are not judging directly about the eidos concerned. The possibility however of transforming an eidetic judgment into a judgment about eidos is always there. The eidetic judgment – to take Husserl's example – 'A color in general is different from a tone in general' may be transformed, through a changed attitude, into the judgment, 'The essence color is a different essence than the essence tone'. Similarly every judgment about an eidos may be transformed into an eidetic judgment, i.e., into a universal judgment about the possible individuals of this essence. In no case, however, is the existence of these individuals presupposed, so that the eidetic judgments never come down to the level of the empirical.

This distinction draws attention to the truth that universality is a derivative characteristic of the essences. The forms 'A triangle' or 'All triangles' are derivative from the original essence 'Triangle in general'.[33] A species or an essence considered in

[32] *Ibid.*, p. 5.
[33] *L. U.*, Vol. II, Part I.

itself is as much singular as universal; only the aspect of spatio-temporal individuation is absent.

In fact one can go further and distinguish between three kinds of eidetic knowledge: a. Knowledge of the 'eidos' itself as the object of such knowledge as the *'Gegenstand-Worüber'*; b. Perception of the 'eidos' in a single real instance. (Husserl recognizes this in *Ideen*, Vol. I, p. 18, as an eidetic perception in a modified sense. In this case an individual is given only as instance or individuation of an essence); c. Perception of the unending totality of possible individuals constituting the extension of the essence. Both b and c give rise to eidetic judgments. Only a gives rise to judgments about the eidos.

6. The arguments thus far may be summed up now. Although it may be true that every fact is an 'index' for an essential structure, yet this only means that the content of empirical perception 'may be' transformed into the content of eidetic perception. Although an individuum may be defined, as Husserl has suggested, as a 'this-there' with a concrete material essence, two points must be borne in mind. First, the 'with' in the above definition should be understood in a sense totally different from that in which one understands such a sentence as 'This is a tree with green leaves'. The 'with' occurring in the definition does not denote real possession. Next, the 'this-there' itself cannot be taken to have another essence 'corresponding' to it. The temporal uniqueness of the real individual cannot be derived from the essences. Husserl in an exceedingly difficult paragraph[34] distinguishes the 'this-there' from the 'last material essence', bringing them both under the common title 'categories of substratum'. Every 'this-there' has no doubt its essence in the sense explained above, but the 'this-there' itself is a category of the real world and not of the realm of essences. We fail to bridge the gulf between facts and essences, between the real and the ideal. The phenomenological discontinuity remains and has to be recognized. This discontinuity sets a limit to all deductive metaphysics. By 'deductive metaphysics' is here meant all those philosophies that attempt to deduce the world of real spatio-temporal facts from non-temporal essences.

[34] *Ideen*, Vol. I, p. 35.

6.1. Husserl has warned, as is well-known, against the reduction of the idealities into real factors. This reduction however is as much unwarranted as the opposite deduction; both fail to recognize that phenomenological discontinuity which separates the two realms. By insisting on this discontinuity we are not indulging in another metaphysical dualism. The dualism or the discontinuity is rather, more strictly speaking, between the two corresponding modes of givenness, or it is a discontinuity between the corresponding 'evidences'.

Things are given in the 'naturalistic attitude'. The 'naturalistic attitude' is the practical attitude. The mode of givenness of things is the practical mode. There is no 'naturalistic' contemplation of the world of things: that would be the height of the intellectualistic prejudice. Perception of things is not a theoretical act; it is inseparably bound up with practice. The world of things is the horizon of actual and possible practice.

6.2. Here in this connection, Husserl's later emphasis on the pre-reflective, prescientific *'Lebenswelt'* as the implicit presupposition of reflective thought is significant. It also reminds us, as Fritz Kaufmann has pointed out in his review of *Problems Actuels de la Phénoménologie* in *The Philosophical Review* (1954), of Dewey's world of 'direct experience'. Husserl rightly raises interesting questions about the possibility of a science of the *'Lebenswelt'* as well as about the a priori structure, if any, of this *'Umwelt'*.[35] Here is besides a point where the researches of the later Husserl merge into those of pragmatists like Dewey, and existentialists like Heidegger. Besides from this point of view there is the need of a fresh understanding and evaluation of Husserl's *'Konstitutionanalyse'* which smacks of deductive metaphysics, but which has to be exhibited in its phenomenological harmlessness, i.e., in such a way as not to conflict with that phenomenological discontinuity which has been emphasized in this paper. These are programs that are far beyond the scope of the present paper.

---

[35] *Die Krisis der europäischen Wissenschaften* (Husserliana, Vol. VI), pp. 28, 36.

CHAPTER XV

GILBERT RYLE'S CRITICISMS OF
THE CONCEPT OF CONSCIOUSNESS*

1. In Chapter VI sec. (2) of his *The Concept of Mind*, (London, 1949) Gilbert Ryle criticises a concept of consciousness which in my opinion is one of the most important of all the different concepts of consciousness to be found in the different schools of philosphy. This is the concept of consciousness as self-intimating, self-revealing, self-luminous etc.. By making this supposedly distinguishing feature of consciousness his main target for criticism, Ryle has done the service of drawing attention to the right point, even if by way of criticism. For Western philosophy as yet had only one clear formulation of a positive distinguishing feature of consciousness: this is what Brentano and Husserl called 'intentionality'. The self-luminousness theory however, implicit though in much of traditional western philosophy, has never come to the forefront except perhaps in Kant's notion of the 'I think' which according to Kant must necessarily be able to accompany all our representations and in Samuel Alexander's notion of 'enjoyment' as distinguished from 'contemplation'. In Indian philosophy, on the other hand, the schools of Mimamsa and Vedanta have made the notion of self-luminousness (*svayamprakāśatva*) of consciousness the cornerstone of their epistemology and metaphysics. Considering the eight pages of Ryle's arguments from the point of view of this Indian tradition, his arguments appear to me to be a curious mixture of insight and misunderstanding to both of which this paper seeks to draw attention.

2. To start with, Ryle's emphasis on the analogy of light seems to hold good also of the Indian discussions of this theme. Just as

* First published in *The Visva Bharati Journal of Philosophy*, *III*, 1966–67.

light reveals other objects while revealing itself, so does consciousness reveal itself while revealing objects other than itself. If another lamp were required for the revelation of light, that would surely lead to an infinite regress. So also, it is argued, if consciousness were not self-luminous but needed something else in order to be revealed, that something else would need other revealing agencies and thus an infinite number of revealing agencies would have to be postulated. As in the case of light, so also in the case of consciousness, the infinite regress can be stopped by admitting some one member as self-luminous, as needing no revealing agency other than itself.

While the analogy of light is so commonplace, it is far from the truth to assert with Ryle that the myth of consciousness is "a piece of para-optics".[1] The Indian philosophers were well aware that while speaking of self-luminousness they were not doing anything more than making use of a highly appropriate analogy. "Consciousness", says Ryle, "was imported to play in the mental world the part played by light in the mechanical world".[2] This division of labour gives a false impression of the real nature of the point at stake. The analogy fails in the long run, for light itself in order to be revealed requires the self-luminousness of consciousness. The self-luminousness of consciousness is admitted not merely to explain the way we apprehend the episodes enacted in the second theatre called mind, but also to explain how anything at all could be known. The distinction between the physical world and the mental world is not essential to this notion of consciousness. Ryle's statement of the notion of self-luminousness owes its inaccuracies to one reason amongst others that he introduces and considers it in the context of a two-world theory which however is not an essential background for the notion. I am not of course denying that many of those who uphold the self-luminousness theory have also upheld the two-world theory.

3. I will now present the self-luminousness theory in the context of Indian philosophical tradition and within such limits as in my opinion are necessary for my present purpose. Then I will

---

[1] *The Concept of Mind*, p. 159.
[2] *Ibid.*, p. 159.

consider the criticisms of Ryle. This will help in clarifying the points I propose to make against Ryle.

The traditional Indian philosophers asked a question which may be formulated as: "How do I know that I know something?" Supposing I know that S is p, the object of my knowledge is the fact that S is p. But how do I know that I know that S is p? There are two groups of answers to this question. There are some, the Nayiyāyikas, who hold that if K_1 is the knowledge of an object O, K_1 is known only by becoming the object of another knowledge K_2. K_2 however need not be known, but can be known if so desired and if circumstances permit. When however it is known, it becomes the object of K_3. This amounts to saying that neither K_1 nor K_2 nor any other knowledge is known by itself. If K_1 is the primary knowledge (seeing, hearing etc.), K_2, K_3 etc. are introspections. A knowledge is the knowledge of its own object and not of any other object. K_1, by hypothesis, is knowledge of O. Hence, argues the Nayiyāyika, only O, and not K_1 itself, is known by K_1. K_1 therefore is not self-intimating. No knowledge can be so for the same reason.

To the above argument of the Nayiyāyika, those who defend the self-luminousness theory reply as follows. To suppose that K_1 can be known only by K_2 and K_2 by K_3 would lead to an infinite regress. My awareness of my knowledge would then depend upon the completion of an infinite series. An infinite number of knowledges has to be postulated. In that case, I would never come to know that I know. We must therefore suppose that the series must somewhere have an end. Wherever we agree to close the series, the last member must be known without being the object of another knowledge, i.e., it must be self-luminous. If such a self-luminous knowledge has at all to be admitted, why not say that K_1 itself is so?

4. Under such circumstances we cannot but wonder as to the real target of one of Ryle's major arguments. In this argument, Ryle insists on the endless regress which the theory he is attacking involves i.e. on the "infinite numbers of onion-skins of consciousness" that the theory under consideration has to postulate. But what precisely is the theory against which this criticism holds good? Not the self-luminousness theory, for this theory has just

the special advantage that it dispenses with the supposed endless regress. And I have in the above paragraph drawn attention to the fact that the Indian defenders of the self-luminous theory attack the Nayiyāyika with the same weapon with which Ryle seeks to deal his last death-blow at the self-luminousness theory.

To decide what precisely is the theory against which Ryle's last argument holds good, let us see how he proves the infinite regress. In his example, K_1 is an inferential knowledge of O. K_2 is the apprehension of K_1, i.e. of the inferring. K_2 to be known must require K_3 and so on *ad infinitum*. The theory which Ryle here criticises differs from the Nayiyāyika's theory in two respects, and these differences place the theory mid-way between the Nayiyāyika's and the Vedantist's theories. Like the Nayiyāyika, the theory criticised by Ryle holds that K_1 is known by K_2 and K_2 by K_3. But unlike the Nayiyāyika, the theory that is being criticised by Ryle takes the higher order knowings in a non-dispositional sense. Whereas all that the Nayiyāyika claims is that K_2 can be, if so desired and if circumstances permit, known by K_3, this theory holds that K_2 is necessarily made the object of K_3. Further, this theory differs from the Nayiyāyika's in the further point that whereas for the Nayiyāyika K_1, K_2, K_3 are succeeding cognitions, for this theory they are simultaneously imbedded in any and every mental state. For the Indian self-luminousness theory, on the other hand, K_1 is actually known (in a non-dispositional sense) but not by K_2 but by itself. K_2, K_3, etc. are uncalled for.

Thus we find that the infinite regress does not vitiate the Indian formulation of the self-luminousness theory, for the very point about the Indian theory is the assertion that K_1 is known without being the object of another knowledge, K_2.

It is also interesting to see that the Nayiyāyika by making the higher order knowings from K_2 onwards merely possible cognitions has a good argument by which he could avoid the charge of infinite regress. For the Nayiyāyika will argue that K_1 alone is required for O to be known, and that K_1 is invariably followed by K_2 while K_2 need not be known unless there is a special desire for it to be known, that when it is known it becomes the object of K_3 and that the same is true of K_3. There is therefore no infinite regress.

The Vedantist of course would try to show that an unknown knowledge is a self-contradiction and that if K_2 is unknown there cannot be any desire on one's part to know it.

It is rather Ryle's version of the self-luminousness theory (which is the Nayiyāyika's theory with the differences that the higher order knowings are not taken to be merely possible and that K_1, K_2, K_3, etc. are taken not to be successive but to be simultaneous) that lies flagrantly open to the charge Ryle urges against it. The self-luminousness theory as formulated by the Indian philosophers however escapes Ryle's death-blow.

Ryle himself is not totally unaware of this truth. For he sees[3] that the self-luminousness theory does not imply that there are two acts of knowing either as synchronous performances or as somehow indissolubly welded together. If this be so, one fails to understand why he ascribes to that theory the view that there is, for example, an apprehension of inferring over and above the inferring of which it is the apprehension.

6. Another argument which Ryle advances against the self-luminousness theory is admitted by him to be merely persuasive. Nevertheless, I will try to find out a reply. The question is, how do we, as ordinary men, vindicate our assertions of fact. Ryle argues that we never appeal in our vindications to 'immediate awareness' or to any 'direct deliverance of consciousness'. We would rather support our statements of fact by saying that we see, hear, smell or taste so and so. Asked if one really knows something, one never replies, Ryle argues, "Oh yes, certainly I do, for I am conscious of doing so".

I imagine the following conversation:

Mr A. – "Look here, there is a bird's nest in the tree!"

Mr B. – "How do you know that?"

Mr A. – "Well, I see it."

Mr. B unless he has been made sophisticated by study of philosophy would not normally ask "How do you know that you are seeing?". But even an unsophisticated person may ask other questions: "Are you sure you are really seeing one?", "Are you sure you are really seeing a bird's nest, or are you seeing some-

---

[3] *Ibid.*, pp. 159–9.

thing else up there?", "Are you sure you are seeing one or are you imagining one?" etc.

The second group of questions is of course answered, and the answer vindicated, without appealing to the self-luminousness of consciousness. Further, Mr. A need not – now I am answering Ryle – vindicate his assertion of the fact that there is a bird's nest up there by appealing to any direct deliverance of consciousness. He says, and need say even on the self-luminousness theory, that he sees one. But the sophisticated question "How do you know that you know?" has to be answered, if we are to avoid an infinite regress, by admitting at some point of the answer that something is known without being an object of another knowledge. The self-luminousness theory says that my knowing that I am seeing is not another act synchronous with seeing or indissolubly welded with it (Ryle, to be fair, sees this), but that my knowing O and my knowing that I am knowing O are one and the same act. The Vedantist is well aware that when the self-luminous consciousness is said to be 'known' by itself, this word 'known' is used in a pickwickian sense and not in the same sense in which one says of a proposition that it is known. That which makes possible all knowledge cannot itself be an object of knowledge: this was also the point Kant wanted to make out against the rationalist psychology of his time.

7. Of all Ryle's arguments, it remains to consider the one appealing to facts like self-delusion. Although the self-luminousness theory does not claim to provide, as has been pointed out, an answer to the question "Are you really seeing one or are you imagining you are seeing one?", yet – it may be argued – does not the very possibility of this question cut at the roots of the theory? For, how, if consciousness be self-intimating, can I be at all deceived about my mental states? How can I at all entertain a doubt about the mental state I am experiencing? How can I ask myself "Am I really seeing or am I imagining I am seeing?"? "If consciousness was what it is described as being", writes Ryle,[4] "it would be logically impossible for such failures and mistakes in recognition to take place".

Replying, let me at once say what I have said before, namely

[4] *Ibid.*, p. 162.

that self-luminousness is not a property of mental states (admitting, provisionally though, the two-world theory) just as it is not a property of non-mental objects. It is the property of awareness, be it the awareness of a physical object or of a mental state, be it awareness of the object seen or of my seeing of it. Awareness itself is not a mental state.

If mental states and non-mental objects are so far on a par, cases of mistaking one physical object for another (e.g., a rope for a snake) and cases of mistaking one mental state for another (e.g. an imagining for a seeing) have equal relevance for the issue at stake. But none of these two groups of cases disproves the self-luminousness theory, for this theory accounts not for the truth of any knowledge but for the fact that I am not only aware of the object known but at the same time am aware of my own awareness, or using Samuel Alexander's phraseology, for the fact that I 'enjoy' my own awareness without making the latter the object of another awareness. False awareness is also an 'awareness of . . .' and this awareness is as much 'enjoyed' as correct apprehension is. Only, the theory would add, nothing – neither physical nor mental – can be known unless this self-luminous awareness were there, that is to say, if consciousness were not self-luminous.

For the same reason, unconscious mental states (to which Freud has drawn attention) present as little difficulty as unknown physical objects.

I should add at the end that the purpose of this paper is not to maintain that the self-luminousness theory as stated here is philosophically invulnerable. My purpose has been to show that Ryle's criticisms do not succeed in exploding this notion.

CHAPTER XVI

ON G. E. MOORE'S DEFENCE OF COMMON SENSE*

1. In this paper I shall critically discuss G. E. Moore's Defence of Common Sense[1] with the purpose of showing that Moore's idea of defending common sense was entirely mistaken. This mistake is based, as I shall try to show, firstly on a mistaken notion about the nature of common sense and, secondly, on a mistaken notion about the relation between common sense beliefs and philosophy. Nothing that I say in this paper regarding the value and the validity of Moore's Defence of Common Sense should be taken as reflecting my opinion about the other aspects of Moore's philosophy.

2. Let me state at the outset that the word 'common sense' is used by Moore in a somewhat unusual sense. Ryle has rightly drawn attention to the fact that 'common sense' is ordinarily used to stand for "a particular kind and degree of untutored judiciousness in coping with slightly out of the way, practical contingencies".[2] To make common sense therefore a partisan in philosophical dispute would appear monstrous to common sense itself. For, 'common sense', in its ordinary unphilosophical use, does not stand for a set of beliefs or a set of propositions like those listed by Moore. Men who possess common sense of course do believe in many or even all of these propositions; but so also do men who, we say, lack common sense. Moore, therefore, when he takes upon himself, as one of his philosophical jobs, the task of defending common sense in the sense of defending a set of

---

* First published in the *Indian Journal of Philosophy*, II, 1960, No. 4, 1–10.
[1] J. H. Muirhead (ed.), *Contemporary British Philosophy* (Second Series), London, 1925, pp. 193-223.
[2] G. Ryle, *Dilemmas*, Cambridge, 1954, p. 3.

propositions in which he along with most of us believes, must be using the word 'common sense' in a very uncommon way.

2.1. In reply to the above, one may quite well agree to dispense with the word 'common sense' while appealing instead to the beliefs that are common to the plain men of Europe and North America! This is in fact what Thomas Reid means when in his Reflections on the Common Theory of Ideas, he says, referring to Berkeley's philosophy:

> If a plain man, uninstructed in Philosophy, has faith to receive these mysteries, how great must be his astonishment! ... After his mind is somewhat composed it will be natural for him to ask his philosophical instructor: Pray, Sir, are there then no substantial and permanent beings called the sun and moon, which continue to exist whether we think of them or not?...[3]

It is the beliefs of 'the plain man, uninstructed in Philosophy' which, it might be suggested, Moore was defending. This however cannot be Moore's intention. For, firstly, Moore certainly does not believe in all that the plain man, uninstructed in philosophy, believes to be true. And he seeks to defend the truth only of some of the beliefs of the plain man. Secondly, the beliefs of the plain man, depending largely upon his religious and cultural background, may – and, in fact, do – include a large number of beliefs which Moore, I presume, would not undertake to defend.[4]

3. Let me therefore pursue this point a little further with a view to bringing out the nature of the beliefs Moore sought to defend. It seems to me that Moore's interest consists as much in defending his belief in certain propositions as in proving certain beliefs of philosophers to be false. Many philosophers have believed in such propositions as 'Time is unreal', 'There are no other selves', 'Matter is unreal', etc.. Moore's purpose is to show that these propositions contradict the beliefs of common sense. Now the truth of the proposition 'Time is unreal' contradicts the

---

[3] I am indebted to my friend Eberhard Bubser for pointing out this passage to me.
[4] When the words 'common sense', 'commonsense beliefs' are used in the rest of this paper, they are to be understood in the light of the remarks in para. 2.

truth of the proposition 'Time is real'. The belief that Matter is unreal contradicts the belief that Matter is real. Since it often happens that what a person is refuting throws light upon what he is at the same time defending, we may presume that Moore seeks to defend the beliefs 'Matter is real', 'Time is real', etc. But of what kind are these latter beliefs? Can we attribute these beliefs to the 'plain man, unschooled in Philosophy'? The plain man, unless he is also an unschooled philosopher, does not bother about such propositions as 'Time is real' or 'Matter is real'. Defending the truth of these propositions may therefore be taken as amounting to defending a certain philosophical theory and not what a plain man believes in.

3.1. In reply to the above criticism, it may be suggested that although the plain man does not say, or explicitly formulate his belief by saying 'Matter is real' or 'Time is real', yet the other propositions[5] which he believes to be true certainly imply the truth of the propositions 'Matter is real' and 'Time is real'. Some examples of these other propositions which the plain man believes to be true are: 'Here is my right hand which I am raising up', 'There exists at present a human body which is my body', 'I was born in the year 1928'. Belief in the truth of these propositions implies belief in the reality of matter, time and space and therefore contradicts the philosophers' beliefs in the unreality of matter, time and space. The contradiction, therefore, which Moore detects subsists, not between the said philosophical beliefs and certain beliefs of common sense, but between the said philosophical beliefs and certain other beliefs implied by the above-mentioned beliefs of common sense. That the said philosophical beliefs are not necessarily incompatible with the truth of the propositions in which common sense believes is admitted by Moore; but he nevertheless reminds us that the philosophical propositions may be understood in such a way that they contradict the common sense beliefs. In other words, although the proposition 'Matter is unreal' is not incompatible with the proposition 'There is a human hand here', the former proposition may be so understood (or formulated, analysed, or interpreted) that belief in it amounts to believing that the latter proposition

---

[5] *Contemporary British Philosophy* (Second Series), p. 200.

is false. It seems to me that in stressing this latter possibility, that is to say, the possibility that the said philosophical beliefs may contradict the said beliefs of common sense, Moore is on the wrong side.

For, first, as I have already emphasized, the said philosophical beliefs do not directly contradict the commonsense beliefs; they contradict only certain other beliefs which are implied by these commonsense beliefs. On no interpretation of them, that is to say, on no interpretation either of the philosophical beliefs or of the commonsense beliefs would they come to a direct conflict. But even as to this indirect conflict, two questions should be raised: first, what is the nature of these other beliefs which are implied by the commonsense beliefs? Secondly, can we at all say that these other beliefs, whatever may be their nature, are implied by the commonsense beliefs? I have already suggested my answer to the first of these questions: these other beliefs are themselves not beliefs of the plain man but are as much philosophical beliefs as the philosophical beliefs which they contradict. So the conflict is between two sets of philosophical beliefs. To the second question, my answer would be in the negative. The said commonsense beliefs do not imply the philosophical beliefs 'Matter is real', 'Time is real', 'Space is real', etc.

3.2. It may be suggested in reply to the above that the proposition 'Matter is real' could be understood in such a manner that it would thereby become an implicate of the commonsense beliefs. With this I agree, but so far as I can see, the proposition 'Matter is real' if suitably interpreted so as to become an implicate of the commonsense beliefs would be, in effect, nothing other than a restatement of these latter beliefs. In that case, to believe in the proposition 'Matter is real' would be the same thing as to believe in all propositions like 'This is a human hand', etc., etc. If the proposition 'Matter is real' is thus nothing but shorthand for a number of propositions in which commonsense believes, then only it is not a philosophical proposition and is also an implicate of commonsense beliefs; but in that case it would not be the contradictory of the philosophical proposition 'Matter is not real'. To sum up : the philosophical proposition 'Matter is not real' contradicts the proposition 'Matter is real' only when the latter proposition is a philosophical proposition, but in that case the proposition 'Matter is real' is not an implicate of the commonsense beliefs and therefore no contradiction could be shown to subsist between these beliefs and the philosophical proposition 'Matter is real'. On the other hand, if the proposition 'Matter is real' is taken to be an implicate of commonsense beliefs, then it would not be a philosophical proposition but would be reduced to a mere shorthand for the innumerable propositions about physical objects in which we believe ordinarily; but in that case it would cease to be the contradictory of the philosophical belief that matter is unreal. Again, no contradiction could be shown to subsist between the philosophical belief that matter is unreal and the commonsense beliefs. It follows that in no case does the philosophical proposition 'Matter is unreal' contradict the commonsense proposition like 'Here is a human hand'. Moore's defence is therefore not called for.

3.3. Nor would it help to insist that what Moore is doing is to defend, not beliefs, but ordinary use of words. For neither of the two propositions 'Matter is real' and 'Matter is unreal' makes an ordinary use of the word 'real'. Both make philosophical uses. Malcolm has drawn attention to the fact the doubt which Moore aims at dispelling by asserting 'I know for certain this is a human hand' is a philosophical doubt and that his use of 'know' in this context is not an ordinary use.[6] What I want to insist on is that in his zeal to defend common sense Moore has ended up by distorting it.

From what has been said before, it would follow that there is no question of the same proposition being true from the commonsense point of view and false from the philosophical point of view.

3.4. I cannot imagine common sense saying 'Time is real', for the assertion 'Time is real' is uttered only when the doubt 'Is time real?' is dispelled. And I wonder if common sense is ever haunted with this last doubt. Common sense, on the other hand, may be haunted, given suitable circumstances, by the doubt 'Is this a real tree?' and this doubt is dispelled by the assertion 'This is a real tree' or by the assertion 'This is only a painted one.'

[6] In *Philosophical Review*, 1949.

4. This brings us to a certain paradox which belongs to what I should like to call the existential situation of the philosopher – a paradox out of which Moore develops a set of arguments against the philosopher who denies the reality of matter and of time. No philosopher, Moore seems to be insisting, has ever been able to hold such views consistently. "One way in which they have betrayed this inconsistency is by alluding to the existence of other philosophers. Another way is by alluding to the existence of the human race, and in particular by using "we" in the sense in which any philosopher who asserts "we sometimes believe propositions that are not true" is asserting... that very many other human beings... have had bodies and lived upon the earth..."[7] The philosopher in the course of his philosophical activity assumes the reality of those very objects that his philosophy regards as unreal. This is indeed a paradox. But what does it point to? Does it show that a philosophical transcendence is not possible? I would rather say that the paradox would not exist if philosophical transcendence of common sense were not possible. Just because there is this paradox, philosophical transcendence is a fact. I am aware that there are philosophers who would deny the paradox and a paradox is denied the moment you resolve it, – either following Moore or following the Absolutist! I for one do not believe that resolution of such paradoxes is either necessary or possible. They are there; they have to be recognized as such. In fact, they provide the tragic ethos that characterizes the existence of the philosopher. They neither call for a rejection of the philosophic pursuit in favour of the certainty of common sense nor do they call for a denial of the common sense beliefs in favour of the philosophic truths.

4.1. I may be told that though common sense has its limitations yet the limitations themselves belong to common sense so that the philosopher could love common sense as Cowper loved England in spite of all her faults.[8] The point that concerns us here is whether it is possible to transcend common sense. Making use of the analogy of the poet's England, let me suggest that al-

---

[7] *Contemporary British Philosophy* (Second Series), p. 203.
[8] I am indebted to my friend and colleague Prof. K. K. Banerjee of Jadavpur University for suggesting this metaphor.

though one loves one's homeland in spite of all her faults, one can transcend that love to reach a wider love of humanity. What however is more important is that one understands one's love only when one can contemplate it from a distance. What I wish to suggest is this: the true character of common sense belief as a belief cannot be revealed to me unless I can look at it from outside, as a neutral spectator – that is to say, unless in so far as I philosophize, I suspend my beliefs, neutralize them as it were, do not live in them, do not let myself to be merged in them, and so on. It is true that I have thereby to experience an existential paradox to which I have just now referred.

There are certain limitations that fall within that whose limitations they are: they fall within it in the sense that you can grasp them while confining yourself to the same level of experience. But there are certain other limitations – which are really fundamental – which you can grasp only when there is a radical transcendence of the level of experience concerned. The inaccuracies, inadequacies, hesitations, ambiguities and the vagueness of common sense belong to the first group of limitations. I would even say that when science corrects common sense, it improves upon limitations of the first kind. Science does not therefore bring about a radical reformulation of the notions of common sense. A radical transcendence, and therefore a fundamental understanding, of common sense requires what has been characterized as a neutralization of common sense beliefs or what Husserl would have called a 'phenomenological bracketing' of them. Moore – should I say even at the risk of appearing audacious? – has not given us a genuine philosophy of common sense, for he has not gone into the roots of common sense beliefs. He has not exhibited these beliefs as beliefs. He has not been able to do this, for he wanted to defend common sense. Thereby he played the role of a partisan and not of an enquirer.

5. In the light of the above remarks on Moore's defence of common sense, it will be now of interest to pay some attention to the very puzzling proof of an external world which Moore has advanced in his British Academy Lecture. After going through Moore's proof, one is left wondering what precisely could have led Moore to advance such a proof. Which philosophers he could

have had in mind, that is to say, to which philosophers was he attributing the view that there is no external world? 'Berkeley!' of course, is the first choice. But as we know, Berkeley certainly did not mean to deny the existence of the external world in the sense in which Moore proves it. Nor was Moore, in trying to give a proof, refuting what Kant called 'problematic idealism', that is to say, the position that we never know for certain that there is an external world. Moore, of course, has something to say against 'problematic idealism'; it is in this context perhaps that he draws the distinction between knowing something and proving something. His main proof however is concerned with showing not that we know for certain but that there is an external world. Presumably, he thought that Berkeley had denied the external world. Whatever that may be, let us go into his proof.

By 'external things', he means 'things outside of our minds'. Things to be met with in space are of course things outside of our minds, though not all things outside of our minds (e.g., pains or visual images of animals) are to be met with in space. Now if Moore can prove that there are two things to be met with in space, it would follow that there are two things outside of our minds. "By holding up my two hands, and saying, as I make a certain gesture with the right hand, "Here is one hand", and adding, as I make a certain gesture with the left, "and here is another", Moore claims to have given a most rigorous demonstrative proof of the existence of the external world.

Moore himself has given expression to his apprehension that what he proves may be accepted as true but may at the same time be declared as unimportant. But quite apart from that, does the proof succeed?

I am aware that in questioning Moore's premiss I am in company with many of Moore's critics. Malcolm[9] has, for example, questioned if Moore is justified in saying 'I know here is a human hand'. I, however, wish to urge a quite different point. I would say that Moore cannot, on the basis of his theory of perception, say with certainty 'this is a human hand'.

Just consider some features of his own analysis. The proposition 'I am now perceiving a human hand' is analysed into (Moore

[9] In *Philosophical Review*, 1949.

says: is a deduction from[10]) two further propositions: 'I am perceiving this' and 'This is a human hand'. He is sure about 'I am perceiving this', but what exactly is known thereby he is not sure of. The analysis which is accepted is that the principal subject of the proposition 'I am now perceiving this' is a sense-datum. And he is besides sure that this sense-datum is not a hand. He finds reasons to doubt – although he himself does not doubt – that this (i.e., to say, the sense-datum) is a part of the surface of the hand.[11] How can he under such circumstances be sure of the proposition 'This is a human hand?' The distinction between 'knowing a proposition to be true' and 'not knowing the correct analysis of the proposition' does not help us here.

5.1. In his essay on Hume's philosophy, written much earlier, Moore admits that it is quite impossible for any one to prove, as against the sceptic, that one knows any external fact. 'I can only prove that I do by assuming that in some particular instance, I actually do one'.[12] On this, Stebbing remarks: 'The notion that we may have a reason, though not a logically conclusive reason for certain statements concerning direct observation, is, I believe, one of Moore's important contributions to philosophy.'[13] Hume showed that demonstrative knowledge of matters of fact is not possible; Moore, I would suppose Stebbing to mean, shows that even our non-demonstrative knowledge of the external world has its own certainty which should not be underestimated just because it is other than demonstrative certainty. This, if it were Moore's contention, would have been ranked as one of his valuable insights. When we turn however to Moore's reply, we are disappointed: Moore rejects this suggestion.[14] I can appreciate why Moore should object to the use of the word 'probable' in connexion with our knowledge of the external world. Stebbing in fact is aware of the misleading associations of this word. Let me call the type of knowledge Stebbing had in mind 'non-demonstrable certainty.'

Instead of emphasizing this 'non-demonstrable certainty' of

[10] *Contemporary British Philosophy* (second series), p. 217.
[11] *Ibid.*, p. 218.
[12] *Philosophical Studies*, p. 160.
[13] In P. A. Schilpp (ed.), *The Philosophy of G. E. Moore*, p. 524.
[14] *Ibid.*, p. 677.

the external world and instead of exhibiting the phenomenological nature and roots of that certainty, Moore proceeds to offer a rigorous demonstrative proof. And no wonder that he should fail. The external world is neither in need of nor is capable of a logical proof. That such a proof is necessary is what the sceptics persuade us to believe though knowing fully well that we would not succeed. Moore has succumbed to their persuasion and has offered a proof that hopelessly fails.

6. To sum up: Moore is wrong in presenting common sense as a party in philosophical disputes. He was misled into thinking that philosophical statements could come in conflict with common sense beliefs. A philosophical understanding of common sense requires a measure of transcendence of the level of common sense; it must be added that even Moore in his distinction between the common sense beliefs and their correct analysis makes room for transcendence. As in his defence of common sense, so also in his proof of an external world, Moore's task is ill-conceived. What is important for us is to realize that there is a common source of the two errors: in his eagerness to combat the speculative philosophers, he misses the proper task of a truly phenomenological philosophy both of common sense beliefs and of our belief in the external world.

PART THREE

CHAPTER XVII

REFLECTIONS ON THE NYĀYA
THEORY OF AVAYAVIPRATYAKṢA*

It is well known that the Nyāya advocates an extreme form of
direct realism and maintains that what we directly perceive are
physical objects and not some intermediate entities called variously by philosophers 'ideas', 'contents' or even 'sense-data'[1].
Gotama's sûtras 2.1.31 – 2.1.36 and Vātsāyana's commentaries
on them contain arguments which may be regarded as constituting a very effective defence of what has come to be called the
physical object language as against the sense-datum language.
Gotama's, as well as his commentator's, direct interest however
is twofold. In the first place, they are out to refute the suggestion that perception is not an independent source of knowledge
but a variety of inference. In the course of this refutation, they are
led to their second point: they try to show that the object of
perception, that is to say, the physical object, is not a mere assemblage of parts but a true unity of some unanalysable kind.
Our task in this paper will be to bring out the relevance of these
arguments in the light of contemporary discussions of the
problem of perception.

It would at once be appreciated that the view that perception
is a kind of inference is logically connected with the view that
what we directly perceive are sense-data and not physical objects.
For on this latter view the transition from the sense-data which
alone are directly given to the physical object which we say we

* First published in the *Journal of the Indian Academy of Philosophy*, Vol. I,
No. 1, pp. 30–41.
['*Avayavipratyakṣa*' = perception (*pratyakṣa*) of a whole (*avayavi*)]
[1] In its theory of *savikalpa* perception, however, Nyāya is led to grant a peculiarly intermediate status to certain epistemic entities. This does not affect the basic
direct realism of the system which is maintained with the help of the theory of *nirvikalpa* perception in which the object is directly given free from all epistemic ad-
juncts.

perceive can be effected only through some kind of inference –
or if you like by some process of logical construction. In any case,
the physical object which we say we perceive is not really perceived but either inferred or 'constructed'. If the modern logical
constructionist claims that the Nyāya refutation of the inferential theory does not affect him for he too abandons inference in
favour of logical construction, we may in that case implore him to
have patience; for the Nyāya has another point directly effective
against him: this is the Nyāya contention that the physical
object is a not further analysable unity. After showing how
these Nyāya arguments constitute an effective plea in favour of
the physical object language, we shall enquire into the precise
nature of the unity characterising the object of perception.

The view which Gotama seeks to refute is thus stated by him
in sûtra 2.1.31: "perception should really be regarded as inference, for we apprehend directly only a part of the object. Our
knowledge of the object is based only on such partial apprehension."[2] I say I perceive the yonder tree. But do I really perceive
the tree? An object is properly said to be perceived by me only when
our knowledge of it is caused by the contact of some sense organ
of mine with that very object. But are my eyes in contact (without taking into consideration that peculiar sense in which the
Nyāya speaks of such contacts) with the entire tree? Certainly
not with the hind part hidden away from my sight, certainly
not with the interior of the trunk, and so on. Only a part of the
tree do I see. Why then do I say that I perceive the tree? What
I actually do is that from this part which I really see I infer that
there is a tree over there, so that my perception of the tree is
really inference. The inference may be implicit or explicit or
associational or a self-conscious process of reasoning; in any case,
the same argument holds good. Further, there may be difference
of opinion as to what exactly the part is. It is quite possible
that Gotama has in his mind the Buddhist theory that the tree,
in fact any object, is nothing but a mere aggregate of atoms, and
this is how Vatsayana interprets the intention of the sûtra. But it
is also possible that the parts are nothing but the various qualities, the colour, the shape, the size, etc. which make up the ob-

---

[2] This is a rather free rendering of the *sûtra* which runs thus: "*Pratyakṣamanu-
mānamekadeśagrahanādupalabdheḥ*".

ject, for as is well known the *dravya*, according to the cepāmkhya is a collection of such qualities (*guṇasamghāta*). Or in conformity with common sense, the parts of the tree may be regarded simply as its trunk, branches, leaves etc. In any case, the point under consideration is, if it is only a part or some parts that I see, what justifies me in saying that I perceive a tree over there.

Gotama and his commentator have advanced the following objections against such a view: –

1. What I call the tree is either the mere assemblage of its parts or it is more than such assemblage. On either alternative the inferential theory would not be tenable. Consider the first alternative that the tree is nothing but a mere assemblage. Only one part of this assemblage is directly seen. What then is inferred? The theory can only hold that from seeing this part, say the front part, we infer the other parts that are not seen. But neither the front part nor the hind part taken by itself is the tree. Hence what is inferred is not the tree but only the unseen part of the tree. My knowledge of the tree thereby has not been proved to be inferential. Similarly on the theory that the tree is more than the assemblage of parts, the inferential theory has no better chance of success. For in order to be able to infer B from A it is necessary either that B must be analytically contained within A or that B must always have been observed together with A. In the present case, only the second possibility is open. And yet since on this theory the whole is never perceived along with the part, the whole could not possibly be inferred from the part that is given. Hence the tree which is a whole that is more than the mere sum of its parts could not possibly be inferred on this theory.

2. We do not directly apprehend the mere part (*Naca eka-deśopalabdhih*), for the whole, the tree itself, is also given through that part. This in fact is the central argument of the Naiyāyika. This thesis has two parts each of which requires separate treatment. In the first place, it has to be shown that the tree – in fact any physical object – is more than a mere assemblage of its parts, that it is something new over and above the parts. But next it has also to be shown that perception of this whole does not require perception of all its parts, so that the whole may be per-

fectly legitimately said to be perceived even if one is not directly perceiving all its parts. The view criticised here (that the tree is not being directly perceived for only a few of its parts are visible) is based on the wrong assumption that we must perceive all the parts of a whole in order to perceive the whole itself. The Nyāya rejects this assumption. In fact the perception of any of its parts may suffice for the perception of the whole.

3. Nyāya therefore takes great pains to prove that there is a whole that is other than the mere sum of the parts. Gotama devotes the sûtras 2.1.33-36 to this point but again returns to it in a later context in the sûtras 4.2.4-12. The commentator Vātsāyana and the later Naiyāyikas develop this theme in great detail, their principal target for attack being the Buddhist. Here we shall only sum up the main Nyāya arguments relevant from our present point of view.

(a) If the tree be regarded as a mere aggregate of atoms, then the atoms being themselves supersensible, the tree itself would remain unsensed. If the tree remains unsensed, so also shall its colour, shape, size, position, etc. We could never also know it as a tree, that is to say, we could never perceive the universal treeness in it. Thus all the *padārthas* such as *dravya*, *guṇa*, *karma*, *sāmānya*, etc. would remain unperceived. But actually we do apprehend *dravya*; we also apprehend its quality, its activity, its class, etc.[3]

(b) I not only apprehend the tree over there but also apprehend it as one object. What could be the proper referent of such a statement as "This is one object and that is another", – asks Vātsāyana.[4] Is the referent of such a statement itself one or many? If it be one, then that would amount to recognising that the whole is one object, and not a mere sum of its parts. If, however, there be only parts, how can a mere plurality be referred to as one object. The sense of unity ('This is one') and the sense of plurality ('These are many') cannot refer to the same object.[5] The former refers to one object, not to a mere aggregate. The latter to an aggregate, but not to a unity. "But" it may be asked,

[3] *Nyāyasûtra* 2.1.34.
[4] Commentary on *Nyāyasûtra* 2.1.35.
[5] Uddyotakara, *Vārtika* on *Nyāyasûrta* 2.1.35.

"do we not refer to a wood or to an army as one object, although the wood or the army really is a mere aggregate of many different things? Why then would it not be possible in a similar manner to refer to a tree as one object though in reality it is a mere aggregate?"[6] To this, the Nyāya replies in the following manner. It is true that we mistake from a distance, or on account of other *doṣas*, a mere aggregate or a plurality for a unity, so that instead of saying 'These are many', we say 'This is one'. Such a sense of unity is no doubt erroneous. But such an erroneous sense of unity is possible, only if there are other cases, where our sense of unity is right.[7] But if, as the Buddhist contends, all sense of unity is erroneous, then even those cases where, all are agreed, a plurality is mistaken as a unity would remain unexplained.[8] Vātsāyana anticipates the modern phenomenalists' view that we do have a right sense of unity, not of course in the case of our apprehension of a tree, but certainly in the case of our apprehension of a sense-datum, and has two replies to offer. First, since we have one instance of a sense of unity being right (e.g. 'This is one sound') and another instance of unity being wrong, i.e. misplaced(e.g. 'This wood is one object'), some satisfactory reason needs to be advanced, before assimilating the case under consideration ('This is one tree') to the one rather than to the other: the phenomenalist has given no satisfactory reason for assimilating it to the latter type. Secondly, the phenomenalist has no satisfactory reason for regarding what we call sound as one entity. Leaving apart Vācaspati's reminder that some of the Vaibhāṣikas in fact did regard even a sound as an aggregate of atoms, we have to remember the extreme difficulty – perhaps impossibility – of identifying a sense-datum as one sense-datum. Even if we are ever rightly able so to identify, the proper procedure would be to assimilate 'This is one sound' type of statement to 'This is one tree' – type rather than go the other way about. Vātsāyana however has his own special reason for regarding 'This is one tree' as a right application of the concept of unity and not as a case of error. For we also say, 'This is a single,

---

[6] *Nyāyasûtra* 2.1.36.

[7] Vātsāyana, "*Atasminstaditi pratyayasya pradhānāpekṣitatvāt pradhānāsidhiḥ*" commentary on *Nyāyasûtra* 2.1.36.

[8] Uddyotakara, "*Mithyāpratyaya apyete na bhavanti pradhānābhāvāt*" *Vārtika* on *Nyāyasûtra* 2.1.36.

big, and banyan tree'; in such a statement as this, bigness, one-ness, and the specific and the generic characters of the tree are apprehended as belonging to the same locus (*samānādhikaraṇa*) – which proves that that which is one is also a tree and is big etc. Further, when we say that 'the two (A and B) are in contact', the contact is apprehended as belonging to the same locus as two-ness: in such a case it would amount to distorting the implication of such statement if we say, instead, that it is really the many parts which are in contact.

(c) Now if there is such a whole that is other than the mere assemblage of parts, how is this whole related to the parts? The Buddhist might argue that since no satisfactory relation is conceivable why not abandon the hypothesis of such a distinct whole?[9] Either the parts are in the whole or the whole is in the parts, no third alternative being conceivable. The part cannot be in the whole for any one part cannot reside in the entire whole, the part and the whole having different extensions. Nor could it be said that a part resides in a certain region (*ekadeśa*) of the whole, for that region would itself be a part of the whole and there are no regions other than the parts. Exactly similar arguments can be used to prove that the whole cannot reside in the parts: the entire whole cannot reside in any one part, the latter being smaller in extension than the former and since the whole does not have regions other than the parts, it cannot also be said that it is one part in one region and another part in another region. Thus no relation between the whole and the parts being conceivable, it would be safer to conclude that the so-called whole is a mere assemblage of parts.

To this Buddhist argument, Nyāya replies as follows. Nyāya, of course, does not accept the position that the parts reside in the whole. This position, seemingly acceptable to common sense, owes its obviousness to the unreflective identification of the whole with the sum of the parts. Once, however, the distinction and the peculiar unity of a whole are admitted, the parts cannot be accommodated within it; for the spaces – as the critic has pointed out – to which the parts may be allotted are themselves parts. The same difficulty, however, does not really vitiate the position that the whole resides in the parts. The critic's question,

[9] Gautama 4.2.6.

"Does the whole in its entirety reside in a part or does it do so only partially?" is ruled out *ab initio*, for the words 'entire' and 'partial' – as Vātsāyana points out – [10] have no application to a thing that is one. The word 'entire' means 'all of many things' and the word 'partial' means 'some amongst the many'.[11] Hence both apply only to a plurality. The whole, according to Nyāya, however, is one and not a mere aggregate; hence there is no question of treating it either in its entirety, or partially.[12] The whole, therefore, is present in each of the parts as well as in their totality.[13]

4. It has now to be shown that perception of all the parts is not a necessary condition of the perception of the whole residing in those parts. If this could be shown, it would follow that the tree may be legitimately said to be perceived even if some of the parts remain unperceived. What is necessary is that some of the parts should be perceived. The argument is simple. Since, as has just been shown, the whole itself, as a distinct entity, is present in each of its parts, the apprehension of a part involves the apprehension of the whole. It cannot be said that I am perceiving only a part or only some of the parts of the tree. True, there are some parts that remain hidden from me. But nevertheless I do perceive the tree through those parts that are exposed to me. Of the parts that are many, some are perceived, and some not. But the tree is one and not many. Being one, if it is perceived, it cannot also be unperceived, nor can it be perceived partially. Hence, I do perceive the tree though I do not perceive all its parts.

We sometimes speak of seeing more or less of a thing. From my window I can see only one side of the school building. I go round the building, see its other sides and say I have now seen more of it. For Nyāya, all such statements are in a sense legiti-

[10] Commentary on *Nyāyasûtra* 4.2.11: *Tavimau kṛtsnaikadeśaśabdau bhedaviṣayau naikasminnupapadyate, bhedābhāvāditi".*

[11] *Ibid.*: *Kṛtsnamityanekasyaśeṣabhidhānam, ekadeśa iti nānātve kasyacidabhidhānam".*

[12] When we speak, however, of the tree in its entirety or in its parts, these words are applied not directly to the tree itself but to the parts, only secondarily to the tree.

[13] There is thus a parallelism between the way the whole resides in each part and the way a universal resides in each instance of it. This parallel justifies the inclusion of both relations under the same type: *samavāya.* (The parallel, however, fails, in that the whole also resides in the totality of its parts; while the universal does not reside in the totality of its instances).

mate, but in another important sense misleading. If from the beginning I know it as a house, I have perceived the whole, and although I might go on increasing my knowledge of its parts, it is the same house which I continue perceiving; I do not, in that sense, come to perceive more of that entity.

What happens when I see the mere edge of a building so that I am not in a position to say what I see, a house or a pillar, a monument or a bandstand?[14] I do see a part of whatever the whole may be. But do I also see that whole? The Nyāya account of such a situation is based on the following important considerations: – Though the perception of a part involves the perception of any one of the wholes residing in that part, it cannot be laid down as a general rule that the perception of a part necessarily involves the perception of a definite whole, resident in it. Let P be a part of W and Q a part of P. Both the wholes P and W are resident in Q. There are also many other wholes P', P'',.... resident in Q. It is quite possible that on perceiving Q I do not perceive W but perceive P or any other of the wholes residing in it. But I must, whenever I perceive Q, perceive it as part of a whole, in case it is so, that is to say, in case a whole is resident in Q.

5. Is it possible to maintain – as the modern sense-datum theorists do – that our perception begins (no matter whether the beginning is understood in the logical or in the psychological sense) with noticing the bare sense-data? Do we not, to start with, perceive a bare patch of colour, and only afterwards come to know of the physical object that is so coloured? Nyāya, it is now apparent, rejects this view. According to Nyāya, we never sense a mere colour, but always perceive a coloured object. The colour is always perceived as characterising the physical object, and the fact of illusory appearance need not lead us to revise this account.

The point, however, to which we want to draw attention especially is this: within the categorial structure of the Nyāya ontology, the perception of a mere property is impossible. The per-

---

[14] This case is different from the case of doubt or error where I perceive a part, no doubt, but there are also certain vitiating factors (doṣas) that render the perception of the whole impossible, or there are conditions that render certain knowledge impossible and give rise, instead, to doubt.

ception of a quality (*guṇa*) is possible only through the *via media* of a substance (*dravya*). A quality is contacted through a relation of *samyukta samavāya*, which is a complex relation entailing a *samyoga* relation with the substance in which the quality is perceived as inhering. To this, one might reply that such a *via media* is necessitated only by the categorial structure of the Nyāya ontology. True; but we may remind the sense-datum theorist that his view that what we sense is a mere colour is no less necessitated by the way he defines both 'sensing' and 'sense-datum'.

Thus according to Nyāya, we do not pass from the part to the whole nor do we pass from the sense-datum to the physical object. The part and the whole, the substance and the quality, are given together though not in the same manner.

II

Thus far it was our task to elaborate the arguments of Gautama and his commentator, with a view to exhibiting their relevance to the contemporary discussions of the problem of perception. What has been said would suffice, it is hoped, to show that the Nyāya distinction between *avayavin* and *avayava* is a most valuable means of rehabilitating the physical object language. It is now left for us to ask what precisely is the nature of the unity of the *avayavin*? The Nyāya, of course, tells us two things about it. It is in the first place something other than the mere assemblage of parts. And secondly the unity of the whole resides in each of the parts in the relation of *samavāya*, while it is wrong to say that the parts reside in the whole. In the following, we shall attempt a phenomenological interpretation of these two points, and in doing so, we shall, of course, depart from the naive-ontological attitude of the Nyāya-Vaiśeṣika system. Before, however, we undertake this, it is necessary to draw attention to certain unsatisfactory features of the Nyāya account.

In the first place, it should be borne in mind – and this is not exactly pointing out a drawback of the theory – that Nyāya does not bring out the exact difference between the mode of perceiving the part and the mode of *perceiving* the whole. One of the ways of doing this *would have been* to say that whereas the part is perceived through the relation of *samyoga*, the whole which resides in the part by the relation of *samavāya* is perceived through the relation ot *samyukta-samavāya*. Nyāya does not say this tor two obvious reasons. Two substances (*dravyas*) cannot, in accordance with the categorial structure of Nyāya ontology, enter into a *samavāya* relation (which by definition is reserved only for certain cases that do not include the case where the relata are two *dravyas* not related as whole and part), and the whole being a *dravya* can only enter into *samyoga* relation with the sense organ. Further the supposition that the whole is perceived through the indirect relation of *samyukta-samavāya* would lead to the following grave difficulty. The part with which the sense organs are said to be in contact is itself a whole some of whose parts are unperceived; this whole, then, it must be said, is perceived exactly like the bigger one of which it is a part, indirectly through the relation of *samyukta samavāya*. In this manner, since every part is a whole, we would be led to the unacceptable position that there is direct contact through *samyoga* only with the last constituents or atoms which are not any more wholes but which, according to Nyāya, are imperceptible.

Nyāya, therefore, holds that both the part and the whole are apprehended through *samyoga*. A whole is contacted through *samyoga*, although not all its parts are so contacted. Inevitably, however, different orders of samyoga would have to be admitted and the privilege of having first-order *samyoga* would be accredited only to the last imperceptible atoms. Though, however, such different orders of *samyoga* would have to be postulated, nothing phenomenologically corresponds to this in the subjective mode of awareness; for in each case, I have the same kind of *anuvyavasāya*, 'I perceive...' The reason for this is that every perceptible part is itself a whole. Since no perceptible substance could have the primary order of *samyoga*, the idea of its absolute givenness, in one of its senses, is here ruled out. This, in effect, means that every whole is perceived through some of its parts; and so on. Though in this manner every whole is perceived through some of its parts, this however is not the same as saying that it is inferred and not perceived. This, in fact, is the only manner in which a substance could possibly be directly perceived.[15]

---

[15] The case, however, with either *guṇas* or universals is different, for these are not wholes made of parts, not *avayavins*. Though these are perceived through some com-

The real difficulty with the Nyāya account does not lie here. It has to be sought in the arbitrary way it seeks to limit the conception of *avayavin*. Firstly, not all conjunctions of parts, it is said, give rise to true wholes. It is only a special kind of conjunction that is regarded as giving rise to a true whole. Now it seems to me that the Nyāya-Vaiśeṣika theory is not quite clear about the precise nature of this special kind of conjunction. It also further seems to me that no strict line of demarcation can be drawn between that conjunction of substances that gives rise to a true whole and that conjunction which does not, for one reason, amongst others, that the Nyāya-Vaiśeṣika philosophy believes in the separability of the parts of even an *avayavin* (For the last mentioned reason, the unity of the *avayavin* cannot be regarded as what has come to be called an organic unity). No strict line of demarcation, in that case, could be drawn amongst physical objects, between genuine wholes and pseudo-wholes. The Nyāya-Vaiśeṣika philosopher supposedly has, in mind, the idea that genuine wholes are *produced* in a manner or in a sense in which the pseudo-wholes are not. What precisely this manner is, in what sense the idea of production applies to one and not to the other case, and how precisely the conjunction of parts in the one case differs from that in the other, – these are questions on which no further light could be thrown except by referring to the way a potter makes a pot or a carpenter a table. Perhaps the maker alone knows the secret, but who then can be sure that some whole has a maker and some others have not? Certainly the separate physical objects are conceived by Nyāya as true *avayavins*, in so far as the system believes in a maker for them all on the analogy of a potter. But why, then, are we debarred from treating the world as a whole as the ultimate *avayavin*? Nyāya avoids this consequence by taking God's authorship of the world to mean not that God has produced the world as a whole, regarded as one single entity, as the potter produces a pot, but only that His authorship pertains to each physical object taken separately.

We thus notice the extreme difficulty of limiting the concept

posite relation like *samyukta-samavāya*, yet in that relation it is given all by itself and is not contacted through any of its parts (though again the *guṇa* is contacted through a substance, and a universal through its instances).

of *avayavin* only to *some* wholes. It cannot be said that to regard the world as a whole as an *avayavin* would conflict with the idea of external relation and the pluralism that are basic to the Nyāya ontology. For if it did then the very admission of the limited *avayavin* would have given rise to the same difficulty though on a lesser scale.

It cannot also be argued that just as we directly perceive a physical object as *avayavin* – for *avayavitva* is rightly held in the theory to be perceptually known – so also we apprehend some of the physical objects as wholes that are not again parts of bigger wholes. In the words of Nyāya, we could say that *carama-avayavitva* is not perceptually determinable. That a given whole is not the part of a bigger whole is not given to perception.

The problem, therefore, with which we are faced is how best to assimilate the central point of the Nyāya conception of *avayavi-pratyakṣa* into a satisfactory theory of perception without limiting it in the way Nyāya does. To this task, then, we now turn.

III

A satisfactory theory of perception must have to avoid the atomistic conception of the given of the Humean-phenomenalistic sort. It has also to avoid the conception of the given which entails that the physical object is inferred but not perceived: this is the view which Gotama and Vātsāyana combat. The physical object is directly perceived, though never all its parts are: this is a point which a sound theory of perception must admit if it is to be honest to phenomena. But there are two directions in which it is possible to extend and amplify the thesis, not in the interest of the theory, but at the dictates of phenomena.

In the first place, it is necessary to ask: what exactly is the mode in which the whole is present in the part? The Nyāya-Vaiśeṣika answer is, of course, "through the relation of *samavāya*". But *samavāya* is also the relation by which qualities are present in substances, and universals in particulars. By including all these cases under one common type, we, of course, economise, but the idea of economy, however indispensable it may be in *constructing a theory*, may sometimes lead to a distortion of the phenomena. What is common to them all is a certain insepara- bility of the relata (*ayutasiddhatva*), but beyond this they are most unlike each other. Hence to say that the whole is present in the parts by the relation of *samavāya*, is not only not very illu- minating but may prove misleading. The whole is indeed present in the parts but not as one thing in another, not as a quality in a substance, nor as a universal in the particular. The whole is pre- sent in the part as the *intended*. The part, *qua* part, is, as it were, saturated with an intention that refers beyond it to the whole. The whole is, ontologically speaking, made up of parts. But phe- nomenologically speaking, it is the fulfilment of the intention awakened by the part. The perception of a part of the wall arouses the intention that demands fulfilment and would not be completely fulfilled short of the perception of all the parts. In this way, we can give sense both to the fact that we know more or less about the whole and to the fact that the whole was given right from the beginning. The whole, as intended, was given right at the outset, but a progressive fulfilment of this intention is possi- ble. Since, however all the parts can never come to be apprehen- ded, a complete fulfilment of this intention is an unattainable ideal, an endless process of approximation. This, however, does not negate the other fact that it is always the same whole that is given as the all-pervading intention.

Secondly, it is necessary to make room for the phenomenon that our perception of a physical object is never that of an iso- lated self-complete atom but is always *out of* a situation, and that likewise it tends to pass beyond itself, or within itself for further determination. Now it seems possible to account for this charac- ter of our perceptual experience if we lift the arbitrary limitation imposed upon the concept of *avayavin*, so that every physical object awakens an intention towards self-transcendence inas- much as it is constituent of a bigger whole. The Nyāya idea of a *samuhālambana* knowledge, though based on an undeniable phenomenon, is inadequate to account for that aspect of per- ceptual experience to which I am drawing attention; for in a piece of *samuhālambana* knowledge, all objects are determi- nately apprehended and possess equal importance, whereas in all perceptual experience there is always, besides the focus (which may contain one or more substantive) a fringe and a tendency of the focus either to pass beyond itself or to determine itself more precisely (corresponding to what Husserl calls the outer and the inner horizons). It cannot be said that the world is atomic and that therefore the supposed continuity and dynamism within perceptual experience is inadmissible, for we cannot argue from what the world is like to what our experience should be like. The correct procedure should be to start from the nature of experience from the phenomenologically descriptive datum and then – if one is still interested in ontology – to base one's conception of the world upon it. It cannot be argued that the supposed continuity – the fringe and the tendency – are not discernible in the linguistic expression of a perceptual knowledge which takes the simple form 'This is a jar'; for linguistic expression is not always a sure index to the nature of experience. It simplifies the datum by limiting itself always to the focus[16] and this simplification, one might suppose, is in part due to the practical interest that hovers around.

A satisfactory theory of perception has to make room for these two phenomenological data: the discreteness and the continuity of our perceptual experience. It is not a phenomenalistic atomism of the Humean-Buddhist type but only a physical object atomism of the Nyāya type that does justice to the former aspect. But a physical object atomism should have to accommodate the other aspect of our perceptual experience; otherwise, it, too, would be faulty by inadequacy. The continuity is no doubt interrupted, as the flow of mental states, in general, is interrupted in deep sleep or in swoon. But in every perception, there is a tendency towards self-transcendence or towards further self-determination, and this intention is imbedded not in our awareness, but in the very object of perceptual awareness, in so far as the objects of perceptual awareness constitute, by virtue of such intentions, one single world.

Before closing this discussion I shall consider only two amongst the many objections that might possibly be levelled against the

---

[16] Nyāya also recognises a similar limitation to the claim of linguistic expression to be index of experience: there is always, as a Nyāya rule runs, an unexpressed qualifier except in the case of universals. See Mohanty, *Gangeśa's Theory of Truth*, Santiniketan, 1966.

theory of perception briefly sketched above. It may be urged that
if the theory is true, then there would be no limit to what is
given, so that it should, by implication, follow that in any perceptual situation the world as a whole is given, which is absurd.
In the second place – and this shall follow from the above – there
would remain no room for any other indirect, say, e.g. inferential,
mode of knowledge. Both the points together lead one to press
the question: what in that case is not given?

As to the first question, my answer would be twofold. It has
been said above that there is no general rule that the perception
of a part necessarily involves the perception of any definite whole
resident in it, though I must perceive some whole resident in it.
Now in that case even if we admit that the world as the largest
whole is resident in every part of it, it would not necessarily
follow that the world as a whole is given in every perceptual
situation. Since the world as a whole is not in fact given, we could
only postulate some form of inadequacy inherent in every perceptual situation to present the world as a whole.

Secondly, saying that every perceptual situation gives rise
to an intention that takes us beyond it does not imply that all
such intentions are fulfilled. In fact, such intentions are more
often than not frustrated owing to the intervention of a stronger
cognitive or other interest.

Finally, it should be recognised that the world as a whole is
not one object amongst others. It is rather the horizon or the
dimension within which perceptions and their intentions are
possible.

It should be clear from the above remarks that the theory of
perception suggested in this paper does not necessarily lead to the
absurdity that everything is all at once given. The distinction
between the given and the not-given is not meant to be obllite-
rated.

CHAPTER XVIII

NYĀYA THEORY OF DOUBT*

I

The Nyāya logic contains a theory of doubt. A preoccupation with the nature, origin and structure of doubt seems out of place in a logical system inasmuch as logic has been taken to be concerned, speaking rather broadly, with formally valid thought abstracted from its psychological context. Now, Nyāya logic – in fact all Indian logic – does not conform to this conception. It is in a broad sense coextensive with, and indeed indistinguishable from, a theory of knowledge, and concerns itself with all kinds of knowledge, the non-propositional and the invalid ones not excluding. In a narrower sense it is of course a theory of inference.[1] But even as a theory of inference, (i) it does not concern itself with the bare form, though some amount of formalism has been developed, and (ii) it does not separate logic from psychology in a way in which western formal logic has done. Consequently, it is as much interested in the psychological conditions of the origin of a certain type of knowledge, say e.g. of inference, as in the conditions of its logical validity.[2]

It is in the light of these remarks about the general nature of the Nyāya logic that we are to understand the reasons for its preoccupation with doubt. For, inquiry (or, as the *Nyāyabhāṣya* says, *pramāṇairarthaparikṣaṇam* i.e. the attempt to determine

---

* First published in the *Visva Bharati Journal of Philosophy*, III, 1966, 15–35.
[1] Vātsāyana for example defines Nyāya as *Pratyakṣāgamāśritamanumānam* (Bhāṣya on NyāyaSûtra 1.1.1.).
[2] What is more, the Nyāya goes to the extent of holding that a formally invalid inference is even psychologically impossible, the socalled *hetvābhāsas* being, not errors in inference, but conditions which render an inference psychologically as well as logically impossible.

the nature of the object with the help of the various sources of true knowledge) presupposes a prior state of doubt; though the Nyāya allows for the case where we make an inference even when there is prior certainty, there being however a special desire to infer. The fact remains however that apart from such cases of intellectual curiosity to provide reasons for what one already knows for certain the most important stimulation for making an inference is provided by a doubt about the presence of the *sādhya* in the *pakṣa* (e.g. of the fire in the hill).

It is further important to bear in mind the fact that for the Nyāya, as for most systems of Indian philosophy, doubt is a species of knowledge, so that if I have a doubt of the form 'Is S p or not?'', most Indian logicians would say that I am having a knowledge – though not a valid one about S. This rather strange contention, so much at variance with both the philosophical and the ordinary usages of the English word 'knowledge' may be accounted for in either of two ways. It may be either that the Indian philosophers, supported by the conventions of the Sanskrit language, are using the word in such a wide sense *as to* include even doubt and error. Or, it may be – and this seems to me to be the more reasonable account – that the Sanskrit word '*Jñāna*' should not be rendered into the English word 'knowledge', so that doubt and error are species of *Jñāna* but not of knowledge. '*Jñāna*' means any conscious state which is characterised by a reference to an object beyond it, and surely doubt and error are states in which we are conscious of something. To be conscious of something amounts, according to the Nyāya, to having a *jñāna* about that object.

There are various classifications of *jñāna*, the most usual one being into *anubhuti* and *smṛti* (memory). The former may conveniently be defined as all *jñāna* other than memory. *Anubhuti* again is usually subdivided into *pramā* (or true) and *apramā* (or false). A true *jñāna* is one in which the object is known exactly as it is, and a false one is one in which the object is known as what it is not.[3] False *jñāna* is either doubt or error. It may be noted that the exact equivalent of the English word 'knowledge', in this scheme, is '*pramājñāna*'. Doubt is a kind of false *jñāna*.

Since it has now been pointed out that '*jñāna*' is not strictly synonymous with 'knowledge', we shall henceforth in this paper

---

[3] Memory also is *apramā*, but not in the sense in which doubt or error is so.

use the word 'knowledge' as if it were so synonymous, and leave the matter at that with the hope that there would be no further scope for misunderstanding.

II

The *Siddhāntamuktāvali* defines doubt as a knowledge which is *ekadharmikaviruddhabhāvābhāvaprakārakam*, i.e. a knowledge which has (two) contradictory *prakāras* — one positive and the other negative – but referring to the same substantive. From amongst the host of definitions to be found in the Nyāya literature, this one may be singled out for its precision and simplicity, and it may be worthwhile to fix upon it. For an explanation of the definition it is of course necessary to prefix a few words about the concept of *prakāra*.[4]

It is well known that according to the Nyāya, knowledge is ontically formless (*nirākāra*) and owes its determinations to its object. It is however capable of being logically analysed. Possibility of such analysis presupposes that knowledge has forms of its own in a quite different sense. But what precisely is this sense? The Nyāya no doubt advocates a direct realism, and holds that knowledge in an important sense has no forms of its own, that it is *nirākāra*, its specific forms being derived entirely from its object. However, the Nyāya also believes in the possibility of analysis of knowledge, which presupposes that knowledge has its constituent logical elements and relations.

In primary unreflective attitude, knowledge is directed towards its object but not towards itself. The content of knowledge is brought to light only in the reflective subsequent attitude. In this reflective awareness, it is the contents of the primary knowledge that are directly intended, whereas the object of the primary knowledge is intended only as ancillary (*pucchalagna*). All such contents of knowledge which reflection discovers are brought under one category, technically called '*viṣayatā*', which again is further subdivided into three sub-categories:

---

[4] For a more detailed account of this and the allied concepts see Mohanty, *Gangeśa's Theory of Truth*, Santiniketan, 1966, Introduction. See also Ingalls, *Materials for the Study of Navya Nyāya Logic*, Harvard, 1951.

'*viśeṣyatā*', '*prakāratā*' and '*samsargatā*'. '*Viśeṣyatā* is the general title for all knowledge contents referring to substantives, '*prakāratā*' for all contents referring to adjectives, and '*samsargatā*' for those that refer to relations.[5]

For illustration, consider the knowledge expressed in the judgment 'This is a pot' (*Ayam ghato*). This knowledge may be analysed, at the first instance, into the following contents:

    (i) a *prakāratā* referring to (the Nyāya would elliptically say, 'attached to') pot-ness;

    (ii) a *viśeṣyatā* referring to the pot (in so far as potness qualifies the pot);

    (iii) a *prakāratā* referring to the pot (in so far as the pot is a determination of the mere this);

    (iv) a *viśeṣyatā* referring to the this (in so far as it is determined by the pot);

    (v) a *prakāratā* referring to this-ness (in so far as it qualifies the this);

and (vi) a second *viśeṣyatā* referring to the this (in so far as it is qualified by this-ness).

Let us now introduce a few symbolical devices with a view to facilitate a schematic representation of these contents in their mutual interrelations.

We symbolise a *viśeṣyatā* by enclosing the name for the corresponding element within the braces { } , and a *prakāratā* by enclosing the name for its corresponding element within the braces ( ).

Thus '{this}' and '(pot)' would read as 'the *viśeṣyatā* referring to this' and 'the *prakāratā* referring to pot' respectively.

If and when a certain *prakāratā* determines or limits a certain *viśeṣyatā* we shall simply write the symbol for the *viśeṣyatā* first and write that for the *prakāratā* after it. Thus '{this} (pot)' would read as 'the *viśeṣyatā* referring to *this* is determined by the *prakāratā* referring to pot'.

Enclosing the whole analysiens by the brackets [ ] and

---

[5] Further elaboration of these concepts, howsoever necessary, would take us beyond the scope of the present paper. See reference given under footnote 4. Be it noted here, to avoid any further misunderstanding, that the epistemic distinction between '*viśeṣyata*' and '*prakāratā*' does not correspond to the ontological distinction between substance and attribute. Nor is it the same as the logical distinction between 'subject' ('*uddeśya*') and 'predicate' ('*vidheya*').

writing 'K' before it, we shall symbolise the knowledge whose logical structure is exhibited within the outermost brackets. Thus 'K [{this} (potness)] is to be read as 'the knowledge whose *viśe-ṣyatā* referring to *this* is limited by the *prakāratā* referring to potness'.

' . ' would symbolise 'and' and '∼' would symbolise 'not'. Thus 'K [{s} (p). {t} (q)]' would read as 'the knowledge whose *viśeṣyatā* referring to s is limited by the *prakāratā* referring to p, and whose *viśeṣyatā* referring to t is limited by the *prakāratā* referring to q'. But 'K [{s} ((p).(q))]' would read as 'the knowledge whose *viśeṣyatā* referring to s is limited by two *prakāratās*, one referring to p and the other referring to q.'

'K [{s} (∼p)]' would read as 'the knowledge whose *viśeṣyatā* referring to s is limited by the *prakāratā* referring to the negation or *abhāva* of p'. But 'K [{s ∼ (p)]' would read as 'the knowledge whose *viśeṣyatā* referring to s is not limited by the *prakāratā* referring to p. 'K [{s} ∼ (∼ p)]' would on the other hand read as the knowledge whose *viśeṣyatā* referring to s is not limited by the *prakāratā* referring to the negation of p'.

The Nyāya defines a *niścaya* or a certain knowledge as one which, not having ∼ p as a *prakāra* has p as a *prakāra* (where, as here, p is a term-variable).[6] Following the symbolic conventions stated above, we may then define a *niścaya* as

$$K [\{s\} (p). \{s\} \sim (\sim p)] \ldots (1)$$

As contrasted with *niścaya*, a doubt may then be defined as a knowledge which has two mutually incompatible predicates (*ekadharmikaviruddhabhāvābhāvaprakārakam*) one of which is the negation of the other. In the case of the doubt 'Is this a man or a lamp-post?', two mutually incompatible predicates are being employed. It is however not sufficient for a knowledge to be called a doubt that it should have two incompatible predicates, for it may be – as in the case of the so-called *samuccayajñāna* – that the two incompatible predicates are referred to two different subjects (e.g. 'This is a man and that is a lamp-post'). If *samucca-yajñāna* is to be represented symbolically as

K [{s} (p). {t} (q)]...(2), a doubt has to be represented as

---

[6] "*tadabhāvāprakārakam tatprakārakamjñānam* (Muktāvali on Kārikā 129).

K [{s} (p). {s} (q)], where p and q are mutually incompatible predicates...(3)

Thus there are two essential components of doubt. In the first place, the predicates must be mutually incompatible. Secondly, they must be referred to the same subject. We shall enquire a little more into each of these.

That the predicates of a doubt should be incompatibles is suggested by the connective 'or.'[7] The *Rāmarudri* defines incompatibility thus: *"virodhaśca tadadhikaraṇāvṛttitvam"*.[8] On this definition, to say that p and q are incompatibles would mean that one of them is never present in the locus of the other. The author of the *Nyāyalīlāvati* is not satisfied with this definition of incompatibility, for in that case the definition of doubt would illegitimately apply to such a case of error as 'This conchshell is yellow' whose analysis may be stated as K [{this} (conchshellness). {this} (yellowness)], where, granted that conch-shells are always white and never yellow, the two predicates are incompatibles according to the definition of incompatibility given above. It is necessary therefore that the two predicates should be logical contradictories, 'p' and '∼ p', one of which is *bhāva* and the other *abhāva*. Doubt in that case would be defined as *'bhāvābhāvaprakārakajñānam'* and symbolically represented, instead of (3), as:

$$K [\{s\} (p). \{s\} (\sim p)]...(4)$$

The adjective *'viruddha'* (incompatible, or opposed) may still be regarded as not redundant inasmuch as there may be cases where 'p' and '∼ p' may be predicated of the same subject without it being a case of doubt, as e.g. in the judgment 'The yonder tree both has and has not contact with a monkey.' In this case, contact with the monkey (*kapisamyoga*) and absence of such a contact may both be rightly predicated of the same thing at the same time, for it may have the contact in one part of it, and absence of it in another part. *Dinakari* therefore suggests that the adjective *'viruddha'* has significance. Even the contradictory

---

[7] *"Vākārathaśca virodha"*, *Kiraṇāvaliprakāśaḥ (Guṇa)*, The Princess of Wales Saraswati Bhavana Texts Series, p. 135.

[8] *Siddhāntamuktāvalī* with *Dinakarī* and *Ramarudrī*.

predicates must be really incompatibles. Doubt then is *viruddha-bhāvābhāvaprakārakajñānam*.[9]

I think, however, that the adjective '*viruddha*' is superfluous. The two predicates 'contact' and 'absence of contact' become incompatibles as soon as the subject is further determined. That the subject of both is to be the same implies, strictly understood, that the two subjects must have the same limitor (*avacchedaka*). Referred to the same tree in the same part of it at the same time, i.e. in the same spatio-temporal limitations, the two predicates would certainly constitute a case of doubt.

This shows the importance of the second component of the definition of doubt, namely, the requirement that the two predicates must be referred to the same subject. The idea of sameness is deceptive. Consider a deliberate contradictory judgment (*āhāryajñāna*) of the form 'This hill without fire has a fire in it' ('*nirbahni parvato bahnimāniti*') whose form is 'S which is $\sim$ p is p.' Here two mutually opposed and contradictory predicates are being referred to the same subject, and yet we do not have a case of doubt. Following *Rāmarudri*, we may say that the analysis of such a case shows its form to be

$$\text{K} \left[\{\{s\} \, (\sim p)\} \, (p)\right] \dots (5)$$

which is different from K $[\{s\} \, (p). \, \{s\} \, (\sim p)]$. The difference, likely to be obvious from a mere inspection of the two schemata, lies in the fact that in the case of (5) $\sim$ p is predicated of mere s whereas p is predicated of s as qualified by $\sim$ p, while in (4) both p and $\sim$ p are predicated of one and the same s.

The definition may nevertheless seem to apply to cases of deliberate contradictory judgments of the form "S is both p and $\sim$ p" which clearly are not cases of doubt. However, such judgments may be regarded as carrying only *śābdajñāna*, so that the *prakāras* are not 'p' and '$\sim$p' themselves but *the property that 'p' and '$\sim$p' are prakāras* (*virodhinānāprakārakatvaprakāraka*). This serves to distinguish a mere *śābda* awareness of a contradiction from a doubt where p and $\sim$p themselves are the *prakāras* (*virodhinānāprakāraka*). This ingenuous distinction drawn by Vardhamāna both in *Līlāvatiprakāśa*[10] and in *Kiraṇāvali-*

---

[9] *Ibid.*, p. 480.
[10] Chowkhamba ed., p. 414.

prakāśa,[11] may have its source in the consideration that a *śabda* knowledge is mediated through a sentence, so that in this case of merely verbal knowledge, 'p' and '∼p' directly qualify the sentence and the fact of their so qualifying the sentence may then be regarded as qualifying the resulting knowledge. In our symbolism, this case may be represented as

$$K [\{s\} . ((p). (\sim p))]...(6)$$

Gadādhara holds that the two contents or *viṣayatās* belonging to a doubt have the following three properties:

(i) One of them is incompatible with the other in the sense that one acts as a hindrance (*pratibandhaka*) to the other:

(ii) nevertheless, the two are co-present;

and (iii) the one content belongs to the knowledge only as qualified by the other, and therefore not as an independent content.[12]

The Naiyāyikas have further discussed the question – not of great importance though – if a doubt has two predicates or four. Added to this is the controversy, touched upon earlier, as to whether in case there are two alternatives they are both positive incompatibles or logical contradictories. We get accordingly three schemata which may be exhibited as follows:

(a) Two positive alternatives theory:

$K [\{s\} (p). \{s\} (q)]$, p and q being incompatibles.

(b) One positive and the other negative alternative theory:

$K [\{s\} (p). \{s\} (\sim p)]$

(c) Four alternatives theory:

$K [\{s\} (p). \{s\} (\sim p). \{s\} (q). \{s\} (\sim q)]$

There seems nevertheless to be something about a doubt which escapes the attempt to analyse it logically. We may grant that the Nyāya is not committing the obvious error of mistaking a doubt-sentence for a propositional one. What the Naiyāyika seeks to analyse is not the sentence, not the proposition certainly in this case – for there is no proposition here – but the *jñāna* as apprehended in reflective awareness. In spite of all this we may

---

[11] *Loc. cit.*, p. 138.

[12] Hence Gadādhara's rather forbidding definition: "*svāvacchinnaprativadhyatānirūpitaprativandhakatva-svasamānādhikaraṇyobhayasambandhena viṣayatāviśiṣṭa-viṣayatāśālijñānam samśayapadārthaḥ*". (*Prāmāṇyavāda Gādādharī*).

nevertheless point out that the above analysis still misses something essential to doubt *qua* doubt.

There were amongst the Naiyāyikas some who sought to reduce
a doubt-sentence to the compresence of two contradictory assertions 'S is p' and 'S is not p'. This view traditionally ascribed to
the author of *Ratnakoṣa* is voiced by Gangeśa, when he in course
of an argumentation with the Mīmāmsakas, contends that doubt
is nothing but such joint predication.[13] Happily, this view is not
shared by Gangeśa himself, for he tells us soon after that doubts
are characterised by *Kotyutkatatva*, i.e. difference in the relative
strength of the alternative predicates. In a mere compresence of
two predications, the question of relative strength of the alternatives would not arise. Vācaspati refers to three possibilities
from this point of view: either the affirmative predicate (p) is
relatively stronger, or the negative predicate ($\sim$p) is the stronger
one, or it may be that both the alternatives are equally strong.[14]
In any case, doubt would involve an oscillation of the mind between the two alternatives: it is this which he has in mind when
Vardhamāna so aptly characterises doubt as *dolāyitānekakotika*,[15]
i.e. as a knowledge where there is, as it were, an oscillation between the alternatives. I think, it is this state of the mind, this
dolāyitatva that is an essential character of doubt and should be
added to the structural analysis explained above, – unless of
course it could be shown that such a character follows from the
structure revealed in (4). I do not know however how this could
be shown.

Distinction should nevertheless be drawn between doubt and
question. Doubt is no doubt one of the sources of enquiry, though
not all doubt is so. There are doubts that are not important
enough and are just set aside and do not initiate any enquiry
whatsoever.[16]

---

[13] "*Viruddhobhayāropasāmagridvayasamājādubhyāropa eka eva bhavati sa eva samśayaḥ*" (*Prāmāṇyavāda*, Darbhanga edition, p. 91).

[14] *Ibid.*, p. 92.

[15] Vardhamana, *Kiraṇāvaliguṇaprakāśa*, p. 130.

[16] Vardhamana, "*Na ca jijñāsājankam jñānam samśayaḥ upekṣanīyasamśayāv-yāpteḥ*" (*ibid.*, p. 183).

III

Having given an outline of the structural analysis of doubt given by the Naiyāyikas, we may now turn to certain ancillary issues concerning it. There is in the first place the question of classifying doubt into various types, and there is secondly the question regarding the causes of doubt. The Naiyāyikas have generally taken up these two issues together and have classified doubt according to its origination. The Naiyāyikas are not all agreed about any of these issues, and Gotama's sûtra on this has been subjected to conflicting interpretations. Vātsāyana, Uddyotakara and Vācaspati differ amongst themselves, not to speak of their differences from the Navya Naiyāyikas. It is difficult to evolve an agreed formula. I give below what seems to me to be an account which cuts across the divergences of opinion about the causes of doubt.

These causes may be divided into two groups: the general causes and the specific causes. By the general causes of doubt we mean those factors which must be present so that any doubt at all may occur. They are in other words causes of doubt *qua* doubt. The specific causes are the causes only of specific kinds of doubt, and are not therefore to be regarded as causes of doubt *qua* doubt. If doubts are to be grouped in accordance with their origination, it is only these latter, namely the specific causes that are to be taken into consideration.

A. The general causes may be brought under two sub-heads, the positive and the negative.

(a) The positive general causes of doubt are two: (i) *dharmi-jñāna* and (ii) *viśesasmṛti*.

(i) In the first place, a doubt *qua* doubt presupposes a knowledge of some sort of the *dharmi*, i.e. the substantive of which the two mutually contradictory predicates are predicates. It should be obvious that this knowledge of the *dharmi* should be a *niścaya* i.e. a certainty, and cannot itself be a doubt, for otherwise the latter doubt would presuppose a further *dharmijñāna*, thus leading to an infinite regress. Consider the doubt 'Is this a man or not?'. Here though the doubter is not sure whether this is a man or not, he has a certain apprehension of the object here before him as a this, and may be along with some other generic characters. Gangesa suggests two reasons why this factor should be regarded as an essential precondition of all doubt *qua* doubt. If *dharmijñāna* were not required for all doubts, there ought not to have been the rule that all doubts must have some substantive.[17] In fact, however, doubts are of the form K [{s} (p). {s} ($\sim$ p)], and not of the form K [(p). ($\sim$ p)]. Further, the property that in doubts one of the alternatives may be stronger than the other (*koṭyutkaṭatva*) cannot be explained otherwise, for in the knowledge K [(p). ($\sim$ p)], 'p' and '$\sim$ p' should have no difference in status; any difference which they may have must be in their relation to the 's' which is being apprehended as 's'.

(ii) Mere *dharmijñāna* is not enough to produce a doubt. Moreover mere knowledge of 's' as 's' does not explain why the doubt should have the predicates 'p' and '$\sim$ p' and not the predicates, let us say, 'q' and '$\sim$ q'. We need therefore another positive, general condition, namely a remembrance of the two alternatives 'p' and '$\sim$ p'. This is what is called *viśeṣasmṛti*, 'p' and '$\sim$ p' being the *viśeṣas* or specific characters. It may also be called *koṭismṛti* for they are also called the *koṭis* or alternatives.

(b) The negative general condition necessary for all doubts *qua* doubt is non-perception of the specific characters as belonging to the substantive (*viśeṣa-adarśana*). Definite knowledge of the presence of any of the specific characters in the substantive is a hindrance to doubt. If the supposed doubter knew for certain that s has p, or if he knows for certain that s has $\sim$ p, then the doubt 'Is s p or $\sim$ p?' would not obviously arise. Hence the absence of such specific knowledge is a necessary condition of all doubt *qua* doubt.[18]

B. While the conditions listed under A are necessary for there being any doubt at all, there are however other special causes of

---

[17] "*Dharmijñānam ca saṃśayahetuḥ, anyathā saṃśaye dharminiyamaḥ koṭyut-katatvam ca na syāt*" (*loc. cit.*, p. 92).

[18] It may be mentioned that both the factors (a) (ii) and (b) are implied in Gotama's sûtra where doubt is characterised as being *viśeṣāpekṣa*, which may mean either *viśeṣādarśana* (*apekṣā=adarśana*) or *viśeṣasmṛtyapekṣa* corresponding to the above two factors respectively. There is a third possible interpretation according to which this expression means "the desire to apprehend the specific characters" (*apekṣā= ākāṅkṣā* or desire); but we cannot include such desire amongst the necessary preconditions of doubt *qua* doubt. There may be doubts even when such desire is absent. Moreover, often the desire to ascertain is a consequence rather than a cause of doubt.

specific types of doubts. Thus doubts may be caused by either (a) perception of the common character (*samānadharmopapatti*), or (b) perception of an uncommon character (*anekadharmopapatti*), or (c) hearing contradictory views expressed by parties opposed over an issue (*vipratipatti*), or (d) reflection on the absence of any concommitance between being experienced and being real and between not being experienced and being unreal (*Upalabdhi-anupalabdhi-avyavasthā*). Let us explain each one of these with suitable examples.

(a) A doubt of the form 'Is s p or not?' may arise from perception of some character common to both 'p' and 'not-p' (provided of course, it is accompanied by perception of s as s, non-perception of the specific characters 'p' and 'not-p', and remembrance of those specific alternatives). By a common character is here meant any character or characters which are present where p-ness is present, but is also present where p-ness is not present, i.e. which may be accompanied either by p-ness or by not-p-ness. Seeing something at a distance (s as a mere this), and perceiving its height, size, shape etc. which could very well belong to a man or to a dead tree trunk, one might doubt 'Is this a man or a dead tree trunk'? If at this stage he could detect any of the specific properties which goes only with manhood, then his doubt would give place to the certainty 'This is a man'. Now it seems clear that in doubts arising from the perception of a common character in the above sense, the alternatives tend to be positive contraries instead of being logical contradictories, a point recognised by Vācaspati when he says that doubts of this kind are characterised by *vidhiprādhānya*.

(b) A doubt may arise also from the perception of an uncommon character. On perceiving some uncommon character in some substantives s, one may be haunted by the doubt what character it shares or has in common with others. The Naiyāyika's favourite example is this: if sound is known merely as possessing soundness (which is its distinguishing and in that sense uncommon character) one may very well doubt if it over and above this possesses eternality or non-eternality, for both are compatible with soundness:

The distinction between cases under (a) and those under (b) is apt to be overlooked. In case (a), one perceives in s a character x which is common in the sense that it *as a matter a fact* accompanies and is consistent with both the alternatives. It accompanies p-ness as well as not-p-ness. In case (b), a character x is perceived in a s such that x belongs to s alone, and x is consistent with both, but not known to accompany either of, p-ness and not-p-ness.

(c) When in course of a disputation, the opposed and contrasting parties put torward their respective theses, a hearer is very likely to be overcome by a doubt as to which of the theses is the correct one. The older Naiyayikas take this as a special case of doubt, where the doubt is *śābda*, i.e. generated by hearing and understanding of the words uttered by the disputing parties. In such a case, of course, doubt arises not in the mind of the disputationists, for each of them is convinced of the correctness of his own contention, but in a neutral observer (*madhyastha*) who is confused by the mere statements of the contradictory positions advocated in the absence of any decisive supporting arguments. There must be absence, in other words, of *anyata-rasādhakahetu*. Such doubt, once it has arisen, cannot be removed by the mere collective judgment (or, *sampratipatti*) of the form 'A holds p to be the case, and B holds not-p to be the case'.[19] What is necessary is the ascertainment which of the two is really the case.

Naiyayikas are divided over the issue whether a doubt arising from this special cause is to be called *śābda* or *mānasa*. The question in other words is: does the doubt arise through hearing, or does it arise through the operation of mind (*manas*)? Raghunātha defends the former alternative and has the older authorities on his side.[20] Viswanatha argues in favour of the latter alternative, and makes use of the premise that *śabda* as a rule is a source of certainty so that by itself it cannot generate doubt.[21] What happens according to him is that the statements of the disputing parties give rise to remembrance of the alternatives. This latter knowledge, then, provided all the other required conditions are present, gives rise to doubt which therefore is *mānasa* and not *śābda*.

---

[19] See *Vātsāyana Bhāṣya* on *Nyāya Sūtra* 2.1.6.
[20] See Phanibhusan Tarkabagish on sûtra 2.1.6. (*Nyāyadarśana* Vol. II).
[21] "*Śabdavyāptijñānādinām niścayamātrajanakatvasvabhāvāt*".

(d) Being an object of experience is not a sure mark of being real. Epistemological objecthood may or may not be accompanied by ontological independence. Both the real water and the water-in-the-mirage are objects of experience. Both the real snake and the illusory snake-in-the-rope are seen. Therefore from the mere fact that something is being experienced one cannot make sure as to whether the experienced something is also real or not. There may therefore arise in such a case doubt about its reality or unreality.

Similarly not being an object of experience is not a sure mark of unreality. The unreal of course may not be experienced. But so also frequently is the real. Not all that is real is experienced. Therefore, from the mere fact that something is not being experienced nothing can be ascertained as regards its reality or unreality. There may therefore arise in such a case doubt about the reality or unreality of what is not being experienced.

Attempts have been made to explain case (d) in other ways. Consider the possibility (d'): Supposing I am having a knowledge which certainly possesses the generic character of experience-ness or *jñānatva*. This generic character however is consistent with, and is accompanied by, either of the two specific characters, the property of having a real object (*sadviṣayakatva*) and the property of having an unreal object (*asadviṣayakatva*). If we do not experience any of these specific characters in the knowledge under consideration there may be a doubt in accordance with rule (a).

However, there is a difference between (d) and (d'). In (d), the doubt concerns the object of the experience under consideration. The object being an epistemological object may or may not be ontologically real. In (d'), on the other hand, the doubt is about the knowledge or experience itself. Its being an experience does not entail either that it is *sadviṣyayka* (true) or that it is *asadviṣayaka* (false).

It has also been contended by others[22] that (d) is a special case of another rule (d''): doubt about the truth of a knowledge gives rise to doubt about the reality of the object of that knowledge (*prāmāṇyasaṃśayāt viṣayasaṃśayaḥ*). Let K be a know-

---

[22] See for example *Dinakari* on *Siddhāntamuktāvali* on *kārikā* 180.

ledge having O for its object. If for any reason I have a doubt of the form 'Is K true or not?' this would generate a further doubt of the form 'Is O real or not?'

There is again a nice point of difference between (d) and (d''). In case of (d) what causes doubt about the reality or unreality of O is not a prior doubt in the truth of K but the perception of the generic character of O as an object of knowledge, this character being consistent with both the reality and unreality of O.

The importance of the rule (d'') – and one reason why it cannot be reduced to any other – is that though a prior certainty about an object (*arthaniścaya*) rules out the possibility of doubt about the same object, nevertheless such doubt may be caused by an intervening doubt in the truth of that initial certainty. The sequence in such cases may be set down thus:

1. Certainty, 'K', about O.   2. Doubt: 'Is K true'?
3. Doubt: 'Is O real?'

In the absence of (2), (3) cannot take place when (1) has already been there, the general rule being that though doubt does not obstruct certainty (for otherwise doubt would never be resolved), yet certainty does exclude doubt except in the case coming under (d'').

(e) Another rule, which according to many comes under the '*ca*' of Gotama's sûtra 1.1.23, is to the effect that a doubt about the pervaded gives rise to a doubt about the pervader (*vyāpy-asandehāt vyāpakasandeha*).[23] Smoke, for example, is pervaded (*vyāpya*) by fire which is the pervader (*vyāpaka*) in relation to it. Wherever there is smoke, there is fire. Smoke is never present in any locus of the absence of fire. If a person who knows this relationship between smoke and fire perceives smoke in a distant hill and recognises the smoke as the *vyāpya* of fire, he would naturally infer, and so arrive at a certainty that the hill also possesses fire. If however such a person, for whatever reason, comes to have the doubt whether what looks like smoke is really smoke or not, he would be led to the further doubt whether the hill possesses fire or not. Of course, here as before in the case of inference, it is necessary that smoke should have been earlier known and in the present recognised to be a *vyāpya* of fire. It

---

[23] See Ingalls, *loc. cit.* for the relation of pervasion or *vyāpti*.

also holds good that certainty about the *vyāpya* of any one of the alternatives of a doubt would necessarily put an end to the doubt. Consider the doubt 'Is this a man or not?' As soon as the doubter comes to perceive clearly such features as hands, feet etc. in the object before him which is being referred to as this, his doubt would give place to the certainty 'This is a man', for the property of possessing limbs is a sure mark of manhood. Hence, the *viśeṣādarśana* or non-perception of specific characters – which is one of the general conditions of all doubt *qua* doubt – must be taken to include non-perception of the marks (or *vyāpyas*) of the specific characters.

IV

In this section we propose to examine Descartes's doubt with the help of the Nyāya theory outlined above. Such a confrontation, it is hoped, will help us to throw light on both the sides, and thereby on the nature of doubt *qua* doubt.

Descartes's doubt applies in the first instance to anything and everything in the world and also to any and every knowledge and experience. In his first Meditation and also in The Principles of Philosophy, Part I, he gives us the grounds of his universal doubt. These grounds are the following:

1. The senses are often found to mislead us. We cannot therefore place absolute confidence in them, for "it would be imprudent to trust too much to what has even once deceived us".[24]

2. Secondly, "in dreams we perpetually seem to perceive or imagine innumerable objects which have no existence".[25]

2a. There are, Descartes argues, "no certain marks by which the state of waking can ever be distinguished from sleep",[26] i.e. from the state of dreaming.

---

[24] Descartes, *The Principles of Philosophy* (Everyman ed.), p. 166.
[25] *Ibid.*, p. 166.
[26] Descartes, *Meditations* (Everyman ed.), p. 81.

3. With regard to the supposedly self-evident truths of mathematics Descartes employs the following two arguments:

a. It is often found that men fall into error even in such matters, and regard as self-evident what is really false.[27]

b. More important for Descartes is this one: We believe that God who created us is all-powerful. We do not however know for certain whether this all-powerful God is not a deceiver. It may therefore be that he created us with the will to deceive us. If on the other hand the creator is not all-powerful then we shall be more imperfect and more likely to be under continual deception.

4. There is a final argument which, as would be clear from the remarks to follow is of the highest importance. We possess a free will and we are therefore free to withhold our assent from whatever is doubtful. In other words, we may suspend our belief in whatever is not "manifestly certain and undoubted".[28]

It seems clear that Descartes's arguments (1) and (2) come under the Nyāya rule (d), i.e. they are really based upon what the Nyāya calls *Upalabdhi-avyavasthā*. In this respect these two really constitute one argument. They appeal to the fact that there is no fixed correlation between being an object of experience and being real. The unreal is as much an object of experience as the real. What is presented through the senses may then be unreal, just as what is presented in a dream may seem to be real. The doubt therefore may be accounted for by (i) perception (mentally) of the generic character of objectivity (*jñānaviṣayatva*) and (ii) uncertainty as to reality or unreality, arising out of the absence of any settled order in such matters.

The argument (2a) however presents great difficulty. What is necessary for the possibility of a doubt of the form 'Am I awake or am I dreaming?' (= 'Is this a dream or is it a waking experience?') is that I should perceive the generic character of experience-ness (*jñānatva*), and yet fail to perceive either of the two specific characters (which in the present case are the property of being a dream and the property of being a waking experience) or their respective marks. The possibility is *a priori* implied therein that there are such marks, and that it is possible to dis-

27 *The Principles of Philosophy*, p. 166.
28 *Ibid.*, p. 166.

NYĀYA THEORY OF DOUBT

tinguish between the two specific characters though in any given case one may fail to do so. Descartes however contends that there are "no certain marks" by which one may be distinguished from the other. If two properties 'p' and 'q' cannot at all be distinguished, i.e. no sure mark exists which could serve the purpose, then there is no question of the non-perception of such marks and hence no possibility of doubt with regard to them. If on the other hand there are such marks though Descartes fails to adduce any then his doubt cannot claim universality. He could then only say that he could not then and there distinguish the one from the other. Moreoever, if no sure mark of dream experience were known to him on what ground could he almost persuade himself to think that he was then dreaming?[29] The point is that a doubt of the form 'Is S p or q?' requires both that 'p' and 'q' are distinct with their respective distinguishing marks and that in a given case there is a non-perception of them. These two conditions defeat the possibility of a universal scepticism.

The argument (3a) is formally of the same type as the first argument and is to the effect that where there is the least chance of error, where in other words there is no *upalabdhivyavasthā* i.e. no rule that only the real is experienced, one may reasonably doubt. This applies as much to sense-perception as to mathematics. And incidentally it may be pointed out that the argument applied to mathematical truths is close to the point of view of the Nyāya logic which does not admit the distinctions between analytic and synthetic, *a priori* and *a posteriori*, self-evident and not-self-evident truths. The subjective possibility of error being always there, there may be doubt regarding the truth of any knowledge whatsoever as also a resulting doubt about the reality of the object of such knowledge.

However, none of the arguments 1-3, though sanctioned by the Nyāya rules, can be used for the purpose of justifying a universal scepticism. For among the necessary conditions of doubt *qua* doubt there is at least one which constitutes a certainty: this is the *dharmijñāna* or knowledge of the substantive. In any particular doubt there must be certainty about the *dharmi*. Basing on the facts of error, we may have two kinds of doubt: the one of the same sort as 'Is this a rope or a snake?', another of the philoso-

[29] *Meditations* (Everyman's ed.), p. 81.

phical kind: 'Is sense-perception valid or not?' or 'Is the world real or imagined?'. It is easy to show that doubts of the second kind are self-stultifying, for they question the very reality of their own respective *dharmis* which they cannot consistently do.

Two other arguments of Descartes remain to be examined. The doubt involved in 3(b) may be restated thus:

'Is God who is known to be all-powerful also a deceiver or not? The doubt so formulated seems to be sanctioned by the Nyāya rule B(b). Here we have an uncommon character belonging to the *dharmi* i.e. being both the creator of the world and all-powerful, and we are left in doubt as to which of the two properties 'being a deceiver' and 'being veracious' – both compatible with the above uncommon character – further belongs to it. Such a doubt, if it comes to happen, would no doubt have a limitless scope with regard to the truth of all our experience. It would not however apply to our belief in the fact that there is an all-powerful creator. The argument is to that extent effective, but loses its force because of the fact that its starting point is a theological belief from which a reflective philosopher may not start.

Descartes's *Cogito* which sets a limit to his doubt may be interpreted as the ultimate *dharmi*, certainty about which is presupposed in any doubt. But it should be pointed out that the 'I' is the *dharmi* only in the reflective judgments of the form 'I know', 'I perceive' etc., but not in the unreflective judgments of the form 'This wall is white', 'The yonder bird is a crow' etc. Doubts being of the form 'Is this wall white or not?', 'Is the yonder bird a crow or not?', they do not presuppose certainty about the 'I' as their *dharmi*. In case however these doubts come to occur through the instrumentality of doubts of the validity of the respective knowledges (as per rule d″), then of course certainty about the 'I' would be presupposed, for the 'I' is the *dharmi* in the latter doubts that have the form 'Did I know rightly or not?'. If Descartes's doubt is to justify certainty about the *Cogito*, then he must be interpreted as having taken to this reflective way of having first doubted the validity (*prāmāṇya*) of our beliefs, and then arrived at the doubt about the reality of the objects of those beliefs. Such an interpretation is amply borne out by Descartes's writings.

One of the chief grounds sustaining Descartes's universal scepticism lies hidden in the last of his arguments. The human will, he writes, is free and so is also free to withhold its assent from whatever is doubtful. It must readily be seen that this argument represents a type of thinking foreign to the Nyāya, and in fact to all Indian philosophy. Withholding assent or doubting as a function of the limitless freedom of the will is not recognised as a possibility in the Nyāya, and therefore the argument (4) does not conform to any of the Nyāya rules.[30] And yet if anywhere it is here that we shall find the sources of a truly philosophical doubt.

With a view to looking closer into the nature of this argument let us ask what is meant by the two expressions "withholding one's assent" and "whatever is doubtful"?

Withholding one's assent means a deliberate, reflective decision not to believe, to suspend or neutralise one's belief, to 'bracket' it as Husserl would say. The motive for doing this – with Descartes, and also with Husserl – is the reflective one of finding a secure basis for human knowledge, a radical foundation, a first principle for the sciences. The Nyāya is operating with a strictly causal-deterministic conception, and within such a framework a doubt could occur only when there are necessary and sufficient conditions for it. The Naiyayika might seek to include this reflective doubt within his own deterministic framework by tracing it to the factor of *icchā* or desire which is recognised by him to overpower others. But I wonder if this would help us to overcome the great difference that subsists between the two conceptions, which may perhaps be brought to light in still another way.

Withholding one's assent to a belief does not exclude making practical use of that belief. Descartes and Husserl, just when they ask us to doubt, or to practise the *epoche*, do not suggest that that would mean giving up and reorientation of our practical behaviour, of our *Lebenswelt* based precisely on those beliefs. On the contrary, Descartes writes:

"... we ought not meanwhile to make use of doubt in the

---

[30] The only rule which bears a certain semblance to the Cartesian case under consideration is the Nyāya rule that the factor of desire (*icchā*) overpowers any other set of factors tending to produce a contrary result.

conduct of life". (The Principles of Philosophy, part I. III.)
And Husserl says the same of his phenomenological *epoche*: the
epoche will not affect the daily course of practical life; it will
only suspend theoretical judgment about the 'being' of the world.

What is excluded is the possibility of making any theoretical
use of the beliefs concerned. I wonder if the Naiyāyika would
approve of this attitude. For him, though ascertainment of the
truth of a belief (*prāmānyagraha*) is not necessary for the appropriate practical behaviour, yet non-apprehension of its falsity is
certainly a necessary condition.[31] Now, on the Nyāya analysis,
doubt in the truth of a knowledge has the form:

K [{this knowledge} (truth). {This knowledge} (falsity)]. In so
far as this doubt has falsity as one of its *prakāras*, the doubt is
an apprehension of falsity in the belief and therefore on the Nyāya
rules would serve as a *pratibandhaka* or hindrance to the appropriate practical behaviour. Normal practical behaviour would
therefore be impeded by a universal scepticism. Descartes and
Husserl do not apprehend this possibility but on the other hand
assure us that their doubt would leave the practical *Lebenswelt*
untouched. There must then subsist *a radical difference* between
the two doubts. They must then be not merely different kinds of
doubts, but as doubts different.

The same radical difference comes to light if we examine what
Descartes means by 'whatever is doubtful'. In one meaning of it,
a thing is doubtful if it is in fact an object of doubt. But, for
one thing, this is not all that is there in the ordinary meaning of
that expression; and, for another, if to be doubtful meant to be in
fact an object of doubt, then Descartes' decision to withhold assent from what is doubtful would be trivial; he would then be
asking us to doubt what is being doubted, which would be utterly
pointless. To be doubtful then means to be a possible object of a
doubt. Now on the Nyāya theory nothing possesses any property or
properties which make it liable to be doubted. Nothing by itself,
i.e. by virtue of any of its own properties, is doubtful. Everything
at the same time is a possible object of a valid knowledge, i.e. a
prameya. Suitable *epistemic* conditions may however produce in a
person doubt about anything. For Descartes, and for the entire
tradition of Western philosophy there is an important sense in

[31] Gangeśa, *Prāmānyavāda*.

which a thing may meaningfully be called doubtful. This is the sense that the thing could have been otherwise, that its contradictory is possible, or that it is, though a fact, a contingent one. If there is any p of which it holds good that both p and not-p are possible then it is doubtful. It is not necessary. It is, as Descartes says, uncertain. From all such things we are entitled to withhold our assent.

It would be obvious that the Nyāya knows no such categorisation of things or facts or propositions into contingent and necessary. It knows, as said before, no distinction between what is *in fact* true but might not have been and what is *necessarily* true, between the *a posteriori* and the *a priori*, or even between analytic and synthetic truths. Bare logical possibility or counterfactual conditionals do not interest it. It gives a logic of facts, and in this sense is extensional, avoiding modal concepts.[32] It would not therefore approve of a universal scepticism, based on the notion of logical possibility.

Should we then say that here is an overall limitation of the Nyāya logic, whose symptoms show themselves in all aspects of it far beyond the narrow subject matter of the present paper? Perhaps it is so. It may also well be the case that doubt (or *saṁśaya*) in one sense is exactly what the Nyāya means by it, and for it the Nyāya logic is well adapted. At the same time, philosophical doubt, doubt in the reflective level, falls beyond its scope. And the two doubts, it may well be, are not only different kinds of doubts but are as doubts different. One and the same logic cannot do justice to both. Descartes may be said to have erred on the opposite side, when he sought to extend the logic of ordinary doubt to philosophical doubt, which is the same as using arguments (1) – (3) to justify the latter.

[32] It should be remembered however that the Nyāya logic is not extensional in the sense that it knows no quantification. But that is an altogether different sense of extensionality.

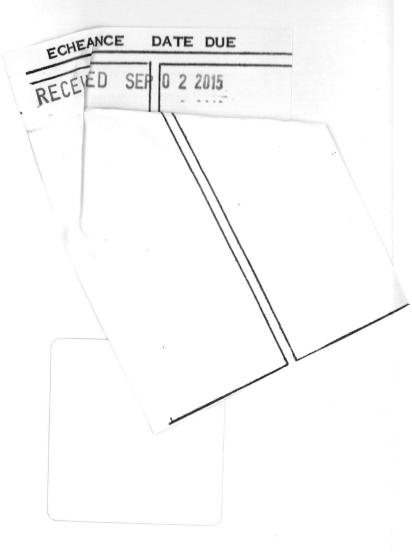

ÉCHÉANCE   DATE DUE

RECEIVED   SEP 0 2 2015